Lecture Notes in Computer S

Edited by G. Goos, J. Hartmanis, and J.

Springer
*Berlin
Heidelberg
New York
Hong Kong
London
Milan
Paris
Tokyo*

Fausto Giunchiglia   James Odell
Gerhard Weiß (Eds.)

Agent-Oriented Software Engineering III

Third International Workshop, AOSE 2002
Bologna, Italy, July 15, 2002
Revised Papers and Invited Contributions

 Springer

Series Editors

Gerhard Goos, Karlsruhe University, Germany
Juris Hartmanis, Cornell University, NY, USA
Jan van Leeuwen, Utrecht University, The Netherlands

Volume Editors

Fausto Giunchiglia
University of Trento
Department of Information and Communication Technology
38050 Povo, Trento, Italy
E-mail: fausto@dit.unitn.it

James Odell
3646 West Huron River Drive
Ann Arbor, Michigan, 48103, USA
E-mail: email@jamesodell.com

Gerhard Weiß
Technische Universität München
Institut für Informatik
Boltzmannstr. 3, 85748 Garching, Germany
E-mail: weissg@in.tum.de

Cataloging-in-Publication Data applied for

A catalog record for this book is available from the Library of Congress.

Bibliographic information published by Die Deutsche Bibliothek
Die Deutsche Bibliothek lists this publication in the Deutsche Nationalbibliografie;
detailed bibliographic data is available in the Internet at <http://dnb.ddb.de>.

CR Subject Classification (1998): D.2, I.2.11, F.3, D.1, C.2.4, D.3

ISSN 0302-9743
ISBN 3-540-00713-X Springer-Verlag Berlin Heidelberg New York

Springer-Verlag Berlin Heidelberg New York
a member of BertelsmannSpringer Science+Business Media GmbH

http://www.springer.de

© Springer-Verlag Berlin Heidelberg 2003
Printed in Germany

Typesetting: Camera-ready by author, data conversion by Olgun Computergrafik
Printed on acid-free paper   SPIN: 10872425   06/3142   5 4 3 2 1 0

Preface

Over the past three decades, software engineers have derived a progressively better understanding of the characteristics of complexity in software. It is now widely recognised that *interaction* is probably the most important single characteristic of complex software. Software architectures that contain many dynamically interacting components, each with their own thread of control, and engaging in complex coordination protocols, are typically orders of magnitude more complex to correctly and efficiently engineer than those that simply compute a function of some input through a single thread of control.

Unfortunately, it turns out that many (if not most) real-world applications have precisely these characteristics. As a consequence, a major research topic in computer science over at least the past two decades has been the development of tools and techniques to model, understand, and implement systems in which interaction is the norm. Indeed, many researchers now believe that in future computation itself will be understood as chiefly a process of interaction.

Since the 1980s, software agents and multiagent systems have grown into what is now one of the most active areas of research and development activity in computing generally. There are many reasons for the current intensity of interest, but certainly one of the most important is that the concept of an agent as an autonomous system, capable of interacting with other agents in order to satisfy its design objectives, is a natural one for software designers. Just as we can understand many systems as being composed of essentially passive objects, which have state, and upon which we can perform operations, so we can understand many others as being made up of interacting, semiautonomous agents.

This recognition has led to the growth of interest in agents as a new paradigm for software engineering. As its very successful predecessors, AOSE 2000 and AOSE 2001 (Lecture Notes in Computer Science, Volumes 1957 and 2222), the AOSE 2002 workshop sought to examine the credentials of agent-based approaches as a software engineering paradigm, and to gain an insight into what agent-oriented software engineering will look like. AOSE 2002 was held at the First International Joint Conference on Autonomous Agents and Multiagent Systems (AAMAS) in Bologna, Italy, in July 2002. Some 49 papers were submitted to AOSE 2002, and 15 of them were accepted for presentation (which is an acceptance rate of 30 %). The submissions followed a call for papers on all aspects of agent-oriented software engineering, and particularly the following:

- Methodologies for agent-oriented analysis and design
- Relationship of AOSE to other SE paradigms (e.g., OO)
- UML and agent systems
- Agent-oriented requirements analysis and specification
- Refinement and synthesis techniques for agent-based specifications

- Verification and validation techniques for agent-based systems
- Software development environments and CASE tools for AOSE
- Standard APIs for agent programming
- Formal methods for agent-oriented systems, including specification and verification logics
- Model checking for agent-oriented systems
- Engineering large-scale agent systems
- Experiences with field-tested agent systems
- System deployment using standards such as FIPA
- Best practice in agent-oriented development
- Market and other economic models in agent systems engineering
- Practical coordination and cooperation frameworks for agent systems
- Standardisations for AOSE
- Reuse approaches for agent-oriented software, including design patterns, frameworks, components, and architectures
- Integration of agent-oriented software into existing business processes and implications for business process reengineering
- Implications of agent-oriented software on organizational and social structures within and between companies (e.g., changes in roles, responsibilities, transparency, business processes, and decision schemes)

This volume contains revised versions of the 15 papers presented at the workshop. Additionally, it contains two invited contributions, by Massimo Benerecetti and Alessandro Cimatti on "Validation of multiagent systems by symbolic model checking," and Jörg Müller and Bernhard Bauer on "Agent-oriented software technologies: flaws and remedies." We believe that this thoroughly prepared volume is of particular value to all readers interested in key topics and most recent developments in the very exciting field of agent-oriented software engineering.

Acknowledgements. We thank the authors, the participants, and the reviewers for making AOSE 2002 a high-quality scientific event. Special thanks also goes to Keith Decker, the AAMAS 2002 workshop chair, for his support, and to Alfred Hofmann at Springer-Verlag for the continued opportunity to publish the AOSE proceedings in the LNCS series.

December 2002   Fausto Giunchiglia
                                                                     James Odell
                                                                   Gerhard Weiß

Organising Committee

Fausto Giunchiglia (Co-chair)
   University of Trento and ITC-IRST, Italy
   E-mail: M.J.Wooldridge@csc.liv.ac.uk
James Odell (Co-chair)
   James Odell Associates, Ann Arbor, MI, USA
   E-mail: email@jamesodell.com
Gerhard Weiß (Co-chair)
   Technical University of Munich, Germany
   E-mail: weissg@in.tum.de

Steering Committee

Paolo Ciancarini, University of Bologna, Italy
Michael Wooldridge, University of Liverpool, UK

Program Committee

Bernard Bauer (Germany)
Federico Bergenti (Italy)
Scott DeLoach (USA)
Marie-Pierre Gervais (France)
Paolo Giogini (Italy)
Olivier Gutknecht (France)
Michael Huhns (USA)
Carlos Iglesias (Spain)
Matthias Jarke (Germany)
Nicholas Jennings (UK)
Catholijn Jonker (The Netherlands)
Liz Kendall (Australia)
David Kinny (Australia)

Manuel Kolp (Belgium)
Yannis Labrou (USA)
Alex van Lamsweerde (France)
Jürgen Lind (Germany)
John Mylopolous (Canada)
Andrea Omicini (Italy)
Van Parunak (USA)
Anna Perini (Italy)
Onn Shehory (Israel)
Morris Sloman (UK)
Eric Yu (Canada)
Franco Zambonelli (Italy)

Additional Reviewers

Paolo Bresciani (Italy)
Jan Broersen (The Netherlands)
Matthias Nickles (Germany)

Benno Overeinder (The Netherlands)
Michael Rovatsos (Germany)
Arnon Sturm (Israel)

Table of Contents

Part IV: Methodologies and Tools

Part V: Positions and Perspectives

Specifying Electronic Societies
with the Causal Calculator

Alexander Artikis[1], Marek Sergot[2], and Jeremy Pitt[1]

[1]Electrical Engineering Department, Imperial College of Science, Technology and
Medicine, SW7 2BT, London, UK, +44 (0)20 75946221
[2]Department of Computing, Imperial College of Science, Technology and Medicine,
SW7 2BZ, London, UK, +44 (0)20 75948218
`a.artikis@ic.ac.uk,mjs@doc.ic.ac.uk,j.pitt@ic.ac.uk`

Abstract. In previous work [1] we presented a framework for the specification of open computational societies i.e. societies where the behaviour
of the members and their interactions cannot be predicted in advance.
We viewed computational systems from an external perspective, with a
focus on the institutional and the social aspects of these systems. The
social constraints and roles of the open societies were specified with
the use of the Event Calculus. In this paper, we formalise our framework with the use of the $C+$ language, a formalism with explicit state
transition semantics. We use the implementation of the $C+$ language,
the `Causal Calculator`, a software tool for representing commonsense
knowledge about action and change, to animate and validate the specifications of computational societies. We demonstrate the utility of the
`Causal Calculator` (by specifying and executing a Contract-Net Protocol) and comment on its functionality regarding the specification of
computational societies.

1 Introduction

Negotiation protocols [2,3] and Virtual Enterprises [4] are two examples of application domains where software agents form computational societies in order
to achieve their possibly competing goals. Key characteristics of such societies
are agent heterogeneity, unpredictable behaviour [5], conflicting individual goals,
limited trust and a high probability of non-conformance to specifications. Consequently, it is important that the activity of such societies is governed by a
framework with formal and meaningful semantics [6]. In order to address such
a requirement we presented in [1] a framework for specifying, animating, and
ultimately reasoning about and verifying the properties of open electronic societies, i.e. computational systems where the behaviour of the (heterogeneous
and possibly competing) members and their interactions cannot be predicted in
advance.

The framework for the specification of e-societies was formalised with the
use of the Event Calculus [7]. In this paper we formalise the framework with the
use of the $C+$ language [8], a formalism with *explicit* state transition semantics.

F. Giunchiglia et al. (Eds.): AOSE 2002, LNCS 2585, pp. 1–15, 2003.

We use the Causal Calculator (CCALC), a software tool that implements $C+$, to execute and, prove properties of, the specifications of open societies.

This paper is structured as follows. First, we briefly describe the $C+$ language and the Causal Calculator. Second, we present the framework for the specification of open e-societies. Third, we specify a Contract-Net Protocol (CNP) [9] with the use of the framework for the specification of e-societies and the $C+$ language. Fourth, we demonstrate the utility of CCALC by executing and 'validating' the specifications of the CNP. Finally, we discuss related work, summarise and comment on the functionality of CCALC regarding the specifications of computational societies.

2   The $C+$ Language

The action language $C+$ [8] enables the representation of properties of actions, including actions with conditional and indirect effects and concurrently executed actions. An *action description* in $C+$ is a set of $C+$ rules that define a transition system of a particular kind. In this section we briefly present $C+$ [1].

The representation of an action domain in $C+$ consists of *rigid* constants, *fluent* constants and *action* constants:

- *Rigid constants* are symbols that represent the features of the system whose value is fixed and does not depend on the state.
- *Fluent constants* are symbols characterising a state. They are divided in two categories: *Simple fluent constants* and *statically determined fluent constants*. Simple fluent constants are related to actions by *dynamic rules* (i.e. rules describing a transition from a state s_i to its successor state s_{i+1}). Statically determined fluents are characterised by *static rules* (i.e. rules describing an individual state) relating them to other fluents (static and dynamic rules are defined below).
- *Action constants* are symbols characterising state transitions. Intuitively, they represent the actions of the agents and the environment.

An *action signature* is a non-empty set σ^{rf} of *rigid* and *fluent* constants and a non-empty set σ^{act} of *action* constants. An *action description* D in $C+$ is a set of *causal laws*. A causal law can be either a *static law* or a *dynamic law*. A static law is an expression of the form

$$\text{caused } F \text{ if } G \tag{1}$$

- Every constant occurring in F or G is rigid or fluent. In other words, F and G are formulas of signature σ^{rf}.
- If F contains a rigid constant then every constant occurring in F, G is rigid.

In a static law fluents F and G are evaluated on the same state of the transition system. A dynamic law is an expression of the form

$$\text{caused } F \text{ if } G \text{ after } H \tag{2}$$

---

[1] We follow the formal and more detailed analysis of $C+$ provided in [8].

- Every constant occurring in F is a simple fluent constant (i.e. F is a formula of signature σ^{rf}).
- Every constant occurring in G is rigid or fluent (i.e. G is a formula of signature σ^{rf}).
- H is any combination of rigid constants, fluent constants and action constants (i.e. H is a formula of signature $\sigma^{rf} \cup \sigma^{act}$).

In a transition from state s_i to state s_{i+1} simple fluent constants in F and rigid and fluent constants in G are evaluated on s_{i+1} and rigid, fluent and action constants in H are evaluated on s_i. F is called the *head* of the static law (1) and the dynamic law (2).

The $C+$ language provides various abbreviations of the causal laws. The abbreviations that will be used in this paper are the following:

- We specify that fluent F is *inertial* as: **inertial** F. This is an abbreviation for a dynamic law of the form: **caused** F **if** F **after** F.
- The fact that action α cannot be executed if G holds is represented as: **nonexecutable** α **if** G which is an abbreviation of **caused** $\perp$ **after** $\alpha \wedge G$.
- The *closed-world assumption* regarding a formula F is represented as: **default** F which is an abbreviation of: **caused** F **if** F.

Any action description in $C+$ defines a *transition system*, a directed graph whose vertices are states and whose edges are labelled by actions. Given an action description D we can define the following:

- A *state* is an interpretation of σ^{rf} that satisfies $F \subset G$ for every static law (1).
- An *action* is a propositional interpretation of σ^{act}.
- A *transition* is a triple (s, a, s') where s is the initial state, s' is the resulting state and a is an action.
- A formula F is *caused* in a transition (s, a, s') if $F \in T_{static}(s') \cup E(s, a, s')$, where:

    1. $T_{static}(s) = \{F \mid \text{static law (1) is in } D, s \models G\}$.
    2. $E(s, a, s') = \{F \mid \text{dynamic law (2) is in } D, s' \models G, s \cup a \models H\}$.

- A transition (s, a, s') is *causally explained* by D if and only if:

    1. $s' \models T_{static}(s')$.
    2. $s' \models E(s, a, s')$.
    3. There is no other s'' such that $s'' \models T_{static}(s')$ and $s'' \models E(s, a, s')$.

The *transition system* described by D is the following directed graph:

- The vertices are the *states* of D.
- An edge from state s to state s' is labelled with action a if the transition (s, a, s') is *causally explained* by D.

3   The Causal Calculator

The Causal Calculator (CCALC), a software system designed and implemented at the University of Texas[2], enables the representation of commonsense knowledge about action and change, and implements the $C+$ language that was described in the previous section [8]. CCALC has been applied to several challenge problems, e.g. [10]. Action descriptions in $C+$ are translated by CCALC first into the language of causal theories and then into propositional logic (via the process of completion of the definite causal theories) [8]. The models of the propositional theory correspond to paths in the transition system described by the original action description in $C+$. The input files of CCALC consist of comments, declarations and $C+$ causal laws regarding some action domain. These files are written in the input language of CCALC. The functionality of CCALC includes, among other things, computation of three kinds of tasks that can be represented as CCALC queries:

– *Prediction.* Given (partial or complete) information about an initial state and a complete sequence of actions, compute the information that holds in the resulting state (if there exists one) of a given transition system (action description) D.
– *Postdiction.* Given partial information about an initial state, (partial or complete) information about a resulting state, and, possibly, a (partial or complete) sequence of actions that leads from the initial state to the resulting one, compute some additional information that holds in the initial state (if there exists one) of a given transition system (action description) D.
– *Planning.* Given (partial or complete) information about an initial state and (partial or complete) information about a resulting state, compute the complete sequence of actions (if there exists one) that will lead from the initial state to the resulting one of a given transition system D.

In all of these computational tasks information (partial or complete) about intermediate states may be provided.

4   Specification of Open Electronic Societies

Artikis et al. [1] present a theoretical framework for providing executable specifications of *open computational societies*. A computational society is considered *open* (in [1]) if the following properties hold: First, the internal architecture of the agents is not publicly known. An open society can have members with different internal architectures. Therefore, open societies are treated as *heterogeneous* ones. Moreover, there is no direct access to an agent's mental state and so we can only infer things about it. Second, the members of the society do not necessarily have a notion of global utility [3]. Members may fail to, or choose not to, conform to specifications in order to achieve their individual goals. In addition

---

[2] http://www.cs.utexas.edu/users/tag/cc/

to these properties, in open societies 'the behaviour of the members and their interactions cannot be predicted in advance' [5].

In this framework the computational systems are viewed from an external perspective, that is to say, we are not concerned with the internal architecture of the agents. Three key components of computational systems are specified, namely the *social constraints, social roles* and *social states.* The specification of these concepts is based on and motivated by the formal study of legal and social systems (a theory of institutionalised power [11] and a theory of normative positions [12]) and traditional distributed computing techniques (state transition systems [13]). In [1] the social constraints and roles are specified by means of a subset of the 'full version' of the Event Calculus [7]. In this paper, we mainly focus on the social constraints and specify them with the use of the $C+$ language; a formalism with explicit state transition semantics. We illustrate the use of $C+$ by specifying a Contract-Net Protocol.

4.1   Social Constraints

We maintain, as in [1], the standard, in the study of social and legal systems, long established distinction between *permission, physical capability* and *institutionalised power* (see e.g. [11]). In other words, there is no standard (built-in) relationship between the actions that an agent is *physically capable* of performing, the actions that an agent is *permitted* to perform and the actions that an agent is *empowered* (by the institution/society) to perform. Accordingly, the social constraints specify the following:

- What kind of actions 'count as' [11] *valid* ('effective', 'meaningful') actions. Distinguishing between *valid* and *invalid actions* enables the separation of meaningful from meaningless activities.
- What kind of actions (valid, invalid) are *permitted.* Determining the *permitted, prohibited, obligatory actions* enables the classification of the agent behaviour as 'legal' or 'illegal', 'social' or 'anti-social', etc.
- What are the *sanctions* and *enforcement policies* that deal with 'illegal', 'anti-social' behaviour.

Valid actions are specified as follows: An action counts as a *valid action* at a point in time if and only if the agent that performed that action had the *institutionalised power* [11] to perform it at that point in time. Differentiating between valid ('meaningful') and invalid ('meaningless') actions is of great importance in the analysis of agent systems. For example, in an auction, the auctioneer has to determine which bids are *valid* and therefore, which bids are *eligible* for winning the auction.

On the second level of specification, the definition of *permitted, prohibited* or *obligatory* actions is *application-specific.* In other words, there is no standard definition of permitted actions — permitted actions may be defined in different ways in various computational societies. The same holds for the specification of sanctions; that is, the definition of sanctions may vary from one computational society to the other.

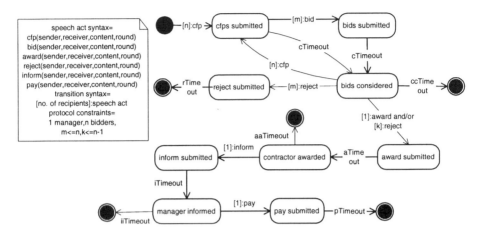

Fig. 1. The UML State Transition Diagram of the CNP [1].

5   A Contract-Net Protocol

In [14] we describe an abstract producer/consumer (APC) scenario where producers sell information to consumers. In this scenario the producers are explorer agents that map out the distribution of oil in their environment and consumers are cartographer agents that initiate Contract-Net Protocols to acquire the maps from the explorers. The main roles of the society that executes the Contract-Net Protocol (CNP) are that of the *cartographer* and that of the *explorer*. A brief description of the CNP (Figure 1) is the following: a manager issues a call for proposals (*Cfp*) for a particular task to a set of bidders. Bidders submit their bids (if they are interested) to the manager. The manager then has three choices: (i) award a particular bid, (ii) reject the received bids, or (iii) issue a new *Cfp* incrementing the *protocol round*[3]. In the first two cases the protocol ends. In the third case the protocol starts again. Actions must be performed according to specified deadlines/timeouts.

Table 1 demonstrates a number of rigid, fluent and action constants and a causal law of the $C+$ representation of the CNP. Each of the constants will be described in the following sections. Two causal laws define when a state transition takes place. The first one states that in order to change state at least one action should take place (we employ an abbreviation provided by the input language of CCALC to represent this law):

$$\textbf{caused } \bot \textbf{ after } \neg d_1 \wedge \neg d_2 \wedge \ldots \wedge \neg d_n \text{ for every action constant } d_i \quad (3)$$

The second one states that at most one action can take place at each time:

$$\textbf{noconcurrency} \quad (4)$$

---

[3] The protocol round is a parameter of the description of the actions that agents perform (i.e. action constant). It is represented by an integer that, initially, is equal to 1 and is incremented by 1 each time a cartographer performs a valid *Cfp*.

Table 1. A partial $C+$ description of the CNP.

Notation:
roleName ranges over { *Cartographer, Explorer* }
agent,agent2,e,c range over { *Cartographer$_1$, Explorer$_1$,..., Explorer$_n$* }
perf ranges over { *Cfp, Bid, Award, Reject, Inform, Pay* }
content,content2 range over a finite set of task descriptions
round ranges over $\mathbb{N}^+$, the set of positive integers

Rigid constant (domain is { *Cartographer, Explorer* }):
Role_of (agent)

Simple fluent constant (boolean domain):
ValidActionHappened(agent, perf, agent, content, round)

Statically determined fluent constants (boolean domain):
Pow(agent, perf, agent, content, round),
Permitted(agent, perf, agent, content, round),
Obliged(agent, perf, agent, content, round),
Sanction(agent)

Action constant (boolean domain):
Valid(agent, perf, agent, content, round)

Causal laws:
inertial c for every simple fluent constant c

The result of these two laws is that in order to change state exactly one action should take place. Such a restriction can be lifted in different specifications of the CNP. We introduce this restriction just to simplify our presentation. A number of the remaining causal laws of the formalisation of the CNP are described in the following sections.

5.1   Social Constraints

Valid Actions. The actions that the agents perform can be classified as *valid* or *invalid*. An action will count as [11] a valid one if and only if the agent that performed that action had the institutional power to perform that action. For example, the specification of valid actions could be represented by a static law of the form:

$$\textbf{caused} \ \ Valid(agent, perf, agent2, content, round) \ \textbf{if}$$
$$Pow(agent, perf, agent2, content, round) \wedge \tag{5}$$
$$Action(agent, perf, agent2, content, round)$$

In (5) *Valid* is an action constant representing valid actions, *Action* is an action constant representing the agents' actions and *Pow* is a fluent constant representing the institutional powers of the agents. Constraint (5) states that if an *agent* performs an action (represented by *Action*) and he has the institution-alised power to perform that action (represented by *Pow*) then this action is considered valid. However, we cannot represent such a constraint in the $C+$ language, since it is not possible to have an action constant both in the head and the body of a causal law[4]. Since it is not possible to specify such a constraint in $C+$, we have defined the following constraint (in order to approximate constraint (5)):

$$\textbf{nonexecutable } Valid(agent, perf, agent2, content, round) \textbf{ if}$$
$$\neg Pow(agent, perf, agent2, content, round) \tag{6}$$

According to constraint (6) a *Valid* action is **nonexecutable** if the agent that performs it does not have the institutionalised power to do so. In other words, an agent can perform a valid action only if he has the power to do so.

In the applications we have in mind we want to keep track of the valid actions as they occur. Therefore, we use *ValidActionHappened*, a *simple fluent constant* to record the fact that a valid action has happened. We are aware that encoding fluents (that represent the history) in a state description in this manner runs counter to the spirit of transition systems. We are currently examining alternative formalisations that avoid this issue.

Since valid actions are determined in terms of institutional powers, it is important to specify these powers. We represent the institutional powers with the use of a statically determined fluent. There are several rules that define ('statically determine') the *Pow* fluents. For example, the power to *Bid* is defined as:

$$\textbf{caused } Pow(e, Bid, c, content, round) \textbf{ if}$$
$$ValidActionHappened(c, Cfp, e, content, round) \wedge$$
$$\neg CTimeoutHappened(round) \wedge \tag{7}$$
$$\forall content2 : \neg ValidActionHappened(e, Bid, c, content2, round)$$

The above law specifies that an explorer (represented by the e variable) has the power to *Bid* if the following conditions hold:

- A cartographer (represented by the c variable) has performed a *Valid Cfp*.
- A *CTimeout* has *not* taken place.
- The explorer has *not* performed a *Valid Bid*.

Only when these conditions hold, will an explorer be empowered to perform a *Bid*. Such a *closed-world assumption* regarding the specification of powers is defined as follows:

$$\textbf{default } \neg Pow(agent, perf, agent2, content, round) \tag{8}$$

In other words, in the absence of information to the contrary (e.g. constraint (7)), no agent is empowered to perform an action.

---

[4] Such a constraint can be represented in the extended $C+$ [15] (see Section 8).

Apart from the actions that agents perform, the specification of the CNP includes a number of additional actions/events, the *timeout events*. These events are *system events*, in the sense that they are performed by a global clock, and are considered valid. The timeout events are represented by a number of action constants. Due to space limitations, we have omitted the representation of these constants and the laws that are associated with them from the presented analysis.

Permitted Actions. We now specify what actions are *permitted* during the execution of the CNP. As for the *Pow* fluent, we represent permitted actions with the use of a statically determined fluent, the *Permitted* fluent. For this variation of the CNP we have specified that an agent is permitted to perform an action *if and only if* he has the power to perform that action:

$$\textbf{default } \neg Permitted(agent, perf, agent2, content, round) \tag{9}$$

$$\begin{aligned} \textbf{caused } &Permitted(agent, perf, agent2, content, round) \textbf{ if} \\ &Pow(agent, perf, agent2, content, round) \end{aligned} \tag{10}$$

The specification of the permitted actions is *application-specific*. In different settings we might specify permissions in a different manner. For example, we might forbid agents in certain circumstances to perform actions even if they are empowered to do so.

Apart from the valid and permitted actions, the specification of the CNP includes definitions of *obligations, sanctions* and *social roles*. We represent obligations and sanctions with the use of *statically determined fluent constants* (as in the case of powers and permissions). We represent social roles [1] with *rigid constants* (see Table 1) on the assumption that the agents do not change their roles (i.e. *Cartographer, Explorer*) during the execution of the CNP. Of course, such a restriction can be lifted in different specifications of the CNP. Due to space limitations, we omit the presentation of the causal laws that are associated with obligatory actions, sanctions and social roles.

5.2   Social States

The *action signature* of the formalisation of the CNP can be specified as:

- $\sigma^{rf} \supseteq \{ValidActionHappened, Pow, Permitted\}$. σ^{rf} is the set of rigid and fluent constants.
- $\sigma^{act} \supseteq \{Valid\}$. σ^{act} is the set of action constants[5].

The action description D of the CNP is a set of causal laws, some of which were presented in the previous sections of this paper. This action description defines a transition system where:

- The vertices are *states* of D, i.e. interpretations of σ^{rf}.
- The edges (s, a, s') are *causally explained* by D.

---

[5] For clarity reasons we omit the parameters of the constants.

Consider a CNP with only two agents, cartographer C and explorer E, and the transition (s, a, s') where:

- $s \supseteq \{Pow(C, Cfp, E, MapUK, 1), Permitted(C, Cfp, E, MapUK, 1)\}$.
- $a = \{Valid(C, Cfp, E, MapUK, 1)\}$.
- $s' \supseteq \{Pow(E, Bid, C, MapUK, 1), \neg Permitted(E, Bid, C, MapUK, 1),$ $ValidActionHappened(C, Cfp, E, MapUK, 1)\}$.

In order to determine whether this transition is an edge of the transition system defined by D we need to determine if this transition is *causally explained* by D (see Section 2). Intuitively, constraints (9) and (10) specify (in this example) that we cannot have a state where an agent is empowered, but not permitted, to perform an action. Because of constraint (10), $T_{static}(s') \supseteq$ $\{Permitted(E, Bid, C, MapUK, 1)\}$. Consequently, $s' \not\models T_{static}(s')$ and (s, a, s') is not causally explained by D. (s, a, s') is not an edge of the transition system defined by D. Similarly, we can determine which state transitions *are* edges of the transition system defined by D.

6   Executing the Specifications

We used the $C+$ language to declare the constants (Table 1) and specify the laws of the formalisation of the CNP. The $C+$ formalisation is translated to the input language of the Causal Calculator (CCALC) in order perform a number of computational experiments with our formalisation of the CNP. For example, constraint (6) is written in the following way in the input language of CCALC[6]:

```
nonexecutable valid(Agent, Perf, Agent2, Content, Round) if
            -pow(Agent, Perf, Agent2, Content, Round).
```

To test our formalisation of the CNP we performed a number of queries to CCALC. The tested formalisation includes four agents; cartographer1 occupies the role of the cartographer and explorer1, explorer2, explorer3 occupy the role of explorer. The task description is mapUK and the protocol can have at most two rounds (1..2).

(Prediction) Query 1. We are in the *bids considered state* (see Figure 1). The following events have taken place: all of the explorers have performed valid bids about mapUK (the protocol round is 1) and the first timeout (i.e. cTimeout) has elapsed. cartographer1 is empowered to perform a new cfp or to award or reject the three bids he has received. In this state, can cartographer1 perform a valid reject to explorer1 regarding mapUK at the first protocol round? If yes, what are the new powers associated with cartographer1? CCALC determines that the valid(cartographer1,reject,explorer1,mapUK,1) action is executable. The resulting state includes the following powers:

---

[6] See [8, 10] for details about the syntax of the input language of CCALC.

```
1: pow(cartographer1, award, explorer2, mapUK, 1);
   pow(cartographer1, award, explorer3, mapUK, 1);
   pow(cartographer1, reject, explorer2, mapUK, 1);
   pow(cartographer1, reject, explorer3, mapUK, 1).
```

(Planning) Query 2. Given the initial state of the CNP, i.e. `cartographer1` is empowered to issue a `cfp` to the three explorers, is it possible to find a state (within 16 steps[7]) where some `explorer` has been awarded some task and `cartographer1` is permitted to `award` some other `explorer`? This question can be represented by the following `CCALC` query:

```
:- query
maxstep :: 1..16;
0: pow(cartographer1, cfp, explorer1, mapUK, 1),
   pow(cartographer1, cfp ,explorer2, mapUK, 1),
   pow(cartographer1, cfp, explorer3, mapUK, 1);
maxstep:
[\/Content \/Agent \/Round |
   validActionHappened(cartographer1,award,Agent,Content,Round)] &
[\/Content2 \/Agent2 \/Round2|
   permitted(cartographer1,award,Agent2,Content2,Round2)].
```

`CCALC` finds no solution within 16 steps. Due to constraints (3) and (4), the maximum number of steps in this CNP is 16. Since there is no solution within 16 steps (starting from the initial state), the following statement holds: In this specification of the CNP it is not possible to reach a state where the agent occupying the role of the cartographer has awarded an agent and is permitted to award another agent.

(Postdiction) Query 3. Initially, `cartographer1` was permitted to issue a `cfp` to `explorer3` regarding `mapUK` at the first protocol round. After one step `cartographer1` is empowered to `award` `explorer1` regarding `mapUK` at the first protocol round. What can we say initially about the powers of `cartographer1`?

`CCALC` finds several solutions. The action (that leads from the initial state to the resulting one) at each solution was `cTimeout`, i.e. the timeout after a `valid` `cfp`. In all of these solutions, the initial state included the following:

```
0: permitted(cartographer1, cfp, explorer3, mapUK, 1);
   validActionHappened(explorer1, bid, cartographer1, mapUK, 1);
   pow(cartographer1, cfp, explorer3, mapUK, 1).
```

6.1 Evaluation

In our experiments (four agents, two task descriptions, two protocol rounds) `CCALC` generated big theories: over 2000 atoms, over 20000 rules and over 30000 clauses. Prediction queries were computed in 45 seconds on a Pentium IV 2GHz,

---

[7] A *step* is a transition from one state to the next. Due to constraints (3), (4), in this specification of the CNP a step takes place when exactly one action takes place.

1GB RAM computer. Increasing the number of agents, task descriptions or protocol rounds (scalability of the formalisation) leads to larger theories that make CCALC compute queries in a less timely fashion.

Based on our formalisation of the CNP and its execution in CCALC, we have reached the conclusion that CCALC does not seem suitable for on-line activities, that is, activities during the actual execution of the societies. On-line activities include, among other things, the compilation of the social states (i.e. what powers, permissions, obligations and sanctions are associated with each member of the society at each time point) during the simulations of electronic societies. The compilation of the social states is performed with the use of prediction queries. The computation of prediction queries, as shown above, is not performed sufficiently fast for on-line activities.

As already mentioned, in previous work [1] we formalised the CNP with the use of a sub-set of the 'full version' of the Event Calculus [7] and implemented this formalisation in the Prolog programming language. This implementation, a software tool called the *Society Visualiser* (SV), can compute prediction queries regarding the Event Calculus specification of the CNP. Given the same experimental settings, the Society Visualiser computed prediction queries sufficiently fast for on-line activities.

Unlike CCALC, the Society Visualiser cannot compute planning and postdiction queries. This limitation of the SV can be lifted by employing an Event Calculus planner [7] (see Section 7 for a use of such a planner in the context of specification of interaction protocols). This is an issue that we have not yet addressed.

CCALC can be used in various settings/configurations with respect to the simulation/actual execution of computational societies. One possible setting is the following: CCALC acting as a central entity in a computational society, monitoring (or even auditing) the execution of the members of the society and producing the social states of the society. In this setting, members of the computational systems can query CCALC in order to determine the powers and normative positions relevant to them and their peers. In a different setting, the functionality of CCALC may be distributed. For example, each member of the computational system may have a module with similar computational capabilitites as CCALC. This module will produce the powers and normative positions of the agent that it belongs to.

7   Related Work

There are several approaches in the DAI literature that come close to the objectives of our work. A few notable examples are work on *e-institutions* [16], work on *commitment protocols* [17] and work on *negotiation protocols* [2].

Yolum and Singh [17] present a formalisation of the *commitment protocols* [6] in terms of the *Event Calculus*. Moreover, they employ an abductive Event Calculus planner [7] in order facilitate the planning of the agents that execute these protocols. Our work is very similar to [17]. We employ CCALC to perform planning as well as prediction and postdiction queries regarding the specifications of computational systems that are formalised in $C+$.

Bartolini and colleagues [2] focus on the specification of *negotiation mechanisms* (rather than *negotiation strategies*) and argue that the *negotiation rules* should be made explicit at the design stage of a multi-agent system rather than being implicitly specified in the minds of the participants of the negotiation protocols. Furthermore, they propose a software framework for automated negotiation that provides several functionalities to the participants of the negotiation protocols. For example, agents can access the negotiation rules at any time in order to determine/modify their strategies.

Our work has similaritites with the work of Bartolini et al. [2]. Negotiation protocols can be viewed as types of 'open computational societies' (as these have been defined in this paper). There is no access to the internals of the participants of the negotiation protocols. Moreover, the participants are negotiating in order to achieve their antagonistic goals. Like [2], our motivation is that the rules (i.e. social constraints) of such computational systems should be explicitly (and formally) defined at the design stage of the computational systems. The software framework for automated negotiation of [2] bears some similarities with the way we use CCALC for the execution of the specifications of the computational systems. In particular, *negotiation hosts* [2] provide similar functionalities to the ones that CCALC provides (especially when CCALC is used as a central entity — see Section 6.1).

A key difference between our work and the work reviewed here is that we explicitly represent the institutional powers of the members of the computational systems and differentiate between institutional power, physical capability and permission. Jones and Sergot [11] pointed out that " 'empowering' is not an *exclusively* legal phenomenon, but is a standard feature of any norm-governed organisation where selected agents are assigned to specific roles (in which they are empowered to conduct the business of that organisation)". The concept of *institutionalised power*, although being a standard feature of any norm-governed institution/society, is not explicitly represented in the reviewed approaches. Singh [18] provides an implicit representation of the concept of institutional power in his work on commitment protocols. Moreover, the reviewed approaches do not differentiate between institutional power, permission and physical power.

8   Summary and Current Work

The functionality of the Causal Calculator (CCALC) regarding the specification of open electronic societies can be summarised as follows:

- CCALC implements $C+$, a language with explicit state transition semantics, support for effects (direct and indirect) of actions and default ('inertia') persistence of fluents from state to state. As shown in Sections 2 and 5.2 an action description in $C+$ defines a transition system of a particular kind.
- CCALC provides a tool that enables the society designers and the agent designers to 'validate' the specifications of the social laws after the design stage.

The validation is mainly performed with planning and postdiction queries. These type of queries enable the designers to prove various properties of the protocols/society specifications (e.g. see Query 2 in Section 6). In this way, agent designers can perform planning queries in an off-line phase (i.e. before the commencement of the actual execution of the societies) in order to determine whether it is desirable or not to deploy their agents in societies.

– CCALC does not seem suitable for on-line activities (i.e. activities during the actual execution of the societies) such as the compilation of the social states (i.e. what powers, permissions, obligations, sanctions, roles are associated with each member of the society at each time point) during the simulations of electronic societies.

Current work includes two main directions. Sergot [15] presents an extension of the $C+$ language that includes direct support for specification of (a version of) the 'counts as' relation for action [11] and a treatment of permitted/forbidden states, actions and paths (in the spirit of [19]). We are currently formalising our framework using extended $C+$ in order to directly use laws of the form (5) and not approximate them with laws of the form (6).

Furthermore, we are investigating ways of improving the computation of CCALC rules resulting from the society specification shown. More specifically, we aim to improve the way CCALC computes prediction queries. In order to do that, we aim to identify and discard the $C+$ laws that are not relevant to the (prediction) query in question. In this way, CCALC will have as input a smaller number of $C+$ laws and will therefore generate a smaller number of rules and clauses (via the process of completion of the definite causal theories [8]).

It is important to note that CCALC is a tool under development and, therefore, some of these issues (large number of atoms and scalability) may be addressed in future versions[8].

Acknowledgements

This work has been undertaken in the context of the EU-funded ALFEBIITE Project (IST-1999-10298). We would also like to thank Vladimir Lifschitz and Joohyung Lee from the Action Group at the University of Texas for their suggestions regarding the $C+$ language and CCALC.

References

1. Artikis, A., Pitt, J., Sergot, M.: Animated specifications of computational societies. In Castelfranchi, C., Johnson, L., eds.: Proceedings of Conference on Autonomous Agents and Multi-Agent Systems (AAMAS). (2002) 1053–1062
2. Bartolini, C., Priest, C., Jennings, N.: Architecting for reuse: A software framework for automated negotiation. In: Proceedings of Workshop on Agent-Oriented Software Engineering (AOSE). (2002) 87–98

---

[8] We used ccalc 2.04b for the computational experiments.

3. Rosenschein, J., Zlotkin, G.: Rules of Encounter: Designing Conventions for Automated Negotiation among Computers. The MIT Press (1998)
4. Hardwick, M., Bolton, R.: The industrial virtual enterprise. Communications of the ACM **40** (1997) 59–60
5. Hewitt, C.: Open information systems semantics for distributed artificial intelligence. Artificial Intelligence **47** (1991) 76–106
6. Singh, M.: A social semantics for agent communication languages. In: Issues in Agent Communication. LNCS 1916. Springer (2000) 31–45
7. Shanahan, M.: The event calculus explained. Artificial Intelligence Today (1999) 409–430
8. Giunchiglia, E., Lee, J., Lifschitz, V., McCain, N., Turner, H.: Nonmonotonic causal theories. (2001)
9. Smith, R., Davis, R.: Distributed problem solving: The contract-net approach. In: Proceedings of Conference of Canadian Society for Computational Studies of Intelligence. (1978) 217–236
10. Lee, J., Lifschitz, V., Turner, H.: A representation of the zoo world in the language of the causal calculator. In: Proceedings of Fifth Symposium on Formalizations of Commonsense Knowledge. (2001)
11. Jones, A., Sergot, M.: A formal characterisation of institutionalised power. Journal of the IGPL **4** (1996)
12. Sergot, M.: A computational theory of normative positions. ACM Transactions on Computational Logic **2** (2001) 522–581
13. Fagin, R., Halpern, J., Moses, Y., Vardi, M.: Reasoning About Knowledge. The MIT Press (1995)
14. Pitt, J., Kamara, L., Artikis, A.: Interaction patterns and observable commitments in a multi-agent trading scenario. In: Proceedings of Conference on Autonomous Agents (AA), ACM Press (2001) 481–489
15. Sergot, M.: The language $(\mathcal{C}/\mathcal{C}+)^{++}$. ALFEBIITE Deliverable D6(2) (2002)
16. Esteva, M., Rodriguez-Aguilar, J., Sierra, C., Garcia, P., Arcos, J.: On the formal specifications of electronic institutions. In Dignum, F., Sierra, C., eds.: Agent Mediated Electronic Commerce. LNAI 1991. Springer (2001) 126–147
17. Yolum, P., Singh, M.: Flexible protocol specification and execution: Applying event calculus planning using commitments. In Castelfranchi, C., Johnson, L., eds.: Proceedings of Conference on Autonomous Agents and Multiagent Systems (AAMAS). (2002) 527–535
18. Singh, M.: An ontology for commitments in multiagent systems: Towards a unification of normative concepts. Artificial Intelligence and Law **7** (1999) 97–113
19. van der Meyden, R.: The dynamic logic of permission. Journal of Logic and Computation **6** (1996) 465–479

Modeling Agents and Their Environment

James J. Odell[1], H. Van Dyke Parunak[2], Mitch Fleischer[2], and Sven Brueckner[2]

[1] James Odell Associates, 3646 West Huron River Drive, Ann Arbor
MI 48103-9489, USA
email@jamesodell.com
http://www.jamesodell.com
[2] Altarum, PO Box 134001, Ann Arbor
MI 48113-4001, USA
{van.parunak,mitch.fleischer,sven.brueckner}@altarum.org
http:// www.erim.org/~vparunak/

Abstract. Without an environment, an agent is effectively useless. Cut off from the rest of its world, the agent can neither sense nor act. An *environment* provides the conditions under which an entity (agent or object) can exist. It defines the properties of the world in which an agent will function. Designing effective agents requires careful consideration of both the physical and communicational aspects of their environment.

1   Introduction

Agents need to operate and exist within an environment. Figure 1 illustrates a common view that agents perceive their environment though sensors as well as effect actions on it. [Pfeifer, 1999; Weiss, 1999; Russell, 1995] For example, a Stock agent can receive an event indicating that quantities of a particular part are low. The agent then decides whether more parts need to be ordered and, if so, put out a general call-for-proposal so that interested vendors can reply. When proposals arrive, the Stock agent will choose and notify the winning vendor. This model implies that agents interact *via* an environment. Even direct communications (such as vender notification) must occur through some medium. In other words, the environment provides the appropriate conditions that enable interaction among agents. This insight, largely overlooked in the design of purely electronic agents, is particularly critical for managing agents that are situated in the physical world.

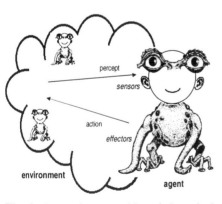

Fig. 1. Agents interact with and through their environment.

F. Giunchiglia et al. (Eds.): AOSE 2002, LNCS 2585, pp. 16–31, 2003.
© Springer-Verlag Berlin Heidelberg 2003

2   What Is an Environment?

One of the key properties of agents is their autonomy. However, autonomy is not an all-or-nothing issue. Practically speaking, agents can neither be totally free of external dependencies nor completely reliant on them. They always depend on external factors to some degree.

> An *environment* provides the conditions under which an entity (agent or object) exists.

In other words, it defines the properties of the world in which an agent can and does function. An agent's environment, then, consists not only of all the other entities in its environment, but also those principles and processes under which the agents exist and communicate. Designing effective agents requires careful consideration of all of these factors when designing their environment.

A canonical example of agents situated in an environment is an ant colony. Ants interact with one another largely through chemicals, called *pheromones*, that they deposit in the environment and then sense to guide their actions. Numerous individual interactions yield the emergent development of paths through the environment. However, the environment is more than just a communication channel. Agents depend both on tangible, physical support and on other agents. Two aspects, then, are critical for agent environments (and the formation of paths): the physical and the communicational.

3   Physical Environment

The particular kind of environment that biological agents (animals and plants) require for survival is referred to as their ecological niche. Edward O. Wilson defines *ecological niche* as: "The range of each environmental variable such as temperature, humidity, and food items, within which a species can exist and reproduce." [Wilson, 1975] While artificial agents can have different requirements for survival, they still require an ecological niche, or physical environment, to support them.

> The *physical environment* provides those principles and processes that govern and support a population of entities.

3.1   Principles of a Physical Environment

The laws of physics provide us with the fundamental truths that are essential to the world in which we live. For example, a physicist could use the study of particle dynamics to describe the causes for motion and the way in which bodies influence each other. For such descriptions, we obtain principles such as the conservation of energy, gravity, sound waves, and fluid dynamics. In Karl Sims' agents, the same principles apply because his "creatures" were bred to swim, run, and fly in a world whose laws of physics are almost identical to ours. [Sims, 1994a, 1994b] In contrast, the ant's environment has its own particle dynamics. For example, ants may only move from one place to an adjacent place; no two ants may occupy the same place at the same time; and yet pheromones may be aggregated when separate ants deposit them at the same place. The concepts of diffusion and evaporation are also part of the agent environment. This makes it possible for pheromones to spread to neighboring places as well as evaporate over time. Similarly, a statement of fundamental qualities is also required for agent environments. Here, each agent-based system must identify and define those fundamental truths forming the ground of its system.

For agents, principles of the physical environment can be thought of as laws, rules, constraints, and policies that govern and support the physical existence of agents and objects. Basic characteristics for an agent environment can include [Weiss, 1999; Russell, 1995]:

- **Accessibility.** To what extent is the environment known and available to the agent? An environment is effectively accessible if the agent can access the environmental state relevant to the agent's choice of action. Another consideration is whether the available resources are ample or restricted.
- **Determinism.** To what extent can the agent predict events in the environment? The environment is deterministic when the next state of the environment can be determined by the current state and the actions selected by the agents.
- **Diversity.** How homogeneous or heterogeneous are the entities in the environment?
- **Controllability.** To what extent can the agent modify its environment?
- **Volatility.** How much can the environment change while the agent is deliberating?
- **Temporality.** Is time divided in a clearly defined manner? For example, do actions occur continuously or discrete time steps or episodes?
- **Locality.** Does the agent have a distinct location in the environment which may or may not be the same as the location of other agents sharing the same environment. Or, are all agents virtually collocated? Also, how is a particular locality expressed (e.g., coordinate system, distance metrics, relative positioning)?

3.2   Processes of a Physical Environment

Formally, an environment can be expressed as a two-tuple [Parunak, 1996]:

$$Environment = <State_e, Process_e>$$

Where, State$_e$ is a set of values that completely define the environment. The structure, domains, and variability of these values are not constrained by this definition, and differences in these features are responsible for much of the interesting variation among different kinds of environments. The state also includes the agents and objects within the environment. *Process$_e$* is an autonomously executing mapping that changes the environment's state, *State$_e$*. "Autonomously executing" means that the process runs without being invoked from any outside entity. In computational terms, an environment has its own virtual CPU. The important feature of this definition of environment is that the environment itself is active. It has its own process that can change its state–which includes the agents and objects within the environment–independently of the actions of its embedded agents[1].

---

[1] The exact nature of the coupling between agents and their environment depends on how state and process are modeled in each: as a discrete-event or time-based dynamical system. The former involves a discrete state with a symbol-manipulation processing style; the later, a continuous state with difference or partial differential equations. See [Parunak, 1996] for more details.

In an agent environment, the primary purpose of these processes is to implement the environmental principle. For example, the gravitational field is a principle that can be implemented with a process that attracts entities in a prescribed manner. In other words, the falling of an apple to earth can be regarded as the process of gravity in action.

In the case of ants, the environment is not a passive conduit for information. Instead, it actively processes pheromones in three ways. It aggregates pheromone deposits from separate ants at the same place (thus realizing a primitive form of information fusion). It evaporates pheromones over time (thus providing a novel form of truth maintenance). Finally, it propagates pheromones to neighboring places (thus disseminating information). Experiments show that these mechanisms are critical to the formation of paths. More generally, environmental activity means that the environment may change even when the agents living in the environment do not take action.

Different physical environments will be required for different kinds of agents–and vice versa. With artificial agents, much more than physics is happening because much of the environment is information intensive. In ant-based environments, the pheromones *are* information. In many defense-related agent systems, the information-intense environment includes satellite telemetry, body- and vehicle-based communications technology, and geographic positioning grids. In agent-based supply chains, information about orders and resources is a major component of the system.

To support the varied information requirements of such agent-based systems, a common processing platform would be useful. This platform would provide a foundation upon which agent applications could build to leverage their own specific environmental requirements. Such a platform–whether the agents are implemented as software, hardware, or a combination of both–would consist of:

- **Application Support** contains the applications, as well as all management and support services for the entities supported by the environment, such as directory and ontology services, query, mobility, security, and firewalls.

- **Communication and Transportation** packages, routes, verifies, and transmits data required for the application support layer. It provides a general-purpose service that has no application dependencies and the type of data does not matter.

- **Physical Linkage** specifies the physical and electrical characteristics of the bus. Typically, this involves the hardware that converts the characters of a message into electrical signals for transmitted messages and electrical signals into characters for received messages. This can include standard physical interfaces such as controllers, actuators, sensors–as well as road networks and pallets.

The processes for an agent's physical environment may be implemented in either hardware or software; however, at some point (Physical Linkage) the environment must be realized in some material form. For example, CAN (Controller Area Network) has developed hardware for Physical Linkage layer. They have also developed software for the Application Support layer that supports CAN controllers and interface devices [http://www.omegas.co.uk/CAN/].

The processes for an agent's physical environment may be implemented in either hardware or software; however, at some point (Physical Linkage) the environment must be realized in some material form. For example, CAN (Controller Area Network) has developed hardware for Physical Linkage layer. They have also developed software for the Application Support layer that supports CAN controllers and interface devices [http://www.omegas.co.uk/CAN/].

Some work has already been done to define the standard services required for agent-based physical environments. The FIPA (Federation of Intelligent Physical Agents) *Agent Platform* defines an abstract architecture for agent deployment and is summarized in Fig. 2. [FIPA, 1998] The existence of layered protocol such as FIPA and ISO shows that people already have an intuition about the importance of relating agents to the rest of the world.

- **Agent management system** (AMS) can be implemented as a single agent that supervises access to and use of the agent platform. The AMS maintains a directory of logical agent names and their associated transport addresses for an agent platform. The AMS is responsible for managing the lifecycle of the agents on the platform and actions such as authentication, registration, deregistration, search, and mobility requests.

- **Agent platform security manager** (APSM) is responsible for maintaining security policies for the platform and infrastructure. The APSM is responsible for run-time activities, such as communications, transport-level security, and audit trails. Security cannot be guaranteed unless, at a minimum, all communication between agents is carried out through the APSM.

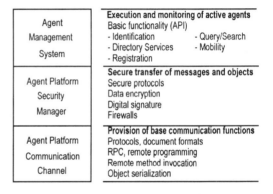

Agent Management System	Execution and monitoring of active agents Basic functionality (API) - Identification - Query/Search - Directory Services - Mobility - Registration
Agent Platform Security Manager	Secure transfer of messages and objects Secure protocols Data encryption Digital signature Firewalls
Agent Platform Communication Channel	Provision of base communication functions Protocols, document formats RPC, remote programming Remote method invocation Object serialization

Fig. 2. The agent platform specified by FIPA.

- **Agent platform communication channel** provides a path for basic interchange between agents, agent services, AMS, and other agent platforms. It must at least support IIOP. Agents can reach agents on any number of other platforms through the Agent Communication Channel. Ways of communicating include using blackboard or message-based communication; point-to-point, multicast, or broadcast; push or pull; and synchronous or asynchronous.

In spite of the acronym, the FIPA architecture focuses almost entirely on the electronic environment, and does not address the physical environment. As such, it does not address the real potential of an active environment to provide emergent system-level behavior. As stated earlier, every agent has an environment. However, such environment can be consciously used in special ways to get more powerful interaction.

A standard that does address the physical environment is the ISO/OSI model, depicted in Fig. 3 [2]. This model describes how communications should occur between computers on any network, and has been adopted as a general "open" network com-

---

[2] Guy Genilloud, Guy has proposed a flexible translation for linking FIPA to OSI via CORBA in [Genilloud, 1997].

munication standard. In principle, anything that conforms to the standard can communicate, electronically, with anything else that conforms to the standard.

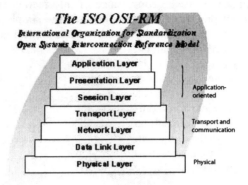

Fig. 3. The ISO 7498 Open Systems Interconnection (OSI) model [ISO 1994].

3.3   Population of a Communication Environment

An environment is an inhabited place; i.e., it is populated. An agent's environment might or might not contain other entities, and it might be open or closed. An environment's population is the totality of entities under its consideration. For the environment of the canonical software ant, this population would consist of food, pheromones, and other ants. For a real-world ant, it would also include earth, twigs, trees, and picnics. For a stock agent in a supply network, it would include physical inventory, road and rail networks, packaging conventions, and so on.

4   Communication Environment

In *individualist* agent environments, agents are viewed as independent entities; whereas in *collectivist* environments, agents are viewed as interdependent. While an agent can operate by alone, the increasing interconnections and networking require a different kind of agent–one that can communicate effectively with other agents. A communication environment provides two things. First, it provides the principles and processes that govern and support the exchange of ideas, knowledge, information, and data. Second, it provides those functions and structures that are commonly employed to enhance communication, such as roles, groups, and the interaction protocols between roles and groups. In short:

> The *communication environment* provides those principles, processes, and structures that enable an infrastructure for agents to convey information.

4.1   Communication, Interaction, and the Social Agent

4.1.1   Communication

Basically, communication is the conveyance of information from one entity to another. The nature of this transfer can range from the simple to the complex. For example, a satellite could periodically send one bit to inform ground control that it is still functioning correctly; in contrast, the information exchanged within the US Senate to negotiate tax cuts can appear quite chaotic. In contrast, broadcasts such as television commercials do not necessarily result in communication. A signal may go out, but if you are not listening or watching, how can the commercial convey information?

(a) Two agents with no communication activity.

(b) One agent transmitting to another, but not communicating.

Figure 4 illustrates the difference between transmission and communication. In Fig. 4(a), neither agent has any transmission activity. Figure 4(b) indicates that the agent on the left transmitted information through the environment, but was not received by the other agent. Communication, however, requires that the information

(c) One agent communicating with another agent (but not interacting).

Fig. 4. Agent transmission versus communication.

transmitted by one agent results in a state change of another (Fig. 4(c)). In the case of television commercials, perceiving its transmission means that your senses have at least detected it. The perception could involve you buying the advertised goods, throwing a shoe at the television screen, or simply choosing to do nothing. Either way, communication has occurred because the act of sensing and deciding involves a state change by the receiver.

4.1.2   Interaction

Proving that communication has occurred, however, requires us to know that the inner state of the receiving agent has in fact changed. We are not advocating that the communication environment possess such mentalistic knowledge–only that such an environment be present so that transmission and communication can occur. However, knowing that a transmission was received can be important to the sending agent. One useful way to determine if communication has occurred is when an interaction results. Figure 5(a) depicts one agent communicating with another. Here, the other agent responds, but the original agent does not receive the responding transmission. (The original agent, then, cannot know for a certainty whether communication occurred.) In other words, there was no interaction between the two agents. *Interaction*[3] requires two-way communication (i.e., a reciprocal effect), as illustrated in Fig. 5(b). Interaction, then, not only defines exchange of information, it confirms that the original transmission was in fact received by the other agent. In other words, the original

---

[3] The action or influence of agents on each other; i.e., having a reciprocal effect.

agent can infer that its transmission was communicated to the other agent as soon as a response is received–even if the response communicates only that the responder did not understand the original message.

4.1.3   Social Environment

In agent-based systems, communication and interaction are commonly employed together. Furthermore, agent-based communication can even involve patterns of interaction, or *interaction protocols*. From simply requesting the price of a product to conducting elaborate contract-bidding activities require that some agree-upon approach be in place to facilitate interactive communication–without which the conveyance of information could easily result useless Babel. Such a situation could be considered *social*.

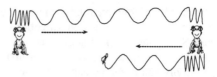

(**a**) One agent communicating with another agent; and the other agent transmitting a response, but not communicating or interacting.

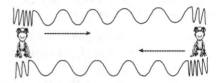

(**b**) Two agents interacting interacting.

Fig. 5. Agent communication versus interaction.

> A *social environment* is a communication environment in which agents interact in a coordinated manner.

As illustrated in Fig. 6, the social environment is a subset the communication environment. In other words, not all communication is social (as defined above), but all social activity requires communication.

4.2   Principles of a Communication Environment

Communication principles provide us with the fundamentals that are essential for interactions, customs, norms, values, commitments, dependencies, and so on, that constitute an agent society. The canonical ant's communication environment is simple: all communications between ants are via pheromones. Here, the communication involves a two-step process: the ant deposits pheromones that act as information for other ants, while the "other ants" query the local environment for the presence of pheromones. In short, these ants participate in a social communication by way of environmental substances, rather than directly with each other. Additionally, some ant societies have multiple kinds of pheromones: one for exploring and one when returning with returning food. The net effect is informing a society of ants about how to find food or home–whichever

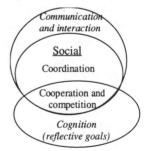

Fig. 6. Social environment: co-ordination–and possibly cooperation, and competition

is useful for any given ant. If an ant is foraging, information about where to find food is useful; if the ant has food, directions on how to get back the colony would be useful. Such interaction is social because it provides the ants with an infrastructure for the colony because it produces coordination among the ants.

Supply-chain agents can have elaborate collaborative protocols acquiring and delivering goods and services along value-adding chains. Defense-related protocols, require different interaction policies at different command levels. Both direct and indirect interaction can be employed as interaction strategies in thee applications.

In rich multiagent societies (MAS), several principles are required to facilitate the communication environment.

− **Communication language** - Agents communicate to understand and be understood. The formal study of communication has three aspects: syntax, semantics, and pragmatics. Agent-based social environments must define the principles required to address these aspects. Additionally, it must define the types of messages that will be employed (e.g., assertions, queries, replies, requests, and denials) and the ontology. Some of the common agent communication languages (ACL) languages include FIPA ACL, and KQML.

− **Interaction protocols** - An agent interaction protocol (AIP) describes a communication pattern as an allowed sequence of messages between entities and the constraints on the content of those messages [Odell, 2000a and 2000b]. Examples of AIPs include the contract net protocol, Dutch auction protocol, and publish/subscribe protocol. FIPA has standardized more than a dozen AIPs [FIPA, 2000].

− **Coordination strategies** - Agents communicate to achieve their goals and the goals of the social group in which they participate. Cooperation, competition, planning, and negotiation are common principles used to perform activities in a shared environment. AIPs can be associated with each of these strategies.

− **Social policies** - The permissions and obligations that dictate acceptable social behavior. They include being able to apply and enforce these policies across distributed agents and systems. The general focus here is on the application and management of policies on agents and groups of agents–not the detailed management of agent lifecycles and areas currently addressed by FIPA agent management specifications. Other considerations for social policy can involve:

  o Implicit *vs* explicit rules; not all rules are specified in advance: i.e., learning what the rules are or adjusting to a change in rules, emergence of rules, unconscious rules, when tradition becomes a social norm, or policy.

  o Different levels: of influence/power (e.g., the ROI on obeying or violating a rule, strength and "evaporation" of rule; rules don't always stick around, rules as memes, language use.)

− **Culture** - a set of values, beliefs, desires, intentions, trust, morality. These can determine the characteristics of the above. FIPA vs. KQML cultural differences; English vs. other different-culture language (e.g., Navajo). Culture also affects language, interaction protocol, and social policies (implicit & explicit).

4.3   Processes of a Communication Environment

An agent's communication environment provides processes that enable agents to interact productively[4]. In particular, it must provide:

– **Interaction management** - managing the interactions among entities to ensure that they are adhering to the selected agent interaction protocol (AIP). AIP adherence can be maintained by those agents participating in the protocol, so that the environment does not need to be involved. However, trusting that each agent can and will adhere to and ensure correct AIP interaction may not be enough to ensure social order. An environment-level control can be implemented as an AIP-manager agent. Did you get what you wanted/needed/expected;

– **Language processing and policing** - where the language parses correctly, it parses correctly but is wrong (evidence or contradictory), or is correct but inappropriate within the agent's context.

– **Coordination strategy services**

  o **Directory service** - locating agents can be supported by white-page (individual), yellow-page (industry), or green-page (offered services) methods. In the physical environment, this directory is used to provide information about where the agent is physically; in the social environment, it provides information about an agent's role or the services that it can provide.

  o **Mediation services** - acting through an intermediate agency. Specialized agents could be established in the environment to act as a communication's intermediary for activities such as transaction management or ontology translation. Environment-level mediation can be implemented using specialized agents.

– **Policy enforcement service** - control of the agent by its environment or social group. The range of possible mechanisms for enforcing policy mechanisms can range from social sanctions to a complete withdrawal of supporting services for the non-conforming agent.

– **Social differentiation** - the process whereby a group or community becomes separate or distinct. To ensure success, groups will institutionalize and employ roles for their members. An agent can play multiple roles in multiple groups.

– **Social order** - the production of a structure of relationships among social agents [Castelfranchi, 2000]. Social order can be the result of formal policies as well as emerge via self-organizing mechanisms. The later is a emergent social pattern of its own, such as the stock market. The former has to do with managing the conditions of an agent society as a whole employing a non-accidental and non-chaotic pattern of interactions. For example, auctions employ strict social patterns. Such a mechanism can be employed to control undesirable emergent patterns that need to be remedied. For example, when stock prices rise or fall by too many points in a session, trading curbs are triggered.

---

[4] The agent communication *channels* are defined as part of the physical environment. The communication *environment* uses those channels to convey information.

4.4   Population of a Communication Environment

As mentioned earlier, a physical environment consists of all those entities in the physical environment. In contrast, an agent's social environment consists of

- those social units in which the agent participates,
- the roles that are employed for social interaction,
- all the other members who play roles in these social units.

Each social unit, or *group*, is a set of agents associated together by some common interest or purpose. There are three reasons for creating groups.

- **Intragroup associations** - Groups are commonly formed to foster or support the interaction of those agents within the group. Here, the group provides a place for a limited number of agents to interact among themselves. For example, such agents might wish to exchange information or seek safety in numbers.

- **Group synergy** - Social units can be formed to take advantage of the synergies of its members, resulting in an entity that enables products and processes that are not possible from any single individual. Corporations, unions, and governments are examples of such social units.

- **Intergroup associations** - Social units also serve as an entity with interactive capability. Here, a group is a set of agents that interact with other sets of agents. Recurrent patterns of interaction define roles, and frequently associated roles are usually considered as defining (sub)groups.

A group can be empty if no agents participate in the group; its collection can also contain a single participating agent or multiple agents. Groups have a separate identity within a larger whole and can be composed of agents, as well as other groups[5]. Furthermore, groups can become social actors influencing group processes and outcomes, as well. For example, most business organizations interact with sector groups such as industry, technology, agriculture, and government; and each of these can influence the other as well as consist of their own subgroups. In this way, an agent social environment can be thought of as a society where agents interact in a more or less ordered community.

A *role* is an abstract representation of an agent's function, service, or identification within a group. In other words, each role is a class of agents that participates in pattern of dependencies and interactions in a prescribed manner. A pattern of dependencies is an important component of a role. For example, if agent A is a customer, there must be some agent B on whom A depends for goods and services, while B depends on A for money. For AIPs, roles define which actions are permitted for a certain class of agents. For example, an agent playing the customer role may request goods, but not supply them; the supplier has the opposite requirements. [Parunak, 2001a]

---

[5] Some debate exists about whether a single agent can be its own group, because each agent can be thought of as having both a social and physical existence. There is another debate about whether or not a group has the status of an agent (holonics vs. AALAADIN).

5   Spatial and Temporal Considerations

An agent's environment–physical or social–must occupy both space and time. Agent populations abide and interact, their processes occur, and their environmental principles are defined over that same temporal space. Agent space and time involves the notion of agent *place*, along with two of its primary attributes: *extent*, and *locality*.

5.1   Place

Each agent environment can be thought of as a whole or it can be subdivided into discrete *regions*. Regions partition the agent's physical environment into smaller physical units–where each region may have different or unique characteristics. For example, a grid structure can be defined for the ants so that discrete locations are provided for both the ants and their pheromones, as well as the ability to form pheromone paths. Region definition can also include geographic-based attributes, such as lakes, hills, roads, and structures. In social environments, regions spatially partition the environment into groups and roles. In contrast, temporal space can define unique characteristics for each place in time.

Region specification can include various constraints. For example, in a physical environment we may wish to specify that no two ants may occupy the same place at the same time; yet, we may permit accumulation of multiple units of pheromones. In a social environment, business organizations might be limited to having one person occupying the role of president at any point in time.

Set theoretic distinctions can be made between membership and set. For example, if Agent A belongs to Organization B and Organization B belongs to a federation of organizations C, A does not necessarily belong to C. However, if an Agent A is an element of Set B and Set B is contained by Set C, then Agent A is also an element of Set C.

The region size is determined based on the design granularity: meter-sized places are unrealistic for small ants; micron-sized regions would push the limits of current technology. For example, Pacific Gas & Electric specifies a longitude and latitude within two meters accuracy called a *geocode*. The geocode place size for PG&E, then, is four-square meters. In combat examples, a similar grid structure and size is also employed.

In another example, SRI proposes a new top-level Internet domain called .geo. [SRI, 2000] In a .geo system, the Earth would be partitioned into cells based on latitude and longitude. Dedicated servers would hold the data registered to Web sites within its geographical domain, as well as maps and other information. As illustrated in Fig. 7, places can be arranged hierarchically so that search engines could direct queries to one type of server, depending on what the Web user was looking for. The Internet user could then query for cardiac bench surgery in North America or men's clothing stores in Ann Arbor, Michigan. In this way, web user would never need to use unwieldy .com addresses; the geo-enabled search engine translate a geographic location into web sites registered at that location.

Geodata Placement

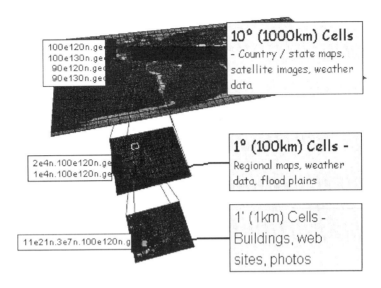

Fig. 7. Places has a hierarchy of geographic placement. [SRI, 2000]

5.2   Extent

Agent environments must exist in some designated area (or volume) in space and time. Region designations can be expressed in various ways: length/width/height, location points indicating the boundary, memory or disk locations, to and from dates, and so on. The shape of physical space can also be considered here. Social space can expressed in terms the degree of interaction. For example, this could include the number of people you work with, the "degree of separation" between one website and any other website. For example, the environment could be a flat plane or a torus space. In other words, agent environments require an extent that defines its size, shape, and boundaries. Effects of boundary conditions can also be addressed here.

5.3   Locality

The ability to locate an entity is an important factor, particularly in agent communication. *Locality* provides the position or situation of a region or entity. Often the locality of the region can become an agent's locality. Locality can be addressed in an absolute and relational manner.

Absolute locators are locators that assign a unique address to each agent or region. Simple two-dimensional grid system employ column-row designations, geospatial systems employ longitude-latitude-altitude designations, and IT systems employ unique identifiers in the form of keys and unique reference IDs.

In contrast, *relational* locality means that an agent's location can be described as relative to another location. For instance in a connected graph, one agent could be related to other agents, which could in turn be related to other agents. Connected graphs such as the web, electric power networks, or networks of colleagues are examples of where entity's location can be described relative to other entities. In a planar environment an agent's relative neighborhood could be based on physical proximity rather than edges between nodes. For example in a simple two-dimensional grid like a checkerboard, one square can be characterized as diagonal to, or to the side of, and so on. This kind of locality is particularly useful when an entity is constrained to interact with the region of the environment that is near it. For example, ant agents may only move from one region to an adjacent region, and their pheromones might "flow" into neighboring regions where pheromone strength lessens the further it travels.

Locality is useful for several reasons. One primary reason is that communicating with an agent requires that the message can actually be delivered to the agent. The sender of a communication may not be required to know where the receiver is physically located, but at some point the communication service must find the receiver to deliver the message. Another reason is to provide location information. For example, a dispatcher agent might need to know the physical location of its various resources to schedule effectively. Lastly, agent movement or interaction may be based on, or limited to, physical proximity. For example, an ant agent may only move to or interact with the region that is immediately adjacent to it. In contrast, a flea or grasshopper-style agent may jump multiple squares in a single bound, but is limited to a maximum of five.

Also, it should be noted that since regions are positioned in an environment, the notion of locality applies to them, as well. Furthermore, an agent's locality can be based on the locality of the region it occu-

Fig. 8. Location-aware computing. [Buderi, 2001]

pies. For example in the .geo example (Fig. 8), each region had an absolute locator within which other entities are contained. In this way, an agent's locality can be defined in a discrete space, instead of locating the agent one large, continuous environment.

Hybrid approaches using absolute and relative locality are also useful. AT&T's "bat" transmitters are a good example of a hybrid approach. "Bats" are small battery-powered ultrasonic transmitters that can be worn on a belt or placed inside objects. They broadcast a uniquely identifying 48-bit pulse to receivers embedded every 1.5 meters in ceilings as illustrated in Fig. 8. (For example, about 800 are placed around AT&T's three-story lab in Cambridge, England.) Based on the known position of each receiver, the bearer's precise position can be calculated. In other words, the transmitters and receivers have absolute locators: the transmitter has an 48-bit ID and the receivers are coordinate-based. Then, based on relative proximity, the coordinates of the transmitter can be derived from the receivers' coordinates.

Using this location information, zones can be established around objects and people. If a person's zone overlaps an object's zone, the person becomes the temporary owner of the device, be it a workstation, digital camera, telephone or anything else.

There is no logging on and everything the user creates–documents, pictures, memos– is automatically stored in the user's personal files. [Baduri, 2001] In other words this technology, known as *location-aware computing*, detects when you're online and what kind of device you're using. Many companies now have development efforts that involve location-based computing: AT&T's Sentient Computing R&D (described above), IBM's Pervasive Computing Division, HP's CoolTown project, the ubiquitous-computing projects at Intel and Xerox. [Want, 2001] Microsoft is another such company with its new HailStorm services platform. When someone tries to get in touch with you, the HailStorm system will detect your network location and level of accessibility: Are you at your desk? In a meeting? In transit? Depending upon the answer, the system will e-mail, page or call you.

6   Postlogue

By 2015, the social computing is expected by some to morph into ecological or symbiotic computing. John Seely Brown, chief scientist of Xerox suggests that structural matter (atoms) and computing (bits) will become inseparable.

> Zillions of sensors, effectors and logical elements (made of organic and inorganic materials) will be interconnected via wireless, peer-to-peer technologies, producing smart, malleable stuff used to build smart appliances, buildings, roads and more. It is during this era that computers disappear. In their place, nearly every physical artifact harbors some computationally based brainpower that helps it know where it was, what was near it, when it was moved and so on. In a way, the inorganic world took on organic properties, using computing to transparently modulate responses to the environment. [Brown, 2001]

References

Brown, John Seely, "Where Have All the Computers Gone?," *Technology Review*, 104:1, February 2001, 2001, pp. 86-87.

Buderi, Robert (2001) "Computing Goes Everywhere,", 104:1, *Technology Review*, pp. 53-59.

Castelfranchi, Cristiano (1998) "Modeling Social Action for AI Agents,", 103:1-2, *Artificial Intelligence*, pp. 157-182.

Castelfranchi, Cristiano (2000) "Engineering Social Order," *Engineering Societies in the Agent World*, Springer, pp. 1-18.

FIPA (1998) *Foundation for Intelligent Physical Agents FIPA98 Agent Management Specification*, Geneva, Switzerland, Oct. 1998. (http://www.fipa.org)

Genilloud, Guy (1997) "Flexible Translation for Integrating CORBA and OSI," *Proceedings of Distributed Object Computing in Telecommunications (DOCT 97)*, Object World, Frankfurt, Germany.

ISO (1994) ISO/IEC and ITU-T, "Information Processing Systems, OSI Reference Model: The Basic Model," Standard 7498-1, Recommendation X.200, 1994.

Odell, James, H. Van Dyke Parunak, and Bernhard Bauer (2000a) "Representing Agent Interaction Protocols in UML," *First International Workshop on Agent-Oriented Software Engineering 2000*, Paolo Ciancarini and Michael Wooldridge, eds., pp. 58-65.

Odell, James, H. Van Dyke Parunak, and Bernhard Bauer (2000b) "Extending UML for Agents," *Proc. of the Agent-Oriented Information Systems Workshop at the 17th National Conference on Artificial Intelligence*, Gerd Wagner , Yves Lesperance, and Eric Yu, eds., Austin, TX, pp. 3-17.

Parunak, H. Van Dyke (1997) "'Go to the Ant': Engineering Principles from Natural Agent Systems," *Annals of Operations Research*, volume 75, pp. 69-101.

Paranak, H. Van Dyke and James Odell (2001a) "Representing Social Structure using UML," *Proc. of the Agent-Oriented Software Engineering Workshop, Agents 2001 conference*, Paolo Ciancarini Michael Wooldridge, and Gerhard Weiss eds., Agents 2001conference, Montreal, Canada, Springer.

Parunak , H. V. D., S. A. Brueckner, J. Sauter, and J. Posdamer [2001b] Mechanisms and Military Applications for Synthetic Pheromones. In *Proceedings of Workshop on Autonomy Oriented Computation*, 2001.

Pfeifer, Rolf and Christian Scheier (1999) *Understanding Intelligence*, MIT Press, Cambridge, MA.

Russell, Stuart and Peter Norvig (1995) *Artificial Intelligence: A Modern Approach*, Prentice-Hall, NJ.

SRI (2000) http://www.icann.org/tlds/geo1/ModCE/E_TLD_POLICIES_FIN.htm

Sims, Karl (1994a) "Evolving Virtual Creatures," *Siggraph Proceedings*, July 1994, pp. 15-22.

Sims, Karl (1994b) "Evolving 3D Morphology and Behavior by Competition," *Artificial Life I. Proceedings*, R. A. Brooks and P. Maes, eds., MIT Press, Cambridge, MA, pp. 28-39.

Want, Roy and Bill Schilit (2001), "Expanding the Horizens of Location-Aware Computing," IEEE Computer, August 2001, pp. 31-34.

Weiss, Gerhard, ed. (1999) *Multiagent Systems: A Modern Approach to Distributed Artificial Intelligence*, MIT Press, Cambridge, MA.

Wilson, Edward O. (1975) *Sociobiology*, (abridged edition), Belknap Press, Cambridge, MA

Validation of Multiagent Systems
by Symbolic Model Checking

Massimo Benerecetti[1] and Alessandro Cimatti[2]

[1] Dept. of Physical Sciences - University of Naples "Federico II", Napoli, Italy
[2] IRST - Istituto Trentino di Cultura, 38050 Povo, Trento, Italy
bene@na.infn.it,cimatti@irst.itc.it

Abstract. Multiagent Systems are increasingly complex, and the problem of their verification and validation is acquiring increasing importance. In this paper we show how a well known and effective verification technique, symbolic model checking, can be generalized to deal with knowldge–level properties of multi-agent systems. The approach is fully amenable to the reuse of data structures used in symbolic model checking, Binary Decision Diagrams in particular, to deal with extremely large state spaces, and could, in principle, be integrated in the muti–agent systems development process. A preliminary implementation of the approach in the NuMAS system shows promising results.

1 Introduction

Multiagent systems and paradigms are increasingly used in different application domains, ranging from e-commerce to safety-critical control systems.

The problem of verification for such formalisms is becoming increasingly important. Recent work focuses on modeling various apects of multiagent systems. For instance, [1] focuses on modeling and validating specification of social laws of agents in electronic societies by employing a tool for causal theories. [12] proposes a model–checking–based approach to validate early requirements in Tropos [14], a novel software developement methodology based upon knowlegde level concepts for the design of multiagent systems. [18] proposes a methodology to translate Agent UML sequence diagrams [21] into a textual form which can then be processed by the Spin model-checker [16]. Similarly, [17] proposes a translation methods from Agent UML protocol diagrams into Promela, the input language of Spin, to check reacability properties of agent protocols.

All this work is essentially limited to model and validate those aspects of multiagents systems expressible by standard validation methodologies for concurrent reactive systems, emerged in mainstreem computer science. On the other hand, both traditional [22] and more recent [14] specification methodologies for multiagent systems employ knowldge level notions, such as beliefs, goals, intentions. Despite this, very little work has been proposed to deal with the problem of validating properties at the knowldge level (see for instance [7, 23]).

This paper proposes a framework to specify and validate, by means of model checking techniques, knowledge level properties of agents, which might, in principle, be integrated in the development process of multiagent systems. In [7] the

F. Giunchiglia et al. (Eds.): AOSE 2002, LNCS 2585, pp. 32–46, 2003.
© Springer-Verlag Berlin Heidelberg 2003

formalism of Multi–Agent Temporal Logic was introduced as a first step towards lifting one of the most successful verification techniques, model checking [9], for the validation of multi-agent systems. Multi–Agent temporal logic combines, within a single framework, the aspects of temporal logic, used to reason about the temporal evolution of finite-state processes, with agent-related aspects such as belief, desire and intention. The algorithms for model checking multi-agent temporal logic presented in [7] is, however, based on an "explicit-state" approach to model checking, that requires the enumeration of each state in the model.

In this paper, we reformulate the theory of multi-agent model checking in order to allow for the use of *symbolic* model checking techniques [19]. The main feature of symbolic model checking is the ability to manipulate *sets of states* rather than single states. Such sets are efficiently represented and transformed by means of Binary Decision Diagrams (BDDs) [8]. Symbolic model checking techniques can often lead to dramatic improvements over the explicit-state approach. The resulting theory allows for a direct reuse of the standard temporal logic model checking techniques, and the related tools, and extends them naturally to deal with the multi-agent aspects of the logic. Symbolic model checking for multi-agent systems has been implemented in the NuMAS system, a symbolic model checker for temporal logic, developed on top of the NuSMV symbolic model checker [24]. The preliminary results are extremely promising, and open up the possibility to verify hierarchical systems.

This paper is structured as follows. In Section 2 we describe Multi-Language Temporal Logic. We present the underlying intuitions, and define the language and the semantics (the Multi-Language Finite State Machine) as an extension of the standard notion of Finite State Machine. Finally we present the general algorithm for model checking. In Section 3 we describe the special case of Multi–Agent Temporal Logic, a logic to model beliefs of agents. In Section 4 we present the model checking algorithm in terms of symbolic, BDD-based data structures and transformations. Finally, in Section 5 we outline the results, discuss related and future work, and draw some conclusions.

2   The Multi-language Temporal Logic

2.1   Language

A basic assumption underlying our work is that the framework should allow to model the fact that processes (or agents) have the ability to predicate over the status of other processes (or agents). The framework we use is therefore based on the notion multiple "views", i.e. distinct but related "theories", each describing the model that a process has about another process (or agent). We use what we call "bridge operators" (such as for instance belief, desire, intention operators) to express the fact that a process predicates over another one. When views are organized in a tree hierarchy, they can be thought of as representing processes which predicate over other agents, at different levels of nesting. Figure 1 depicts the case of a hierarchical structure of the views, which is the case we focus on in the paper. The idea there is to associate to each (level of) nesting of bridge operators a process evolving over time. Each view corresponds to a

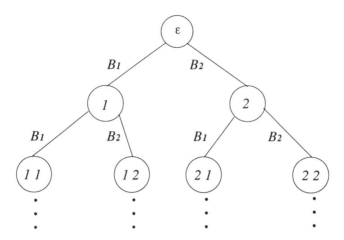

Fig. 1. The structured views for a two-processes multi-language system.

possible nesting of bridge operators. For instance, when analyzing the session of an authentication protocol (see e.g. [3]), it should be able to express the fact that principal 1 believes that its peer 2 believes that it is talking to 1. In the following, we will refer to the entities (e.g. processes) as agents. Without loss of generality, we will limit the ascription capabilities to "belief", and consider only the case of at most one bridge operator among two views. (In the general case, belief, desire and intention can coexist in the framework.)

In the following, let $I = \{1, ..., n\}$ be the set of process indexes. Formally, we call a view any element of I^*, i.e. the set of finite strings of process indexes (including the empty string ϵ). Intuitively, each view denotes a theory in figure 1. We associate a language $\mathcal{L}_\alpha$ to each view $\alpha \in I^*$. Intuitively, each $\mathcal{L}_\alpha$ is the language used to express what is true (and false) in the process of view α.

The language of each view has the following structure. First, in each view α, we have a set of atoms (propositions) of the language. With P_α we denote a subset of the atoms of α, called *local atoms*. In each view, *bridge operators* $\mathcal{B} = \{\mathbf{B}_1, ..., \mathbf{B}_n\}$ are used to construct *bridge atoms*, special propositional atoms obtained by applying any bridge operator $\mathbf{B}_i$ to any $\phi \in \mathcal{L}_{\alpha i}$, resulting in $\mathbf{B}_i \phi$. Intuitively, bridge atoms are used to state a relation on what holds in different views. The formulae of a view are built with the standard applications of the boolean connectives $\neg$ (negation) and $\vee$ (disjunction). Furthermore, in order to express statements on the temporal evolutions of the agents, we allow for the use of the temporal operators of CTL [11], a propositional branching-time temporal logic widely used in formal verification. The temporal operators are $\mathsf{EX}\,\phi$ (ϕ might hold at next time instant), $\mathsf{E}\,(\phi\,\mathsf{U}\,\psi)$ (it might be the case that ϕ holds at a certain time future and until then ψ holds), and $\mathsf{EG}\,\phi$ (ϕ might hold for all future time instants). Temporal operators are compactly characterized by $\mathsf{E}\,(\phi\,\mathsf{U}\,\psi) \leftrightarrow (\psi \vee (\phi \wedge \mathsf{EX}\,\mathsf{E}\,(\phi\,\mathsf{U}\,\psi)))$ and by $\mathsf{EG}\,\phi \leftrightarrow (\phi \wedge \mathsf{EX}\,\mathsf{EG}\,\phi)$. A thorough description is presented in [11].

Given a hierarchy of views, we define a *Multi-Language Temporal Logic language* (MLTL–language) as the smallest CTL language containing, for each α, the set of local atoms P_α and the bridge atoms $\mathbf{B}_i\phi$, for any formula ϕ of $\mathcal{L}_{\alpha i}$.

2.2 Semantics

In the following we generalize the basic notion of Finite State Machine, which is the basis for CTL model checking, to the case of multiple languages, in order to extend CTL model checking to Multi-Language temporal logics.

In model checking, a process is modeled as a Finite State Machines (FSM), i.e. a tuple $F = \langle S, J, R, L \rangle$, where S is a finite set of states, $J \subseteq S$ is the set of *initial states*, the transition relation R is a total binary relation on S, and $L : S \to 2^P$ is a *labelling function*, which associates to each state $s \in S$ the set $L(s)$ of atomic formulae true at s.

Intuitively, a FSM is associated with a *computation tree* of states, originating from the set of initial states and constructed by recursively applying the possible transitions. Each path in computation tree represent a possible temporal evolution of the process represented by the FMS. If there is a path in the tree that leads to a state s we say that s is *reachable* in the FSM. MLTL is intended to formalize processes able to predicate over other processes via bridge operators. We interpret a MLTL language on *Multi-Language Finite State Machines* (MLFSM). Intuitively, a MLFSM is a finite set of FSMs, one for each view, together with FSM–FSM connections, called *compatibility relations*, that take into account cross-view relationships, corresponding to the connections between processes captured by bridge operators.

A basic requirement for model checking is to retain finiteness. Therefore, we impose the following restrictions (a thorough discussion of the motivations can be found in [7]). First, the number of views is assumed to be finite. This can be done e.g. by fixing the maximal depth on the nesting of operators. Second, we distinguish the bridge atoms of a view between *explicit* and *implicit* bridge atoms. For each bridge operator $\mathbf{B}_i$ of a view α, there is a finite set of the explicit bridge atoms, $Expl_{\alpha,i} \subset \{\mathbf{B}_i\phi \in \mathcal{L}_\alpha\}$ that contains those bridge atoms of view α which are explicitly given semantics in a MLFSM. The set of implicit bridge atoms $Impl_{\alpha,i} = \{\mathbf{B}_i\phi \in \mathcal{L}_\alpha\} \setminus Expl_{\alpha,i}$ may be infinite. Implicit bridge atoms are given semantics in terms of the explicit ones, by means of compatibility relations.

A compatibility relation $\mathcal{C}_{\alpha,i} \subseteq Expl_{\alpha,i} \times S_{\alpha i}$, constrains the truth of explicit bridge atoms of a view α to the truth values in the views αi. Depending on the "kind" of bridge operator being considered, the compatibility relation may have different properties. In Section 3 we define what constraints the compatibility relations need to satisfy so as to give bridge operators the correct semantics of belief operators. Consider Figure 2, on the left. Two views, ϵ and i, are shown. For the sake of simplicity, the temporal aspects of the associated FSMs (e.g. transitions) are omitted. In ϵ, there are three explicit bridge atoms, $\mathbf{B}_i\phi$, $\mathbf{B}_i\psi$ and $\mathbf{B}_i\sigma$. Each dashed line collects the states of ϵ that have a given explicit belief in their labeling. For instance, $\mathbf{B}_i\sigma$ is in the labeling of 1 and 2, while $\mathbf{B}_i\phi$ is in the labeling of 2, 3, 5 and 6. In general, this association induces a partitioning of

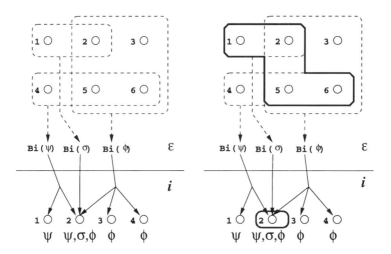

Fig. 2. Explicit bridge atoms, compatibility relation, and model checking.

the set of states in S_ϵ. The multiple-edge solid arrows depict the compatibility relation for each of the explicit bridge atoms. For instance, $\mathcal{C}_{\alpha,i}$ associates to $\mathbf{B}_i\psi$ the set of the states $\{1,2\}$, while $\mathcal{C}_{\alpha,i}(\mathbf{B}_i\sigma)$ is $\{2\}$, and $\mathcal{C}_{\alpha,i}(\mathbf{B}_i\psi)$ is the set $\{2,3,4\}$. The underlying intuition is that when we are in state 4 of ϵ, then we must be either in 1 or in 2 in view i. In general, if process α is in state s, then process αi may be in any of the states compatible with all the explicit bridge atoms (of the form $\mathbf{B}_i\phi$) which are true at s itself.

To summarize, a MLFSM is a triple $\langle\{F_\alpha\},\{Expl_{\alpha,i}\},\{\mathcal{C}_{\alpha,i}\}\rangle$. The first element associates to each view α a FSM F_α with labeling for the set of local and explicit bridge atoms of α. The second element associates to each view a sets of explicit bridge atoms $Expl_{\alpha,i}$. The third element associates to each view α and belief operator $\mathbf{B}_i$ a compatibility relation $\mathcal{C}_{\alpha,i}$. In the following we assume that a MLFSM $\mathcal{M}$ is given.

The notion of satisfiability in a MLFMS is based on the standard notion of satisfiability of CTL formulae in an FSM at a state [11]. This machinery applies unchanged to the local atoms and explicit bridge atoms of a view: the denotation of such an atom is defined in terms of the labeling function associated to the view. The main extension is the interpretation of implicit bridge atoms, based on the interpretation of the corresponding bridge operator through the compatibility relation.

Notice that, even though the notion of MLFSM presented above is very general and does not commit to any particular interpretation of bridge operators, in this paper we mainly concentrate on beliefs. Therefore bridge operators will essentially be interpreted as belief operators. To illustrate the notion of satisfiability in a MLFSM, let us consider the implicit bridge atom $\mathbf{B}_i(\phi\wedge\psi\wedge\sigma)$. The idea is that it is satisfiable in a state s of ϵ if and only if its matrix $(\phi\wedge\psi\wedge\sigma)$ is satisfiable in all the states associated with the explicit beliefs labeling s. For instance, $\mathbf{B}_i(\phi\wedge\psi\wedge\sigma)$ is true in state 1, since $(\phi\wedge\psi\wedge\sigma)$ holds in all the states associated with $\mathbf{B}_i(\sigma)$, i.e. $\{2\}$. $\mathbf{B}_i(\phi \wedge \psi \wedge \sigma)$ is not true in state 4, since $\mathbf{B}_i\psi$ labeling 4 is associated with $\{1, 2\}$ in i, and 1 does not satisfy $\phi \wedge \psi \wedge \sigma$.

Let us call $TrueExpl_{\alpha,i}(s)$ the set of explicit bridge atoms of view α, of the form $\mathbf{B}_i\phi$, which are true at s $(TrueExpl_{\alpha,i}(s) = Expl_{\alpha,i} \cap L(s))$. The states of view αi compatible with s are those states belonging to the intersection, over the explicit bridge atoms true at s, of the sets of states compatible with $TrueExpl_{\alpha,i}(s)$. We extend the compatibility relation to a relation over a *set* of explicit bridge atoms $\mathcal{E} \subseteq Expl_{\alpha,i}$ as follows:

$$\mathcal{C}_{\alpha,i}(\mathcal{E}) = \bigcap_{\mathbf{B}_i\phi \in \mathcal{E}} \mathcal{C}_{\alpha,i}(\mathbf{B}_i\phi)$$

Therefore, the set of states of αi compatible with a state s of α will be simply denoted by $\mathcal{C}_{\alpha,i}(TrueExpl_{\alpha,i}(s))$. We can now define the notion of satisfiability in a MLFSM as an extension of the standard notion of FSM satisfiability (see [11]). The definition runs as follows:

Definition 1. (Satisfiability in a MLFSM) *Let $\mathcal{M}$ be a MLFSM, α a view in I^*, $F_\alpha = \langle S_\alpha, J_\alpha, R_\alpha, L_\alpha \rangle$ the FSM of view α, and $s \in S_\alpha$ a state. Then, for any formula ϕ of $\mathcal{L}_\alpha$, the satisfiability relation $\mathcal{M}, \alpha, s \models \phi$ is defined as follows:*

1. *$\mathcal{M}, \alpha, s \models p$, where p is a local atom or an explicit bridge atom, if and only if $F_\alpha, s \models p$ (same as FSM satisfiability);*
2. *satisfiability of propositional connectives and CTL operators: the same as FSM satisfiability;*
3. *$\mathcal{M}, \alpha, s \models \mathbf{B}_i\psi$, where $\mathbf{B}_i\psi$ is an implicit bridge atom, if andonly if, for all $s' \in \mathcal{C}_{\alpha,i}(TrueExpl_{\alpha,i}(s))$, $\mathcal{M}, \alpha i, s' \models \psi$.*

Furthermore, $\mathcal{M}, \alpha \models \phi$ if and only if, for every $s \in J_\alpha$, $\mathcal{M}, \alpha, s \models \phi$.

2.3   MLTL Model Checking

The model checking problem for MLTL is the problem of determining whether a given MLTL formula is true in a given MLFSM. In [7], a model checking algorithm has been presented based on the idea of labeling the states of a MLFSM with subformulae of the formula to be model checked. In Figure 3 we present a new model checking algorithm for MLTL, based on a set-theoretic approach, which allows for a symbolic implementation by means of BDDs (see Section 4). The algorithm is based on the reformulation of satisfiability in a MLFSM in terms of sets of states, rather than of a single state. In particular, we compute the denotation $[\![\phi]\!]_\alpha$ of the input formula ϕ in the view α, i.e. the set of states of the FSM of α in which ϕ is true. The algorithms assume that the MLFSM $\mathcal{M}$ is a global, read-only data structure. The top level algorithm MLMC(α,ϕ) takes in input a view of $\mathcal{M}$ and a MLTL formula. It computes the denotation ϕ in α, written $[\![\phi]\!]_\alpha$, by calling MLMC-EVAL(α,ϕ) in Line 1. It returns TRUE if the formula is true of the FSM of the view (i.e. it is true at all the initial states of the FSM) (Line 2), FALSE otherwise. The algorithm MLMC-EVAL(α,ϕ) computes

---

Algorithm 1.1 MLMC(α,ϕ)
1   $[\![\phi]\!]_\alpha = $ MLMC-EVAL(α,ϕ);
2   **if** $J_\alpha \not\subseteq [\![\phi]\!]_\alpha$ **then**
3   **return**(FALSE);
4   **return**(TRUE);

Algorithm 1.2 MLMC-EVAL(α,ϕ)
   ▷ $\mathcal{M} = \langle \{F_\alpha\}, \{Expl_{\alpha,i}\}_{i \in I}, \{\mathcal{C}_{\alpha,i}\}_{i \in I} \rangle$
1   **case** ϕ **of**
2   local or explicit bridge atom: $[\![\phi]\!]_\alpha = $ LABELING-EVAL(α,ϕ);
3       $\mathbf{B}_i\psi$ implicit bridge atom:
4               $[\![\psi]\!]_{\alpha i} = $ MLMC-EVAL($\alpha i,\psi$);
5               $\mathcal{C}_{\alpha,i}^{-1}([\![\psi]\!]_{\alpha i}) = \{\mathcal{E} \subseteq Expl_{\alpha,i} \mid \mathcal{C}_{\alpha,i}(\mathcal{E}) \subseteq [\![\psi]\!]_{\alpha i}\}$;
6               $[\![\phi]\!]_\alpha = \{s \in S_\alpha \mid TrueExpl_{\alpha,i}(s) \in \mathcal{C}_{\alpha,i}^{-1}([\![\psi]\!]_{\alpha i})\}$;
7       $\neg\psi : [\![\phi]\!]_\alpha = S_\alpha \setminus $ MLMC-EVAL(α,ψ);
8       $\psi \vee \gamma : [\![\phi]\!]_\alpha = $MLMC-EVAL($\alpha,\psi$) $\cup$ MLMC-EVAL(α,γ);
9   EX ψ: $[\![\phi]\!]_\alpha = $ EX-EVAL(α,MLMC-EVAL(α,ψ));
10   EG ψ: $[\![\phi]\!]_\alpha = $ EG-EVAL(α,MLMC-EVAL(α,ψ));
11   E $(\psi \cup \gamma)$: $[\![\phi]\!]_\alpha = $ EU-EVAL(α,MLMC-EVAL(α,ψ),MLMC-EVAL(α,γ));
12 **end case**
13 **return**($[\![\phi]\!]_\alpha$);

Fig. 3. The MLTL model checking algorithm.

the denotation $[\![\phi]\!]_\alpha$ of the input formula in the input view α. The algorithm is an extension of the CTL symbolic model checking algorithm [19], and implements the definition of satisfiability in MLTL, recursively descending the structure of the formula being evaluated. Lines 7 and 8 take care of the boolean connectives, while lines 9 to 11 take care of the temporal operators, by implementing fix point computations based on the equations presented in previous section. For lack of space, the reader is referred to [19] for the definition of such routines. Line 2 takes care of the base case of local and explicit bridge atoms, whose denotation is derived from the labeling function of F_α. Lines 3-6 take care of the crucial case of implicit bridge atoms. First (Line 4), we compute the denotation in view αi of the argument of the implicit bridge atom $\mathbf{B}_i\psi$, i.e. ψ. This is a simple recursive call to MLMC-EVAL($\alpha i,\psi$), with input the appropriate view below α and the formula ψ. This results in a set of states of αi. Then, following Item 3 of Definition 1, we compute the set of states of view α which satisfy $\mathbf{B}_i\psi$:

$$\mathcal{M}, \alpha, s \models \mathbf{B}_i\psi \text{ iff for all } s' \in \mathcal{C}_{\alpha,i}(TrueExpl_{\alpha,i}(s)), \ \mathcal{M}, \alpha i, s' \models \psi$$

We are, therefore, interested in collecting all the states of α which satisfy the right-hand side of the condition above. Those are the states s such that all the states of αi compatible with s (i.e. $\mathcal{C}_{\alpha,i}(TrueExpl_{\alpha,i}(s))$) satisfy ψ. What we are looking for are the states s such that $\mathcal{C}_{\alpha,i}(TrueExpl_{\alpha,i}(s))$ is included in the set of states of αi satisfying ψ. We can do that in two steps, by observing the following. The intersection of the states of view αi compatible with each element of $\mathcal{E} \subseteq Expl_{\alpha,i}$ consists of a set of states of αi compatible with $\mathcal{E}$. Such a set is intuitively the set of states in which view αi is supposed to be, when α is in any of the states satisfying all the explicit bridge atoms in $\mathcal{E}$. As a consequence, when α is in any of the states satisfying $\mathcal{E}$, the view αi cannot be in any state outside $\mathcal{C}_{\alpha,i}(\mathcal{E})$ (it can only be in a subset of it). Then, any state of α satisfying $\mathcal{E}$ also satisfies any implicit bridge atom $\mathbf{B}_i\psi$ whose argument ψ is true in all the states in $\mathcal{C}_{\alpha,i}(\mathcal{E})$. Therefore, when we need to compute the states of α satisfying the $\mathbf{B}_i\psi$, the first step is to compute all the subset of explicit bridge atoms which are compatible only with states which satisfy the formula ψ. This set is denoted $\mathcal{C}_{\alpha,i}^{-1}(\llbracket\psi\rrbracket_{\alpha i})$, and is defined as follows:

$$\mathcal{C}_{\alpha,i}^{-1}(\llbracket\psi\rrbracket_{\alpha i}) = \{\mathcal{E} \subseteq Expl_{\alpha,i} \mid \mathcal{C}_{\alpha,i}(\mathcal{E}) \subseteq \llbracket\psi\rrbracket_{\alpha i}\} \tag{1}$$

Then, the second step is to collect all the states of α which assign true to any of the subsets of explicit bridge atoms just computed, namely all the states s such that $TrueExpl_{\alpha,i}(s) \in \mathcal{C}_{\alpha,i}^{-1}(\llbracket\psi\rrbracket_{\alpha i})$. The union of all those states of α constitute the denotation of $\mathbf{B}_i\psi$. These are exactly the steps computed in Lines 5 and 6. Line 5 computes the first step, namely the intersection $\mathcal{C}_{\alpha,i}^{-1}(\llbracket\psi\rrbracket_{\alpha i})$ defined above. Line 6 computes the second step, namely the denotation $\llbracket\mathbf{B}_i\psi\rrbracket_{\alpha}$, by collecting the set of states s in α whose set of true explicit bridge atoms (i.e. $TrueExpl_{\alpha,i}(s)$) belongs to $\mathcal{C}_{\alpha,i}^{-1}(\llbracket\psi\rrbracket_{\alpha i})$.

Let us consider now the right part of Figure 2, that depicts the application of the model checking algorithm to the implicit bridge atom $\mathbf{B}_i(\phi\wedge\psi\wedge\sigma)$. The first step is to compute the $\llbracket(\phi \wedge \psi \wedge \sigma)\rrbracket_i$, i.e. $\{2\}$. Then, we collect every state s of ϵ such that all of the states of i associated to it by the the explicit beliefs holding in s are contained in $\{2\}$. This set of states is $\{1, 2, 5, 6\}$, i.e. the union of $\{1, 2\}$, corresponding to the states labeled by $\mathbf{B}_i\sigma$, and $\{5, 6\}$, corresponding to the states labeled by both $\mathbf{B}_i\psi$ and $\mathbf{B}_i\phi$. Indeed, in this example $\mathcal{C}_{\epsilon,i}^{-1}(\llbracket\phi \wedge \psi \wedge \sigma\rrbracket_i) = \{\{\mathbf{B}_i\sigma\}, \{\mathbf{B}_i\psi, \mathbf{B}_i\phi\}\}$. The example also shows that, in order to "invert" the compatibility relation, it is not sufficient to analyze one set of explicit beliefs, but it is necessary to analyze a set (representing the union) of sets (representing the intersection) of explicit beliefs (e.g. $\{\{\mathbf{B}_i\phi, \mathbf{B}_i\psi\}, \{\mathbf{B}_i\sigma\}\}$). The first set, $\{\mathbf{B}_i\phi, \mathbf{B}_i\psi\}$, is part of the result since the intersection of the states associated to $\mathbf{B}_i\phi$ and $\mathbf{B}_i\psi$ is contained in the set $\{2\}$. The second set, $\{\mathbf{B}_i\sigma\}$, is in the result since all the states associated with $\mathbf{B}_i\sigma$ are contained in the set $\{2\}$.

3 The Multi–agent Temporal Logic

3.1 Language and Semantics

In [7, 3, 6] the Multi-Agent Temporal Logic has been presented and applied to the model checking of multi-agent systems and security protocols. As we shall see, MATL is essentially a particular case of Multi-Language Temporal Logic, where the meaning of bridge operators is that of epistemic operators. MATL was designed to express properties of agents specified following the BDI paradigm [22].

In this paper we will restrict ourselves only to beliefs. In MATL the notion of agent (and its beliefs) is built incrementally over the notion of process. Suppose we have a set I of agents. Each agent is seen as a process having beliefs about (itself and) other agents. The main difference with MLTL is that MATL is a MLTL in which each bridge operator $\mathbf{B}_i$ is given the semantics of a belief operator. Therefore the MATL formula $\mathbf{B}_i\phi$, means that agent i believes ϕ. Under this intuition, each view in Figure 1 corresponds to a level of nesting of the belief operators. ϵ represents the view of an external observer (e.g., the designer) which, from the outside, "sees" the behavior of the overall system. The beliefs of agent 1 correspond to the view 1 and are modeled by a process playing 1's role in the system. The beliefs of agent 2 (the view 2) are modeled similarly. The beliefs that 1 has about (the behavior of) agent 2 correspond to the view 12 and are modeled by a process modeling 2's role in the system as seen by agent 1. Things work in the same way for any arbitrary nesting of belief operators.

The semantics of MATL is given by means of particular MLFSMs, called Multi–Agent Finite State Machines (MAFSM), again defined as triples of the form $\langle \{F_\alpha\}, \{Expl_{\alpha,i}\}, \{C_{\alpha,i}\}\rangle$. What makes a MLFSM a MAFSM is the particular structure of the compatibility relations between adjacent views.

Definition 2 (MAFSM). *A MLFSM $\mathcal{M}$ is a MAFSM if for every view α, every explicit bridge atom $\mathbf{B}_i\phi$ of α and every $s \in S_\alpha$ the following conditions hold:*

1. *if $\mathbf{B}_i\phi \in L(s)$, then $s' \in C_{\alpha,i}(TrueExpl_{\alpha,i}(s))$ implies that s' is reachable in $F_{\alpha i}$ and $\mathcal{M}, \alpha i, s' \models \phi$.*
2. *if $\mathbf{B}_i\phi \notin L(s)$, then there exists some reachable state s' of $F_{\alpha i}$ with $s' \in C_{\alpha,i}(TrueExpl_{\alpha,i}(s))$ and $\mathcal{M}, \alpha i, s' \models \neg\phi$*

Condition 1 tells us what are the states in view αi which are compatible with a given state s (satisfying $TrueExpl_{\alpha,i}(s)$), according to the semantics of beliefs, namely that the argument of a beliefs true at a state must be true in all the states reachable from it via compatibility relation. Condition 2, on the other hand, tells us what are the states of view α which actually comply to the semantics of beliefs, i.e. the states which assign truth values to explicit belief atoms in accordance with the semantics of the belief operator. Indeed since $p \supset p \vee q$, it would be unreasonable to allow for a state satisfying the (explicit) belief atom $\mathbf{B}_i p$, yet not satisfying the (explicit) belief atom $\mathbf{B}_i(p \vee q)$ at the same time. This is the kind of situation that this condition prevents. Indeed, let us suppose there is a state s of a view α satisfying $\mathbf{B}_i p$. By Condition 1 of Definition 2, any reachable state s' of view αi compatible with s must satisfy p. By Condition 2 of Definition 2, for s not to satisfy the explicit belief atom $\mathbf{B}_i(p \vee q)$, there must be a reachable state s'' in view αi compatible with s and which does not satisfy $p \vee q$. But, according to Condition 1, all the states compatible with s must satisfy p and, consequently, $p \vee q$ as well, which is impossible.

On the other hand, the definition of MAFSM allows for a state s of a view α satisfying both $\mathbf{B}_i p$ and $\mathbf{B}_i \neg p$. This happens when s is not compatible with any state in view αi (i.e. when $C_{\alpha,i}(TrueExpl_{\alpha,i}(s))$ is empty). This corresponds to the situation where process α, when in state s, ascribes inconsistent beliefs to process αi. Notice however that this kind of inconsistency is of a different nature from the one ruled out by Definition 2. Indeed, allowing a state s not to satisfy $\mathbf{B}_i(p \vee q)$ while satisfying $\mathbf{B}_i p$ would make the specification of α itself inconsistent, while allowing both $\mathbf{B}_i p$ and $\mathbf{B}_i \neg p$ would not. It is clearly possible, though, to rule out also the latter situation, by adding the additional constraint that every state s must be compatible with a non-empty set of the view below (i.e. $\mathcal{C}_{\alpha,i}(TrueExpl_{\alpha,i}(s)) \neq \emptyset$). This would amount to interpret the belief operator $\mathbf{B}_i$ as a modal operator complying to the modal axiom schema D. In the paper, though, we stick to the interpretation of belief operators as operators in modal K.

Finally, notice that, being every MAFSM a MLFSM, the notion of satisfiability in a MAFSM carries over as in MLFSM. Similarly, we can employ the MLTL model checking algorithm in order to check a MATL formula on a MAFSM. In both cases, the only difference is that the semantic structure we work on is now a MAFSM. In Section 2.3 we assumed that the semantic structure on which we execute the Model–Checking algorithm is already given. It is indeed possible to define a synthesis procedure that automatically constructs the suitable MAFSM from a set of independently specified FSMs and a selected set of explicit beliefs, which would lead to significant savings in the modeling phase. Persenting this procedure is out of the scope of this paper (but see [2] for a datailed description).

4   Symbolic Model Checking of Multi–agent Temporal Logic

4.1   Symbolic Model Checking

Model checking is a technique for verifying that a certain system (e.g. a communication protocol, a hardware design), represented as a finite state machine, satisfies a certain property (e.g. deadlock freedom, response to interrupt), expressed as a temporal logic formula. Model checking either provides the guarantee that the system satisfies the property, or returns a *counterexample*, i.e. a description of a system behavior that violates the property, thus pinpointing for the designer bugs which are often judged extremely hard to find with traditional techniques such as testing. *Symbolic* model checking [19] is a particular form of model checking, where the exploration of the FSM is based on the manipulation of sets of states, represented symbolically by means of formulae in propositional logic. In turn, the representation and manipulation of such formulae is based on Ordered Reduced Binary Decision Diagrams (in short BDDs), a canonical form for propositional formulae (see [8] for an overview). This allows for a compact representation and efficient exploration of FSMs of extremely large size, as it is often the case in the case of systems of practical utility. In the following we do not describe the implementation details underlying Binary Decision Diagrams, and we confuse propositional formulae with their BDD representation.

A FSM is represented symbolically with BDDs by introducing a set of (distinct) BDD variables, called *state* variables, one for each atom in P. In the following we write $\boldsymbol{x}$ to denote the vector of state variables. The basic intuition underlying symbolic model checking is to represent a set of states Q by means of a propositional formula $\xi(Q)$ in the state variables $\boldsymbol{x}$. The association ξ is built as follows. The labeling function of the FSM associates a state to a set of atoms holding in it. This is an assignment to the propositional variables. Therefore, a set of states Q is naturally associated with a propositional formula $\xi(Q)$ whose models are exactly the labelings of the states contained in Q. The empty set of states is represented by the formula $False$. The set of states labeled by the atomic proposition ϕ is simply the formula ϕ, while the set of all the states, i.e. $2^{\mathcal{P}}$, is represented by the formula $True$. This clearly shows one of the source of efficiency of the symbolic representation, i.e. that the cardinality of the represented set is not directly related to the size of the BDD. Set theoretic transformations are naturally represented by propositional operations, as follows:

$$\begin{aligned}
\xi(\mathcal{S}\backslash Q) &\doteq \xi(\mathcal{S}) \wedge \neg\xi(Q) \\
\xi(Q_1 \cup Q_2) &\doteq \xi(Q_1) \vee \xi(Q_2) \\
\xi(Q_1 \cap Q_2) &\doteq \xi(Q_1) \wedge \xi(Q_2)
\end{aligned}$$

Each of these operations (e.g. conjunction, negation, disjunction) has a direct counterpart in terms of BDDs: for instance, every time two BDDs are conjuncted, the BDD representation for their conjunction is constructed and returned.

The transition relation of the FSM is a pair-tuple composed of a *current* state (the initial state of the transition), and a *next* state (the resulting state of the transition). To represent transitions, we use another vector $\boldsymbol{x}'$ of propositional BDD variables, called *next state* variables, that represent the value of the propositional atoms after the transition. In the following, we call $\boldsymbol{x}$ *current* state variables to distinguish them from next state variables. With $\xi'(Q)$ we denote the construction of the BDD corresponding to the set of states Q, using each variable in the next state vector $\boldsymbol{x}'$ instead of each current state variables $\boldsymbol{x}$. If Φ is a BDD and $\mathbf{v}$ is a vector of BDD variables, we write $\Phi(\mathbf{v})$ to stress that the BDD Φ depends on the variables in $\mathbf{v}$. We write $[\boldsymbol{x}'/\boldsymbol{x}]$ for the substitution of the current state variables with the next state variables.

A transition is represented as an assignment to $\boldsymbol{x}$ and $\boldsymbol{x}'$. The transition relation R of a FSM is simply a set of transitions, and is thus represented by a formula in the variables $\boldsymbol{x}$ and $\boldsymbol{x}'$, where each satisfying assignment represents a possible transition. Notice that the symbolic representation allows to simulate the application of all transitions to all the states in a given set. For instance, the BDD of the states that can be reached with one transition from a certain set of states Q, called the image of Q, is obtained with the following computation, based on the following operation of quantification: $\exists\boldsymbol{x}.(R(\boldsymbol{x},\boldsymbol{x}') \wedge Q(\boldsymbol{x}))[\boldsymbol{x}'/\boldsymbol{x}]$. The set of reachable states of a machine is obtained by iterating the application of images to the set of initial states, until convergence is reached, i.e. the set of the newly introduced states is empty.

4.2   MLTL Model Checking

We generalize this machinery to the Multi-Language case as follows. For each of the FSM_α in the MLFMS, we use vectors of propositional variables $\boldsymbol{x}_\alpha$, $\boldsymbol{x}'_\alpha$, corresponding to the local and explicit bridge atoms of the FSM, and we have propositional formulae J_α and R_α for initial states and the transition relation of FSM_α, respectively. We write $b_\alpha^i \subseteq x_\alpha$ for the vector of variables corresponding to the explicit bridge atoms of FSM_α of the form $\mathbf{B}_i\phi$. The compatibility relation $\mathcal{C}_{\alpha,i}$ can be represented symbolically with the same mechanism of the transition relation. Since $\mathcal{C}_{\alpha,i}$ is a relation between the explicit bridge atoms in α and the states in αi, it can be seen as a BDD:

$$\mathcal{C}_{\alpha,i}(b_\alpha^i, x_{\alpha i}) \doteq \bigvee_{\langle \mathbf{B}_i\phi \,.\, s_{\alpha i}\rangle \in \mathcal{C}_{\alpha,i}} (\xi([\![\mathbf{B}_i\phi]\!]_\alpha) \wedge \xi(s_{\alpha i}))$$

where $\xi([\![\mathbf{B}_i\phi]\!]_\alpha)$ is the BDD representing the denotation in α of $\mathbf{B}_i\phi$ (i.e. the set of states satisfying $\mathbf{B}_i\phi$), while $\xi(s_{\alpha i})$ denotes the BDD representing the single state $s_{\alpha i}$.

Each satisfying assignment to $\mathcal{C}_{\alpha,i}(b_\alpha^i, x_{\alpha i})$ corresponds to a pair the compatibility relation. Notice that the resulting BDD depends only on a limited subset of the x_i, namely only on the propositional variables corresponding to bridge atoms. The other variables in x_i are irrelevant and, thanks to the reduced form of BDDs, they are automatically simplified away.

Since the formulation of the model checking algorithm given in section 2 is based on the manipulation of sets of states, the symbolic implementation closely follows its structure, with each set theoretic operation being implemented in terms of the corresponding BDD manipulation primitive. The algorithm traverses the structure of the formula being model checked, computing bottom-up the denotation of each subformula. Each denotation is a set of states of one of the FSMs in the MLFSM, and is represented by the corresponding BDD. The base case for a local or explicit bridge atom ϕ (line 2 in figure 3) is handled by simply returning ϕ, i.e. the BDD of the corresponding propositional variable. The cases at lines 6 and 7 for propositional connectives (e.g. $\psi \vee \gamma$) are handled by applying the corresponding BDD transformation (e.g. BDDOR) to the BDDs returned by the recursive evaluation of the arguments ($[\![\psi]\!]_\alpha$ and $[\![\gamma]\!]_\alpha$). The cases of the temporal operators are treated as in standard CTL symbolic model checking. The denotation for $\mathsf{EX}\,\psi$ is the set of the states that can reach the denotation of $[\![\psi]\!]_\alpha$ in one transition of FSM_α. The symbolic representation of this set is obtained via a computation based on existential quantification, called relational product, of the form $\exists x_\alpha'.(R_\alpha(x_\alpha, x_\alpha') \wedge [\![\psi]\!]_\alpha(x_\alpha'))$. Notice how a relational product is a one step logical operation, that allows to explore the FSM in terms of sets of states. This avoids the explicit enumeration of all the transitions applicable to all the states in $[\![\psi]\!]_\alpha$.

The denotation of $\mathsf{E}\,(\phi\,\mathsf{U}\,\psi)$ is computed by means of a least fix point, where the expansion step is given by an EX computation and the termination test is checking if the BDD representing the frontier, i.e. the set of *new* states added to the denotation, is *False*. The case for EG *is* a greatest fix point, implemented in a similar way. The basic step is computing the denotation in α for an implicit bridge atom of the form $\mathbf{B}_i\psi$, at lines 3 to 5 of the algorithm. Line 3 is simply the recursive call that returns the BDD corresponding to $[\![\psi]\!]_{\alpha i}$, representing the set of states of αi where ψ holds. The steps at lines 4 and 5 are computed in terms of a single set of BDD transformations, defined by the following equation:

$$[\![B_i(\psi)]\!]_\alpha(\boldsymbol{b}_\alpha^i) \doteq \forall \boldsymbol{x}_{\alpha i}.(\mathcal{C}_{\alpha,i}(\boldsymbol{b}_\alpha^i, \boldsymbol{x}_{\alpha i}) \supset [\![\psi]\!]_{\alpha i}(\boldsymbol{x}_{\alpha i}))$$

First, we compute the BDD corresponding to the implication of the BDDs for the compatibility relation and for the denotation of ψ. Then, we perform a universal quantification of the state variables of view αi. This results in a BDD in the propositional variables $\boldsymbol{b}_\alpha^i$, that correspond to the explicit bridge atoms with bridge operator $\mathbf{B}_i$. Each assignment to the $\boldsymbol{b}_\alpha^i$ variables identifies a partition in the set of states of view α (see figure 2), that are indistinguishable with respect to the information conveyed by view αi. Each assignment to $\boldsymbol{b}_\alpha^i$ is such that all the assignments to $\boldsymbol{x}_{\alpha i}$, as associated by the compatibility relation, satisfy the BDD representing $[\![\psi]\!]_{\alpha i}$.

5   Results and Conclusions

In this paper we have presented a new approach to the validation of multi-agent systems, based on the use of Multi-Language FSM to describe the system, modal temporal logic specifications to described the properties, and a decision procedure based on model checking techniques. The main contribution is the reformulation of the framework in terms of symbolic, BDD-based data structure, that allow to deal with extremely large. The algorithm described in the paper have been implemented in the NuMAS system, a tool for model checking multi-agent systems. NuMAS, an acronym for "NuSMV for Multi-Agent Systems", is built on top of the NuSMV system, a symbolic model checker available at http://nusmv.irst.itc.it/. NuMAS has been preliminarily tested on the well-known Three Wise Men puzzle, and the Andrews authentication protocol. The results, not presented here for lack of space, are extremely promising. Here we only remark that, even for a very simple example, the state space of the system grows extremely large because of the combined effect of the interaction between bridge and temporal operators.

This work builds upon the theory of Multi-Agent Model Checking [7, 4], where an algorithm for multi-agent model checking is presented in form of "explicit-state", i.e. based on the manipulation of single states. In [3, 6] the potential applications to security are shown, while [5] shows its applicability to the validation of e–commerce protocols. In this work we show how to extend the framework in terms of *symbolic* model checking. The notions of multiple views and multiple languages are mostly inspired by the works by Giunchiglia and his collaborators in the field of Multi-Language Systems [15, 13]. Other related works use combinations of modal temporal logics [23], although the mechanization is not based on symbolic model checking techniques. [20] present an automata theoretic approach to temporal modal logic (restricted to the case of single nesting of beliefs), applied to the specification of knowledge-based systems. We are currently working at the optimization of the algorithms, by tackling more complex case studies. Directions of future research will include the definition new decision procedures for modal logics, based on the automated choice of the basic bridge atoms, and on the lazy evaluation of the compatibility relation. Finally, we will investigate the extension to Model Checking of hierarchical systems.

References

1. A. Artikis, M. Sergot and J. Pitt. Specifying Electronic Societies with the Causal Calculator. In this volume.
2. M. Benerecetti and A. Cimatti.Symbolic Model Checking for Multiagent Systems. In the Proceedings of the *First Workshop on Model Checking and Artificial Intelligence* (MoChArt–02), Lyon, France, July 21–22 2002.
3. M. Benerecetti and F. Giunchiglia. Model checking security protocols using a logic of belief. In *Proceedings of the Sixth International Conference on Tools and Algorithms for the Construction and Analysis of Systems (TACAS 2000). March 27th - April 1st, 2000, Berlin, Germany*. Lecture Notes in Computer Science, N. 1785, 519–534. Springer-Verlag, 2000.
4. M. Benerecetti and F. Giunchiglia. Model Checking-based Analysis of Multiagent Systems. In the Proceedings of the *First Goddard Workshop on Formal Approaches to Agent-Based Systems* (FAABS'00), April 5–7, Greenbelt, USA. Lecture Notes in Artificial Intelligence, pp. 1–15, volume 1871, Springer.
5. M. Benerecetti, M. Panti, L. Spalazzi and S. Tacconi. Verification of Payment Protocols via Multi–Agent Model Checking. In the Proceedings of the *Fourteenth International Conference in Advanced Information Systems Engineering*, Lecture Notes in Computer Sciences, pp. 311–327, volume 2348, Springer.
6. M. Benerecetti, F. Giunchiglia, M. Panti and L. Spalazzi. A logic of belief and a model checking algorithm for security protocols. In *Proceedings of FORTE/PSTV, IFIP*, Kluwer Academic Publication, Pisa, Italy, October 2000
7. M. Benerecetti, F. Giunchiglia and L. Serafini. Model Checking Multiagent Systems. *Journal of Logic and Computation, Special Issue on Computational & Logical Aspects of Multi-Agent Systems*, 8(3):401–423, 1998. Also IRST-Technical Report 9708-07, IRST, Trento, Italy.
8. R. E. Bryant. Graph-Based Algorithms for Boolean Function Manipulation. *IEEE Transactions on Computers*, C-35(8):677–691, August 1986.
9. E.M. Clarke and E.A. Emerson. Synthesis of synchronization skeletons for branching time temporal logic. In *Logic of Programs: Workshop*. Springer Verlag, May 1981. Lecture Notes in Computer Science No. 131.
10. E.M. Clarke, E.A. Emerson and A.P. Sistla. Automatic verification of finite-state concurrent systems using temporal logic specifications. *ACM Transactions on Programming Languages and Systems*, 8(2):244–263, 1986.
11. E.A. Emerson. Temporal and Modal Logic. In J. van Leeuwen, editor, *Handbook of Theoretical Computer Science*, volume B, pages 995–1072. Elsevier Science Publisher B.V., 1990.
12. A. Fuxman, M. Pistore, J. Mylopoulos and P. Traverso. Model checking early requirements specification in Tropos. In *Proc. of the 5th IEEE International Symposium on Requirements Engineering*, Toronto, CA, August 2001.
13. C. Ghidini and F. Giunchiglia. Local Models Semantics, or Contextual Reasoning = Locality + Compatibility. *Artificial Intelligence*, 127(2):221–259, April 2001.
14. F. Giunchiglia, J. Mylopoulos and A. Perini. The Tropos Software Development Methodology: Processes, Models and Diagrams. In this volume.

15. F. Giunchiglia and L. Serafini. Multilanguage hierarchical logics (or: how we can do without modal logics). *Artificial Intelligence*, 65:29–70, 1994.
16. G.J. Holzmann. *Design and Validation of Computer Protocols*. Prentice Hall, 1991.
17. M–P. Huget Extending Agent UML Protocol Diagrams In the Proceedings of the *First Workshop on Model Checking and Artificial Intelligence* (MoChArt–02), Lyon, France, July 21–22 2002.
18. J–L Koning and I. Romero–Hernandez. Generating Machine Processable Representation of Textual Representation of AUML. In this volume.
19. K.L. McMillan. *Symbolic Model Checking*. Kluwer Academic, 1993.
20. R. van der Meyden and M. Y. Vardi. Synthesis from Knowledge-Based Specifications. In Proceedings of the *9th International Conference on Concurrency Theory* (CONCUR'98) LNCS No. 1466, Nice, Sept 1998, pp. 34-49. Springer Verlag.
21. J. Odell, H.V.D. Parunak and B. Bauer. Extending uml for agents. In G. Wagner, Y. Lesperance and E. Yu Eds.: Proceedings of the *Agent–Oriented Information Systems* Workshop at the 17th National Conference on Artificial Intelligence, Austin, Texas, ICue Publishing (2000).
22. A. S. Rao and M. P. Georgeff. Modeling rational agents within a BDI architecture. In J. Allen, R. Fikes, and E. Sandewall, editors, *Proceedings of the 2nd International Conference on Principle of Knowledge Representation and Reasoning*, pages 473–484. Morgan Kaufmann, 1991.
23. A. S. Rao and M. P. Georgeff. A model-theoretic approach to the verification of situated reasoning systems. In *Proceedings of the Thirteenth International Joint Conference on Artificial Intelligence (IJCAI-93)*, pages 318–324, Chambéry, France, 1993.
24. A. Cimatti, E.M. Clarke, F. Giunchiglia and M. Roveri. NuSMV: a new Symbolic Model Verifier. In N. Halbwachs and D. Peled, editors, *Proceedings Eleventh Conference on Computer-Aided Verification (CAV'99)*, number 1633 in Lecture Notes in Computer Science, pages 495–499, Trento, Italy, July 1999. Springer-Verlag.

Patterns in Agent-Oriented Software Engineering

Jürgen Lind

iteratec GmbH, Inselkammerstr. 4, D-82008 Unterhaching, Germany
jli@agentlab.de
©2002, Jürgen Lind, agentlab

Abstract. In this paper, I will show how the now popular concept of software patterns can be used in agent-oriented software engineering. To this end, I will present a possible structure of a pattern catalog for agent-oriented patterns and introduce a pattern description scheme that accounts for the specific needs of agent patterns. Then, I will provide two examples for how this scheme can be used to describe actual agent patterns.

1 Introduction

Patterns are everywhere. In all fields of our daily life, we use existing patterns to solve recurring problems or we develop new patterns for future use. Generally speaking, a pattern is a general solution to a specific recurring design problem. It explains the insight and good practices that have evolved to solve the problem and it provides a concise definition of common elements, context, and essential requirements for a solution. Patterns were first used in [1] to describe constellations of structural elements in buildings and towns.

Several templates for software design patterns have been developed. The first attempt to bring the idea of software patterns into the broad public was undertaken by the "Gang of Four" (GoF) [8]. Their template is used for patterns that describe constellations of classes that solve common software design problems of relatively small scope. A similar approach is taken by a group of Siemens employees [6] who also provide a section. that discusses component structures of relatively large scope. What is common to these two approaches is the fact that they deal with very general problems that are to be found in almost any (sufficiently large) software system. In their second volume [21], the Siemens people therefore deal with patterns for large scale problems in greater detail. The idea of Software Architecture as a field of software development that can specifically benefit from a pattern oriented approach is also discussed in [22]. Due to the great success of the early attempts to semi-formalize the description of software patterns, international conferences are conducted every year to enhance the information interchange in the pattern community; the best known of these conferences is the [17].

Bringing together agents and other fields of software engineering might be difficult as the advantages of agent technology are still not widely recognized. In [7], for example, the entire agent approach is presented as a singular patterns among others. Clearly, this view on agents is much too limited and coarse grained and more elaborate pattern schemata for agents are necessary.

F. Giunchiglia et al. (Eds.): AOSE 2002, LNCS 2585, pp. 47–58, 2003.
© Springer-Verlag Berlin Heidelberg 2003

In the agent world itself, several attempts to introduce patterns and pattern languages have been made. In [12], for example, a concrete pattern for layered agent architectures is presented using am ad-hoc pattern description scheme and without providing and outline for the organization of a agent-oriented pattern catalog. Similarly, [25] provides a collection of best practices but without adhering to a particular description scheme. In [10] and [11], a large collection of agent interaction schemata and generic role models is presented where each role and its relations to other roles are expressed in terms of CRC cards. Further approaches to introducing patterns into the agent world are to be found in [2] or [24]; an interesting approach for using agent patterns in a real world scenario is described in [13].

In summary, however, one must clearly admit that the idea of developing a standardized pattern catalog for agent-based systems has not been investigated in depth and that such an attempt is necessary in order to advance the development of agent-based applications.

2   Pattern Catalog Structure

The first problem in developing a pattern catalog for software patterns is to find an adequate structure of this catalog such that the patterns are grouped together in meaningful categories. In [8], for example, the patterns that are discussed are classified into three classes: *creational patterns* deal with object creation, *structural patterns* describe the composition of classes and objects and *behavioral patterns*, finally, capture interaction between classes and objects. The approach taken in [6] differentiates between three categories of patterns: *architectural patterns* that describe fundamental structural organization schemata for software systems, *design patterns* that capture the refinement of subsystems or components or the relations between them, and *idioms*, finally, that are low-level implementation patterns specific to a particular programming language.

For agent patterns, I suggest using a catalog structure that follows the view oriented approach presented in [14]. The views that are introduced there are used to model the entire system from different perspectives where each of these perspectives captures a set of related aspects. The views that are proposed are as follows:

Interaction. Interaction is a fundamental concept for a system that consists of multiple independent entities that coordinate themselves in order to achieve their individual as well as their joint goals. In this view, interaction within the target system is seen as a generalized form of conflict resolution that is not limited to a particular form such as communication. Instead, several generic forms of interaction exist that can be instantiated in a wide variety of contexts. The developer is encouraged to analyze the target problem with respect to the applicability of these generic forms before designing new forms. The most popular example for interaction is of course a communication protocol, simply because communication protocols have been studied for quite some time. However, multiagent systems that simulate physical environments or real physical multiagent systems such as robots or machines have many other possibilities of interaction besides communication and these forms of interaction must be allowed for in a general purpose method as well.

Role. The role view determines the functional aggregation of t'
capabilities according to the physical constraints of the
abstraction that links the domain dependent part of the ap$_k$
nology that solves the problem under consideration. In my vie
one or more role descriptions and an architecture that is capable ⌐
role models which makes it important to aggregate the basic capabil⌐
to physical constraints.

Architecture (System, Agent, Agent Management). The Architecture view is ⌐
jection of the target system onto the fundamental structural attributes with respect ⌐
the system design. The major aspects that are dealt with in this view are the system
architecture as a whole and – due to the size and complexity of this particular aspect
– the agent architecture. The system architecture is described according to various
aspects and includes things such as agent management or database integration. The
required agent architecture is characterized according to the requirements of the
problem to be solved and it is strongly recommended that the system developer
should at first try to select one of the numerous existing architectures before trying
to develop a new architecture from scratch.

Society. A society is a structured collection of entities that pursue a common goal.
The goal of this view is to classify the society that either pre-exists within the
organizational context of the system or that is desirable from the point-of-view
of the system developer. According to this classification and to well defined quality
measures for the performance of the target society that depend on application specific
aspects, a society model is developed that is consistent with the roles within the
society and that achieves the defined goals.

System. This view deals with systems aspects that affect several of the other views
or even the system as a whole. The System view, for example, handles the user
interface that controls the interaction between the system and the user(s) whose the
task specific aspects are usually the input specification and the output presentation
whereas task independent aspects deal with the visualization of the system activities
in order to enable the user to follow the ongoing computations and interactions. Other
aspects that are described in this view are the system-wide error-handling strategy,
performance engineering and the system deployment once it has been developed.

Task. In the Task view, the functional aspects of the target system are analyzed and a
task hierarchy is generated that is then used to determine the basic problem solving capabilities of the entities in the final system. Furthermore, the nonfunctional
requirements of the target system are defined and quantified as far as possible. Note
that this view does not assume that a multiagent approach is used for the final system
and therefore provides a rather high-level analysis of the problem.

In the case of a compiler application, for example, the basic functional requirement is
that the system translates a program specified in a high-level language to a particular
assembly language. The quality of the resulting code or the maximal tolerable time
for the compilation are nonfunctional requirements and the basic problem solving
capabilities are for example lexical analysis or code generation.

Environment. In this view, the environment of the target system is analyzed from the developers perspective as well as from the systems perspective. These two perspectives
usually differ as the developer has global knowledge whereas the system has only

al knowledge. In the RoboCup domain, for example, the developer has access ɔ the complete state of the system and its environment and this state is completely deterministic from this point-of-view. From the perspective of the individual agent within the system, on the other hand, only parts of the environment are accessible and the state transitions appear to be nondeterministic because of ongoing activities that cannot be perceived by the agent.

The advantage of using this collection of views as the categories of the agent patterns is that it adheres to a decomposition of the target software system that has shown to be quite effective in developing agent-based applications [14]. Still, the above collection of views should serve solely as a starting point as it is not yet clear whether a sufficient number of patterns can be found for each view. If it is difficult to find patterns for a particular view, the best idea is probably to abandon the respective view as a pattern category as it may be too volatile. A sufficient degree of stability is a prerequisite for successful pattern extraction.

3 A Pattern Description Scheme

Pattern description schemata are collections of aspects that, when taken together, fully capture a software pattern. The major advantage of such schemata is that they introduces a structured way to understand, explain and reason about patterns. Furthermore, they allows for a more effective communication among software engineers because a particular pattern description scheme provides the language to talk about patterns. In the existing literature, several general purpose schemata have been proposed, e. g. in [8] or in [6]. These two schemata are rather similar, suggesting that there might exist something as a "canonical" scheme that can be used for different pattern catalogs. Still, however, I do not think that a single, general pattern description scheme is adequate for all categories of patterns, simply because it is too general. Furthermore, I also believe that pattern schemata for agents must be more complex than "normal" patterns because the usually deal with problems of coarser granularity. Therefore, I suggest to split up the pattern description scheme into two parts: a general part that deals with the generic properties of a pattern and a view-specific part that handles those aspects that are characteristic for the view the pattern belongs to two. In Table 1, I have summarized the resulting scheme, the view specific aspects will extend the last point mentioned there.

4 Examples

In this section, I will demonstrate how the pattern description scheme from Table 1 can be used for agent-oriented software patterns. Due to the limited space, however, I shall restrict myself to some introductory remarks only.

4.1 Agent Architecture Patterns

The first example that we will discuss in this section stems from the architecture view and deals with the agent architecture. According to [14], the agent architecture defines a

Table 1. Description Fields in MASSIVE

Name	A crisp name that captures the essential idea underlying the pattern
Aliases	other names that might be used for this pattern
Problem	What problem is solved by the pattern
Forces	Which aspects of the problem are the forces that led to the development of the pattern? What are the prerequisites for using the pattern?
Entities	The entities that participate in the pattern. The name of the slot is chosen to avoid technical terms such as "class" or "object" to avoid a premature limitation on a particular implementation.
Dynamics	How do the entities of the pattern collaborate to achieve their goal.
Dependencies	Does the pattern require any specific environment before it can be applied?
Example	A simple, abstracted example for how to use the pattern.
Implementation	Hints on how the pattern may be implemented.
Known Uses	Examples of systems where the pattern has been applied successfully.
Consequences	What are the consequences of using the pattern? Does the pattern determine design decisions in other places of the system?
See Also	References to other patterns that solve similar problems or that can be beneficially combined with this pattern. Also, where are potential conflicts with other patterns.
View category specific fields	Additional fields that are specific for a particular category and that do not make sense for other categories.

structural model of the components that constitute an agent as well as the interconnections of these components together with a computational model that implements the basic capabilities of the agent. In addition to the general purpose pattern fields, we will use the following view-specific fields that are used to capture the characteristics of a particular agent architecture.

Resource Limitations. This aspect of the characterization describes the resources that are available to a single agent within the multiagent system. If an agent has a very limited amount of processor time or memory space, it is impossible to use an agent architecture that requires, say, the resources of a Unix process. However, this point can also be viewed from a different angle. If the individual agent has to deal with very complex problems, a simple architecture may not be able to cope with the resource requirements of the architecture because it was not designed for heavy weight problems.

Control Flow. The aim of this requirement is to characterize the control flow that is needed within the agent. First of all, the designer should decide whether a sequential flow of control is sufficient or if the agent is required to do several things at the same time and thus needs some parallel action execution model. In the second case, a concurrent architecture that in most case is much more complex then a sequential architecture must be chosen.

Also, the designer must decide about the required flexibility of the control flow. In a more static setting, the flow of control can be explicitly hard-coded into the architecture while in a dynamic context, the flow of control is likely to undergo changes and must therefore be described implicitly e.g. in plan scripts that are interpreted at run time and that can be changed while the agent is in operation.

Knowledge Handling. In MASSIVE, the knowledge representation within the target system is defined in the Task view. In the Architecture view, the knowledge structures that are defined there must be characterized in order to decide which architectural features are necessary to effectively handle these structures. For example, it an important distinction whether the agents knowledge is stored explicitly in a knowledge base or is it encoded implicitly into the agent code. Similarly, the knowledge structures may be represented in a symbolic manner using some sort of logical formulae or in a sub-symbolic form.

Reasoning Capabilities. The reasoning capabilities of the agents define the most important property and often determine the overall complexity of the agent architecture. For example, an agent may be forced to plan its actions if it is not a purely reactive agent, or it may use some utilitarian reasoning mechanisms to chose among several possible actions. Another important issue is the ability for an agent to learn from past experiences or the agent may be used to fulfill special tasks such as theorem proving etc.

Autonomy. The degree of autonomy that is required by the agent defines how the agent interacts with its environment. A reactive agent simply responds to external stimuli by reproducing a pre-defined behavior when a particular stimulus is given by the environment. A pro-active agent, on the other hand, can become active without external trigger and then perform some action that satisfies the goal. Pro-active agents are usually more complex and their behavior is not always predictable.

User Interaction. The more interaction the agent has with the user, the more elaborate the user interface has to be in order to provide convenient means for input and output data. Furthermore, an advanced user interface agent will perform user profiling and try to learn the users preferences from his or her input/output behavior.

Temporal Context. This aspect characterizes the agents lifetime. Obviously, an agent with only a limited activation time will need another form of persistence mechanism – if any at all – then a long-running agent. Persistence refers to the ability of the agent to maintain knowledge structures over time and over unavoidable down-times due to service failures such as hardware or software crashes. However, the amount of information that is collected by the agent over its lifetime can become very large and must be handled in an effective manner. Thus, the architecture must provide means to manage the data handling process.

Decision Making. This attribute characterizes the way in which the agent comes to its decisions during its reasoning processes. While some authors claim that rationality is an inherent property of any agent [19], there are others who consider architectures that support emotional decision making as an alternative [5]. There are two main fields for a potential application of emotional architectures. First, they can become valuable tools to implement lifelike characters and avatars that represent a human user in networked environments. Second, the notion of emotions can be used to express complex heuristics for advanced software agent in a natural way. However, the development of the basic technology is still in its beginnings and does not play a relevant role until now. Still, the developer of a particular application may want to consider these ideas if they are appropriate for the problem in question.

We will no see a concrete example on how this scheme can be used to describe a particular agent architecture pattern. I have chosen the InteRRaP architecture as presented in [16] because it is well documented and therefore the pattern description scheme can be applied easily. Obviously, though, a complex thing such as a generic agent architecture requires a lot more space then that available in this paper. Therefore, the following paragraphs are solely intended to demonstrate how one might start with a pattern that captures the InteRRaP architecture; this is illustrated by the dots that appear in almost any field.

Name. InteRRaP

Aliases. none

Problem. InteRRaP defines an agent architecture that supports situated behavior where the agents are able to recognize unexpected events and react timely and appropriately to them. Second, the InteRRaP architecture enables the agents to show goal-directed behavior in a way that the agent decides which goals to pursue by which means. Third, InteRRaP is designed in a way that the agents can act under real-time constraints and act efficiently with their resources. Fourth, InteRRaP agents must be able to interact with other agents in order to achieve common goals.
...

Forces. InteRRaP was originally designed to bridge the gap between reactivity and deliberation on th one hand and interaction and coordination on the other. InteRRaP is rather heavy-weight architecture that should not be used in a system context with many agents with little resources. Ideally, only a single instance of an InteRRaP agent should run on a single computational node. Additionally, as InteRRaP implements a BDI architecture [18], it must be possible to model the problem domain in terms of BDI concepts.
...

Entities. The major architectural abstraction of the InteRRaP agent architecture is *layering*. InteRRaP consists of three layers that serve different purposes:

Behavior Based Layer (BBL). This layer implements the reactive behavior of the agent, i.e. this layer reacts to external requirements without any explicit reasoning, thus it reacts very fast.

Local Planning Layer (LPL). This layer performs the planning process of an individual agent, it is also responsible to monitor the plan execution of the agents current plan.

Social Planning Layer (SPL). This layer is responsible for the coordination with the other agents within a multiagent system. The coordination with the other agents is achieved with explicit negotiation protocols.

These layers mainly serve two purposes. First, the represent different functionalities that compete for the resources of the agent. Second, the layering allows for better conceptual abstractions in terms of the agents knowledge representation and by restricting access to particular pieces of information to a particular layer.
...

Dependencies. none

Example. [left out for brevity]

Implementation. [left out for brevity]

Known Uses. Examples for the use of InteRRaP agent architecture can be found in [16] and [9].

Consequences. InteRRaP agents in their strict form rely on modeling the agent behavior and the domain knowledge in terms of specific concepts that stem from the knowledge and plan representation schemata used. This can easily become a complex task even for domains with limited complexity. Alternatively, a light-weight version of InteRRaP agents should be used that does not strictly implement the original design and that uses a custom knowledge and plan representation scheme, making it easier to implement domain specific concepts. An example for this approach can be found in [15].

. . .

See Also. BDI agents [4], layered architectures [12]

Control Flow. The control flow of an InteRRaP agent is guided mainly by two principal ideas: *Bottom-up activation* where control is shifted up a layer if the current layer is not competent to deal with the situation (and, of course, a higher layer exists); and *Top-down execution* where each layer uses operational primitives defined at the next lower layer to achieve its goals.

Each layer runs in a (potentially) infinite control loop that is independent from the other layers and that uses the bottom-up activation to hand over the flow of control to the next higher level and town-down execution either to receive operations to execute or to demand the execution of commands from the lower level.

. . .

Resource Limitations. As the InteRRaP architecture is rather complex, the agents that are implemented using the architecture will be rather heavy-weighted. Therefore, the computational resources that are available for a single agent must not be too limited in order to allow for a satisfactory performance of the agent. As the final resource requirements depend on a particular implementation of the generic architecture, no further details with respect to resources are possible.

Knowledge Handling. The InteRRaP agent architecture has a layered knowledge base where the beliefs of an agent are stored hierarchically; this restricts the amount of available information to a particular control layer.

The knowledge is stored using a knowledge representation scheme that consists of *Concepts*, *Types*, *Attributes Features* and *Relations*.

. . .

Reasoning Capabilities. InteRRaP uses the *Assertional Knowledge Base (AKB* to represent the agents current knowledge, its beliefs and its goals in terms of the concepts discussed in the **Knowledge handling** section of this pattern. The AKB offers three types of interface services: *assertional services* that allow to assert new beliefs into the knowledge base, i.e., to create instances of concepts and relations, and to change the values of attributes of existing concept and relation instances, *retrieval services* that provide access to beliefs that are actually stored in the AKB, and *active information services*, finally, that offer a possibility to access information from the knowledge base upon demand.

. . .

The main reasoning capabilities of InteRRaP agents are based on a planning mechanism known as *planning from second principles* [20], [4]. The planner is viewed as a black box, that is given a problem description and that then returns a plan that solves the problem. In InteRRaP, planning and plan execution are interleaved to cope with the dynamic environment of the agents. InteRRaP agents have a *plan library* that represent collections of plans for particular domain specific problems. The plans are represented in a special language allows the agent developer to link domain specific patterns of behavior with an abstract plan.

...

Autonomy. The degree of autonomy exhibited by InteRRaP agents is domain dependent.
User Interaction. [generic architecture, not applicable]
Temporal Context. [generic architecture, not applicable]
Decision Making. [generic architecture, not applicable]

4.2   Interaction Protocol Patterns

The second example that we will discuss in this section are patterns for the interaction view. Here, we have the situation that the most important view-specific aspects of an interaction pattern are already covered in the part of the pattern description that deals with general aspects. These parts are the *roles*, the *messages* and the *temporal ordering* of the message exchange. In the general description scheme, the roles and the messages can be discussed in the "entities" section and the temporal ordering of the messages is part of the "dynamics" of the pattern. However, in order to point out the specific meanings of the three major concepts, I think it is a better idea to remove the fields from the general part of the description scheme and to add the three new fields to the view-specific part. That way, the special semantics of the filed names are emphasized.

To demonstrate how a concrete interaction protocol pattern might look, we will now briefly present a pattern description for the well-known Contract-net protocol as introduced in [23]. Remember that the following paragraphs serve as example only and therefore, the field contents contain introductory aspects only. Furthermore, we will only consider the simple Contract-net variant without task refinements etc.

Name. Contract-net
Aliases. none
Problem. Allocate a particular task to one out of several potential contractors while minimizing the local costs.
Forces. The Contract-net protocol is a one-to-one copy of the behavior shown by participants in market. The idea is to have the participants calculate their local cost for performing a particular task and then announcing the resulting cost to a manager who decides on the task assignment. This leads to an optimal resource allocation in the case of independent tasks. If inter-dependencies between tasks exist, the task allocation process can get caught in local minima.
Dependencies. Using the Contract-net protocol for a task allocation process requires that there exist several potential contractors with comparable abilities. For optimal performance, the Contract-net also requires independent tasks.
Example. [omitted]

Implementation. See [14], Appendix C.
Known Uses. See [15].
Consequences. If the tasks are not independent from each other, the Contract-net protocol is likely to lead to sub-optimal solutions as it can get stuck in local optima. To escape from local optima, additional mechanisms may be necessary (see *See Also* below).
See Also. Simulated Trading [3] as used in [15].
Roles. The Contract-net protocol has two roles: the *manager* and the *bidder*. The manager is responsible for putting together a task description that tells the potential bidders what to do. In closed agent societies, the task descriptions are usually given is some proprietary format; in open agent societies, some sort of standard must be applied. The second task of the manager is to determine the set of possible bidders. This can be achieved by broadcasting the task announcements to all possible receivers or by performing a pre-selection of already known candidates. While the first approach ensures that all potential contractors are reached, it is not very resource effective and can lead to unnecessary computations on the bidders side. Thus, a pre-selection of candidates is usually advantageous. The task of a bidder is to compute the cost for performing the announced task and to send an offer (if the bidder can fulfill the task at all) to the manager. If the manager grants the task to a particular bidder, the bidder guarantees task completion within the constraints provided by the task announcement.
Messages. The Contract-net has four messages: *call for bids*, *bid*, *grant* and *reject*. The *call for bids* message is issued by the manager and contains the task description. The bidders reply to this message with *bid* message if they can perform the task. If not, no message is sent to the manager. After completing the bid collection phase, the manager selects the best bid and sends a *grant* to the successful bidder; the other bidders receive *reject* messages.
Temporal Ordering. See Figure 1.

In this section, we have seen two (short) examples on how a pattern catalog could be developed. These examples show that it is possible to describe agent-oriented patterns in a standardized way and thus to make them available as solutions for recurring problems ins agent system development.

5 Conclusion

Software pattern have shown to be useful tools in many areas of software development; in this paper, a starting point for introducing patterns into agent-oriented software engineering has been presented. The approach integrates with the MASSIVE method but it is not limited to that particular development method. The basic idea that was discussed is to develop a pattern catalog that is structured according to the view-oriented decomposition of the final system as it is suggested in the MASSIVEmethod.

In forthcoming research, the suggested view system must be evaluated for its usefulness as a pattern catalog structure and the pattern description scheme must be analyzed with respect to its adequacy for capturing all relevant aspects of agent patterns. The most important task, however, is to start to collect agent patterns and to make them widely available.

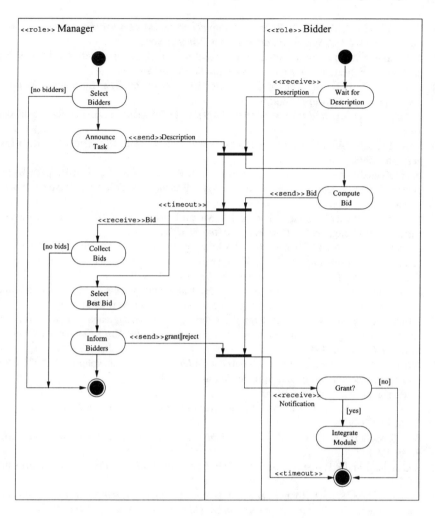

Fig. 1. Contract-net

References

1. Christopher Alexander. *The timeless way of building*. Oxford University Press, 1979.
2. Yariv Aridor and Danny B. Lange. Agent design patterns: Elements of agent application design. In *Proceedings of the Agents-98*, 1998.
3. A. Bachem, W. Hochstättler, and M. Malich. The Simulated Trading Heuristic for Solving Vehicle Routing Problems. Technical Report 93.139, Mathematisches Institut der Universität zu Köln, 1993.
4. M. E. Bratman, D. J. Israel, and M. E. Pollack. Toward an architecture for resource-bounded agents. Technical Report CSLI-87- 104, Center for the Study of Language and Information, SRI and Stanford University, 1987.
5. Alastair Burt. Emotionally Intelligent Agents: The Outline of a Resource-Oriented Approach. In *Proceedings of the 1998 AAAI Fall Symposium Emotional and Intelligent: The Tangled Knot of Cognition*, 1998.

6. F. Buschmann, R. Meunier, H. Rohnert, P. Sommerlad, and M. Stal. *Pattern-oriented Software Architecture Vol 1: A System of Patterns*. John Wiley & Sons, 1996.

7. A. Rodrigues daSilva and J. Delgado. The agent pattern: A design pattern for dynamic and distributed applications. In *Proceedings of the EuroPLoP'98*, 1998.

8. E. Gamma, R. Helm, R. Johnson, and J. Vlissides. *Design Patterns: Elements of Reusable Object-Oriented Software*. Addison-Wesley, 1994.

9. C. G. Jung. *Theory and Pratice of Hybrid Agents*. PhD thesis, Universität des Saarlandes, 1999.

10. E. A. Kendall. Agent Analysis and Design with Role Models. Technical report, British Telecom, 1998. Volume I: Overview.

11. E. A. Kendall. Agent Analysis and Design with Role Models. Technical report, British Telecom, 1998. Volume II: Role Models for Agent Enhanced Workflow and Business Process Management.

12. Elizabeth A. Kendall, Chirag V. Pathak, P.V. Murali Krishna, and C.B. Suresh. The Layered Agent Pattern Language. In *Proceedings of the PLoP'97*, 1997.

13. Holger Knublauch and Thomas Rose. Werkzeugunterstützte Prozessanalayse zur Identifikation von Anwendungsszenarien für Agenten. In *Verteilte Informationssysteme auf der Grundlage von Objekten, Komponenten und Agenten*. GI, 2001.

14. Jürgen Lind. *Iterative Software Engineering for Multiagent Systems - The* MASSIVE *Method*, volume 1994 of *Lecture Notes in Computer Science*. Springer, May 2001.

15. J. Lind, J. Böcker, and B. Zirkler. Optimising the Operation Management with a Multi-Agent Approach - Using TCS as an Example. In *Proceedings of the World Congress on Railway Research (WCRR)*, 1999.

16. Jörg P. Müller. *The Design of Intelligent Agents: A Layered Approach*, volume 1177 of *Lecture Notes in Artificial Intelligence*. Springer-Verlag, Dec 1996.

17. Pattern languages of programs, 2001. `http://jerry.cs.uiuc.edu/~/plop/`.

18. A. S. Rao and M. Georgeff. BDI Agents: from theory to practice. In *Proceedings of the ICMAS-95*, 1995.

19. S. J. Russell and E. H. Wefald. *Do the Right Thing : Studies in Limited Rationality*. MIT Press, 1991.

20. R.C. Schank and R.P. Abelson. *Scripts, Plans, Goals, and Understanding*. Hillsdale:Erlbaum, 1977.

21. D. Schmidt, M. Stal, H. Rohnert, and F. Buschmann. *Pattern-oriented Software Architecture Vol 2: Patterns for Concurrent and Networked Objects*. John Wiley & Sons, 2000.

22. Mary Shaw. Patterns for Software Architectures. In James Coplien and Douglas Schmidt, editors, *Pattern Languages of Program Design*, volume I, 1995.

23. R.G. Smith. The contract net protocol: High-level communication and control in a distributed problem solver. *IEEE Transactions on Computers*, 1980.

24. Yasuyuki Tahara, Akihiko Ohsuga, and Shinichi Honiden. Agent system development method based on agent patterns. In *Proceedings of the ICSE99*, 1999.

25. M. J. Wooldridge and N. R. Jennings. Pitfalls of agent-oriented development. In *Proceedings of the Agents-98*, pages 385–391, 1998.

Concurrent Architecture
for a Multi-agent Platform

Michael Duvigneau, Daniel Moldt, and Heiko Rölke

Universität Hamburg, Fachbereich Informatik
Vogt-Kölln-Straße 30, 22527 Hamburg, Germany
5duvigne,moldt,roelke@informatik.uni-hamburg.de

Abstract. A multi-agent system has a high degree of concurrency. Petri nets are a well-established means for the description of concurrent systems. Reference nets are higher level, object-oriented Petri nets. With Renew (REference NEt Workshop), there exists a tool to model and execute reference nets with seamless Java integration. So, reference nets can be used to design executable multi-agent systems while hiding the sometimes annoying details of concurrent implementations in traditional programming languages. The technique is currently used to implement a FIPA-compliant agent platform for multi-agent systems (called CAPA) focused on retaining a maximum level of concurrency in the system.

1 Introduction

Multi-agent systems implicate a high degree of concurrency: Agents operate independently from each other and can engage themselves in several tasks simultaneously. But most conventional programming languages and therefore the agent frameworks built upon them have only restricted support for concurrent systems. A lot of syntactical or management overhead is needed when implementing concurrent systems using such techniques, which blurs the view on the essential concurrency and synchronisation concepts. So, the sequential view of conventional programming languages leads to systems which do not provide maximum concurrency – it would be better to use a technique where concurrency is the basic assumption, and where it can be explicitly restricted when inappropriate.

Petri nets provide a graphical-intuitive model with formal and precise semantics to handle concurrency and synchronisation. With the extensions of higher level nets, e.g. colored Petri nets, object oriented nets or reference nets, nets can be used to model multi-agent systems efficiently. In our approach we mainly use reference nets [11] because of their object-oriented character, their support of the "nets within nets" paradigm, and the availability of the tool Renew (Reference Net Workshop, [10]) which is able to execute reference nets with seamless Java integration in its simulation engine.

The Mulan (Multi Agent Nets) architecture presented in [14] uses reference nets to describe four levels of multi-agent systems from the overall system view down to the agent-behavior modeling protocols. Although the Mulan model can

F. Giunchiglia et al. (Eds.): AOSE 2002, LNCS 2585, pp. 59–72, 2003.
© Springer-Verlag Berlin Heidelberg 2003

be executed using the Renew tool, some practical features needed for interoperability with other agent platforms are missing. This is due to the conceptual character of Mulan, where the inter-platform communication structures are modeled as a net, allowing cross-platform communication between agents within the net simulation only. To enable the agents to communicate with agents on other platforms, either located at another host or implemented differently (or both), the conceptual platform net of Mulan needs to be extended by a platform implementation oriented along the specifications generated by FIPA (Foundation for Intelligent Physical Agents, [4]). The architecture of this agent platform, called CAPA (Concurrent Agent Platform Architecture), is the subject of this paper.

2   Reference Nets and Concurrency

As the basic technique for modeling agent systems we use reference nets which are a special kind of high-level Petri nets[1]. In this contribution it is assumed that the reader has some knowledge about Petri nets in general. However, the relevant features of Petri nets and reference nets for this paper will be sketched in the following. These are folding, concurrency, and some net extensions.

The basic net formalism of C/E-nets (Condition/Event-nets) comprises all basic features of nets: sequence, synchronisation, conflict, and concurrency. These concepts are also present in more abstract definitions like P/T-nets (Place/Transition-nets) or reference nets. Concurrency can be found in Fig. 1, where the transitions a and b can fire independently, simultaneous firing included.

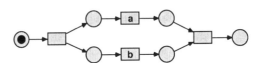

Fig. 1. Concurrent transitions in a C/E-net

In Fig. 2 the concept of folding is shown. Folding can clarify net drawings by combining similar structures of a net into one (parameterised) structure. The net in Fig. 2a can be fold in two different ways: the result in Fig. 2b drops some information and stays at the level of P/T-nets while the net in Fig. 2c preserves all information by distinguishing the two tokens by colors.

Fig. 3 shows the folded net of Fig. 1. It is important to notice that even if the structure of the resulting net in Fig. 3 seems to be sequential the behavior remains fully concurrent as the net from Fig. 1.

In our approach agents are represented by net instances as a specific feature of reference nets. The static structure of a drawn net can be considered to be a

---

[1] An introduction to the capabilities of reference nets and their usage is given in [9]. The documentation shipped with Renew [10] provides a more detailed description of syntax and features of reference nets. The full reference net formalism, including its theoretical foundations, is explained in [11].

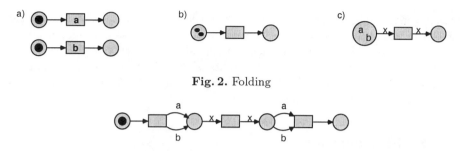

Fig. 2. Folding

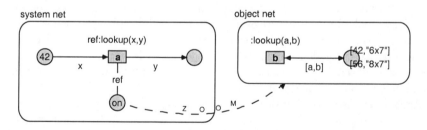

Fig. 3. The net of Fig. 1 folded as a colored net

class while net instances are objects of the type of the related static net model. Each instance has its own local marking, representing the state of the object. Several instances therefore introduce concurrent behavior if they have at least one activated transition each. Even more concurrency can be found if there are (folded) concurrent parts in the net, which is the usual case for us. The instances can be agents.

Reference nets allow communication between the instances by synchronous channels. In Fig. 4 the main concepts can be seen. The transition in the system net can use the reference ref to synchronise itself with transition b of the object net through the synchronous channel :lookup. Both transitions have to fire synchronously – if either one is not activated, the other cannot fire, too. The information flow through the channel is bidirectional, so that transition b in this example can bind the second channel parameter based on the first parameter bound by transition a, resulting in the variable y bound to "6x7". Synchronous channels are the means for agents to communicate with their environment and other agents.

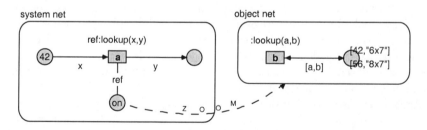

Fig. 4. Net instances communicating through a synchronous channel

The IDE (Integrated Development Environment) used for our approach is Renew in combination with the Mulan architecture. This allows to build models and systems at the same time, since reference nets are directly executable within the Renew simulation engine. Based on the agent concepts each net instance can be replaced by or connected to Java objects.

The new agent platform, called CAPA (Concurrent Agent Platform Architecture), is designed and implemented under the guideline of keeping the level of concurrency as high as possible. The seamless Java integration of the Renew tool allows to implement the agent platform in a mixture of Java and reference nets. Therefore, the advantage of reference nets in handling concurrency and synchronisation can be combined with the flexibility of the object-oriented programming language when working with abstract data types or using the functionality provided by Java's huge class library.

3 Multi-agent Nets

The multi-agent system architecture Mulan [8] is based on the "nets within nets" paradigm [17], which is used to describe the natural hierarchies in an agent system. Mulan is implemented in Renew. Mulan has the general structure as depicted in figure 5 [2]: Each box describes one level of abstraction in terms of a system net. Each system net contains object nets, which structure is made visible by the ZOOM lines[3].

The net in the upper left describes an agent system, whose places contain agent platforms as tokens. The transitions describe communication or mobility channels, which build up the infrastructure. This is just an illustrating example, the number of places and transitions or their interconnection has no further meaning.

By zooming into the platform token on place p1, the structure of a platform becomes visible, shown in the upper right box. The central place agents hosts all agents, which are currently on this platform. Each platform offers services to the agents, some of which are indicated in the figure[4]. Agents can be created (transition new) or destroyed (transition destroy). Agents can communicate by message exchange. Two agents on the same platform can communicate by the transition internal communication, which binds two agents, the sender and the receiver, to pass one message over a synchronous channel[5]. External communication (external communication) only binds one agent, since the other agent is bound on a second platform somewhere else in the agent system. Also mobility facilities are provided on a platform: agents can leave the platform via the transition send agent or transitions could enter the platform via the transition receive agent from another platform.

Agents are also modeled in terms of nets. They are encapsulated, since the only way of interaction is by message passing. Agents can be intelligent, since they have access to a knowledge base. The behavior of the agent is described in terms of protocols, which are again nets. Protocols are located as templates on the place protocols. Protocol templates can be instantiated, which happens for

---

[2] This is just a simplified version, since for example only some nodes are shown and all synchronous channels are omitted.

[3] This zooming into net tokens should not to be confused with place refining.

[4] Note that only mandatory services are mentioned here. A typical platform will offer more and specialised services, for example implemented by special service agents.

[5] This is just a technical point, since via synchronous channels provided by Renew asynchronous message exchange is implemented.

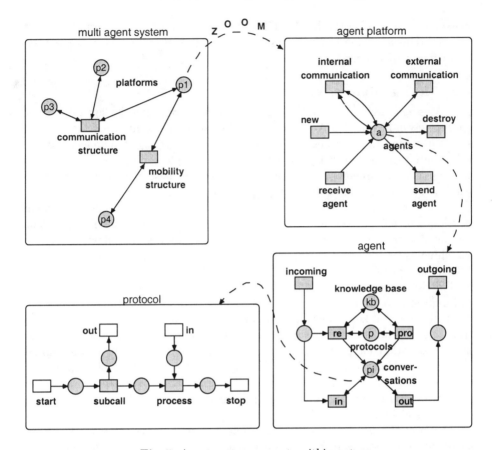

Fig. 5. Agent systems as nets within nets

example if a message arrives. An instantiated protocol is part of a conversation and lies in the place conversations. The detailed structure of protocols and their interaction have been addressed before in [8], so we skip the details here.

4 Concurrent FIPA-Compliant Multi-agent Platform

Mulan is extended by a FIPA-compliant agent platform, called CAPA (Concurrent Agent Platform Architecture), in order to allow cross-platform communications. The new platform replaces the conceptual platform net described in the previous section. The implementation tries to keep the highest level of concurrency by taking advantage from the possibility of mixing reference nets with Java code.

To comply with the FIPA-2000 set of specifications, CAPA has to provide for its agents the management and directory services AMS (Agent Management System) and DF (Directory Facilitator), a local Message Transport System (MTS), and an interface for communication with external platforms, the Agent Communication Channel (ACC). FIPA-agents communicate using asynchronous messages expressed in the FIPA ACL (Agent Communication Language), so an internal representation for such messages is useful to simplify the message interpretation of the agents.

4.1 Message Representation

ACL Messages are represented internally by objects following the key-value-tuple concept given in the "FIPA Abstract Architecture" [4]. Many other information structures used in messages, for example of the FIPA agent management ontology, are represented using the same key-value-tuple concept. In combination with an similar value-tuple concept (without keys), these representation classes can be used for several content languages and ontologies[6].

A subsumption relation is defined upon both tuple classes to allow the agent developer to use pattern matching in a similar way he can use the unification mechanism included in reference nets. The possibility to use flexible pattern matching saves the agent developer a lot of work when it comes to the analysis of incoming messages.

For the implementation of the tuple classes there are two alternatives: Both techniques, Java code or reference nets, could be used. The reference net implementation of a key-value-tuple would be easy, since the formalism allows to store the key-value-pairs as tuples in places. The pairs could be retrieved by using unification for pattern matching with the key component of the tuples. The Java implementation could build up upon existing classes implementing the java.util.Map or List interfaces.

The main disadvantage of the net implementation is due to the lack of type-checking and inheritance when using reference nets with synchronous channels as interface: the net implementation would not be able to catch many of the small careless mistakes made by a developer while he is sketching his agents.

But the decision for a Java implementation has its drawbacks, too. A mutable, Map-based implementation of a container class has to be protected against concurrent modifications. The synchronise feature of the Java language, which could solve some of the concurrency-related issues, does not combine well with the synchronisation scheme of Petri nets, because its text-based locking scheme cannot be used to lock an object's monitor across several transitions.

Nevertheless, CAPA message representation is currently done in Java, for the advantage of type checking and inheritance, allowing for convenience methods that simplify the agent developer's work. The synchronisation problem is delegated to the agent implementation – it has to avoid access conflicts. An alternative solution could be the use of immutable representation objects where instead of every modification a new object gets instantiated.

4.2 Internal Interface to the Message Transport System

The interface between agents and the internal message transport system consists of two synchronous channels (as depicted in Fig. 6). The agent has to provide

---

[6] The reduction of different languages and ontologies to a generic tuple concept has been inspired by the JAS architecture (see [6]).

two uplinks, namely :receive(message) and :send(message), to which the transport system connects via appropriate downlinks. The downlinks of the system net need a reference to be established, this can be obtained through a test arc from the active agents place. While the :send channel can be activated for any message/agent combination, the :receive channel should only be triggered if the message's receiver entry matches the receiver reference used to establish the channel.

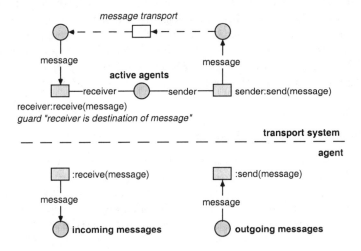

Fig. 6. The internal message transport interface

The transport system interface could be specified alternatively by declaring two Java methods. The transport system has to provide send(message) while the agent offers a receive(message) method. But there is one main difference between the synchronous channel interface and the Java-style interface: The bidirectional information flow through a synchronous channel allows the same reference direction to be used for the receive as well as for the send channel. The object or net instance modeling the agent does not need a reference to the transport system to send its messages. Instead, the environment of the agent connects to the agent by using its reference from the platform management. Despite of the "backward" direction of this connection, the agent can trigger the send channel to the transport system at any time by putting a message in its outgoing message place[7].

The advantage of having an asymmetric relation between the agent platform and agents is a simple security aspect: Since the agent does not have a reference to the transport system or any other component of the platform implementation, it cannot abuse these references. Further, the platform can easily install a guarding instance between the agent and the transport system (without a need

---

[7] Here it is assumed, of course, that the platform acts as cooperative environment for the agent and does not block the channel – but uncooperative behavior would be possible for the platform regardless of the reference direction.

to reconfigure the agent), which checks all inbound and outbound transmissions for permission.

A look at the concurrency aspect of the synchronous channel interface shows that it is not restricted in any way. A synchronous channel can be established between any pair of activated transitions at any time, including the possibility of synchronising one pair of transitions several times at once, if there is a sufficient number of input tokens (e.g. messages) available. So any agent can send several messages at one time as well as several agents can send their messages simultaneously (the same holds, of course, for message delivery) – unless one of the involved nets restricts the concurrency. On the transport system side of the interface, the implementation takes care not to restrict the concurrency (for example by using test arcs to fetch the agent references). If an agent implementation wants to reduce the concurrency, it can do so without affecting other agents.

4.3   Message Transport System

The Mulan platform net distinguishes between internal (between agents on the same platform) and external (cross-platform) communication (see Fig. 5). Currently, CAPA's internal message transport system does not make this distinction (this behavior may be subject to changes). So, all messages – wherever they come from – are passed to the central **MessageTransportService** which provides the functionality of the ACC from the "FIPA Transport Service Specification" [4].

The transport system architecture is defined by two Java interfaces, one of which is the already mentioned **MessageTransportService**, the other declares the functionality of individual **Transport** protocol implementations. The **MessageTransportService** inspects the message's envelope, determines all possible **Transports** based on the envelope's destination addresses and tries the **Transports** until one of them succeeds in forwarding the message. The internal transport net mentioned before is hooked into the transport system as one **Transport** offering the message transfer to all local agent addresses.

The default implementation of the **MessageTransportService** interface is provided by the net depicted in figure 7. This figure shows executable "source code" taken from the current implementation. The channel uplinks :transportMessage, :getDescription, :addTransport and :removeTransport act as method bodies for the Java method declarations from the **MessageTransportService** interface. To avoid cluttering the graphical representation with large code blocks, some functionality is moved into a Java class called **ACCHelper**. The methods of this class are all static and – with the exception of **tryTransport** which possibly forwards the message – free from side-effects.

The main part of the drawing looks like a sequence of loops. This rather sequential than concurrent impression is in fact correct with respect to the handling of one single message. The steps of extracting an address from the message envelope, determining a **Transport** capable of reaching that address and letting the **Transport** try to forward the message have to be done in this specific order. As the FIPA Transport Service Specification suggests, multiple addresses from

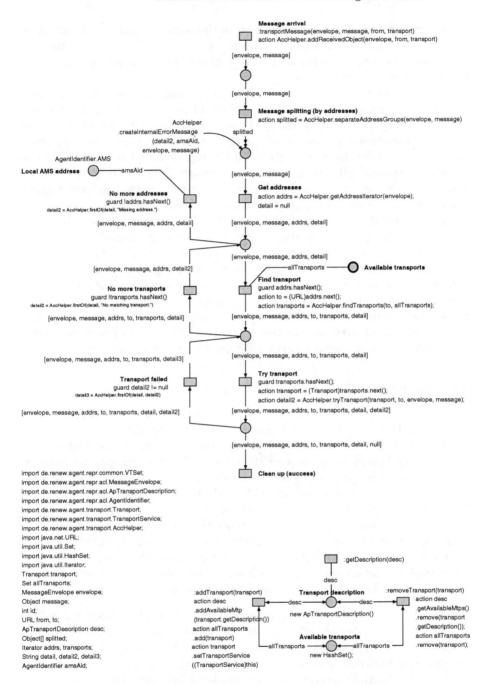

Fig. 7. MessageTransportService implementation

a message envelope also have to be tried in the sequence given in the envelope to respect the agents' preferences. And the goal of not duplicating a message unnecessarily enforces the sequential usage of multiple Transports which could be able to forward the message.

But the inherent concurrency of Petri nets comes to effect immediately if more than one message is in the system. Since all places not storing the message tuple itself (e.g. all side conditions) are connected to transitions by using test arcs, full concurrency is available. This even holds for the split parts of multi-cast messages: After the transition labeled Message splitting has produced several [envelope, message]-pairs (one for each addressee) from the original envelope through a flexible output arc (with two arrow tips)[8], these pairs are handled completely independent from (and concurrent to) each other.

The independency of different message handling "threads" could be represented by creating one individual instance of a (nearly unmodified) message transport net for every message. Such an implementation would come rather close to the Java concurrency concept where an instance of Thread must be used to handle each message in order to reach the same level of concurrency. But in Renew, the folding of several net instances into one net instance is possible without a reduction in concurrency and avoids many net instantiations. The flexible output arc used for message splitting helps in this mission because it allows the folding of the creation of a dynamical number of net instances.

4.4   Management and Directory Services

The Agent Management System (AMS) and the Directory Facilitator (DF) are implemented as pure Mulan agents and run in CAPA like any other application-specific agent. For each of the service functions required by the FIPA Agent Management Specification there exists a protocol net which gets instantiated when a message requesting this function is delivered to the agent. The database of agent descriptions managed by AMS and DF is stored in their knowledge bases and updated by their reactive protocols.

The implementation of both agents relies heavily on the refined default implementation of the Mulan agent concept. This implementation, which serves mainly as a proof of concept with practical use, can easily be replaced by any other implementation conforming to the internal message transport interface. The current implementation consists of three basic nets:

– An agent net implements the message transport interface described before. Further it provides the glue between the knowledge base, the protocol factory and the application-specific protocols. Incoming messages which belong to running conversations are directly forwarded to the protocol instance responsible for the conversation. All other incoming messages are handled by the protocol factory (see below).

---

[8] Flexible arcs are based upon the ideas used by Reisig in [15]. They transfer a dynamic amount of tokens, determined as a function of other input tokens. The exact semantics for reference nets are described in the manual shipped with Renew [10].

- A knowledge base net provides basic, key-value-tuple-like knowledge management. This net allows the agent's protocols to create, read and modify values for given keys. While concurrent read access is allowed, a modification of any key currently requires exclusive access to the whole database. However, the granularity of exclusive access can be changed by providing a different implementation, for example based upon a database engine.
- A protocol factory net chooses protocols to instantiate based upon incoming messages. The subsumption relation defined on the internal message representation objects enables the factory to choose a protocol in accordance to the most specific matching message pattern – allowing the agent developer to specify fall-back protocols associated to a general message pattern. The instantiation of reactive protocols can occur concurrently – as often as incoming messages are available.

  Pro-active protocol instantiation is handled by the protocol factory, too. But since a pro-active transition without preconditions can fire any number of times (even concurrent to itself), the pro-active protocol instantiation is currently restricted to a one-time-shot for practical reasons.

Based upon these three nets, any number of application-specific protocols can run simultaneously. Synchronisation between running protocols appears indirectly, when knowledge base modifications occur.

In the case of the AMS's and DF's directory functions, the search protocol can run any number of times concurrently, because it requires read access only. The other protocols modify the knowledge base by adding, removing or changing entries in the directory. Therefore, all instances of these protocols contain – along with some other preliminary transitions – one transition which requires exclusive knowledge base access (excluding all read-only protocols, too).

5   Related Work

In [8], the Mulan approach has been compared with several other Petri net based agent models, like those of Sibertin-Blanc et.al. [2], Fernandes and Belo [3], Miyamoto and Kumagai [12], or Xu and Shatz [18]. The graphical models of UML [16] and the agent-oriented extensions proposed by AUML [13] do not provide all aspects covered by the reference net/Mulan approach in one diagram type: mainly the exact operational semantics are missing.

Other FIPA-compliant agent platform implementations and agent development environments exist, like FIPA-OS [5] or JADE [7]. CAPA implements again technical features of those platforms that have to be implemented by each FIPA-compliant agent platform, like message representation or transport protocols. The main difference to those platforms is that CAPA does not need to worry about task scheduling, threads or other means to provide concurrency to agents – due to the existing Renew/Mulan-environment.

The effort of JAS [6] to create a Java interface framework for FIPA-compliant agent platforms would be interesting to adopt by CAPA. Unfortunately, the JAS effort was not grown enough when the main parts of CAPA were written to integrate it from the beginning. However, there are some conceptual differences between CAPA and JAS in how agents access platform services.

6   Conclusion

The Mulan architecture extended by the CAPA platform forms an agent framework that provides concurrency at all architectural levels throughout the whole system. A software engineer designing a multi-agent system based on this framework can use as much of the concurrency as desired. The engineer gains freedom in modeling the important concurrency aspect of multi-agent systems explicitly.

And the Mulan/CAPA framework is suitable for practical use. The platform has reasonable performance for our test scenarios and is able to host agents relying on the FIPA-proposed communication structure. This has been proved by the implementation of a popular board game as a multi-agent system based on the framework in a student project at the University of Hamburg.

These features are due to the approach of specifying a FIPA compliant agent platform by using higher level Petri nets, whereas the specification can serve as executable implementation with assistance of the Renew simulation engine. The same approach is available to developers doing agent-oriented software-engineering: They can use an efficient, fast and intuitive modeling technique for concurrent systems at an abstract level – and get an executable implementation in the same step.

The graphical representation of reference nets provides an intuitive means with formal background and precise semantics for modeling concurrency and synchronisation, which both are vital concepts within multi-agent systems. So concurrency aspects can be modeled and discussed explicitly during agent development, as it has been done during the development of CAPA.

The tight integration of Java into Renew allows to integrate Java-implemented parts into the multi-agent system. The element shift from reference nets to Java or from Java to reference nets leads to an abstraction mechanism that combines components from the different implementation techniques at the object or agent level. The result is a clear decomposition of the system or model, using aggregation as main relation concept.

The combination of Java and Renew as base technologies for the agent platform has a couple of other advantages. The independency from technical platforms provided by the Java runtime system allows the agent platform to run in many technical environments. Java's object-oriented type system and huge class library make the development and integration of application-specific functionality into the agent system easier.

The simulation of the running system by the Renew engine is animated and can be inspected interactively, hence allowing validation of the built models and systems. Using Petri nets for modeling multi-agent systems paves the way to use existing methods and tools for formal Petri net analysis. These tools and methods allow the developer to analyse and verify specific sub-cases of the nets which have already been drawn during the development process.

In the context of Mulan, the support of agent mobility has already been tried out, with weak and strong notions[9]. CAPA is able to support different mobility levels – a weaker mobility where the agent has to stop all activities and extract its knowledge base before it can move is possible as well as transparent serialisation of a running agent net instance with complete state transfer.

CAPA is on the way to become a FIPA-compliant agent platform. The required communication infrastructure is already available, but it is currently lacking a FIPA-compliant transport protocol. The platform is designed and implemented with the integration of such a transport protocol in mind, but the concrete implementation of the protocol has not been done yet. Therefore, the interoperability with other FIPA-compliant platforms could not be tested up to now, but will be done soon.

The protocol-driven agent model described in section 4.4 is not mandatory for the use of CAPA. As long as it offers the synchronous channels required by the internal message transport interface, any agent model – reactive or deliberative – can be implemented and inserted into the agent system.

The future plan for the Mulan, CAPA, and Renew combination is to provide a fully FIPA-compliant agent platform integrated into an IDE for the graphical development of agents and multi-agent systems.

References

1. L. Bettini and R. De Nicola: Translating Strong Mobility into Weak Mobility. In G. P. Picco, editor, Mobile Agents, volume 2240 of LNCS, p. 182 pp. Springer 2001
2. W. Chainbi, C. Hanachi, and C. Sibertin-Blanc: The Multi-agent Prey/Predator problem: A Petri net solution. In P. Borne, J.C. Gentina, E. Craye, and S. El Khattabi, editors, Proceedings of the Symposium on Discrete Events and Manufacturing systems, Lille, France, 1996. CESA'96 IMACS Multi-conference on Computational Engineering in System Applications.
3. J.M. Fernandes and O. Belo: Modeling Multi-Agent Systems Activities Through Colored Petri Nets. In 16th IASTED International Conference on Applied Informatics (AI'98), pp. 17–20, Garmisch-Partenkirchen, Germany, Feb. 1998.
4. Foundation for Intelligent Physical Agents (FIPA). Specifications. 2001. Represented at http://www.fipa.org.
5. FIPA Open Source (FIPA-OS). 2001. Available at http://fipa-os.sourceforge.net.
6. Java Agent Services Specification (JAS). 2001. Available at http://www.java-agent.org.
7. F. Bellifemine, G. Rimassa, A. Poggi, T. Trucco, G. Caire and F. Bergenti: Java Agent Development Framework (JADE). 2002. Available at http://sharon.cselt.it/projects/jade.
8. M. Köhler, D. Moldt, and H. Rölke: Modeling the behaviour of Petri net agents. In J. M. Colom and M. Koutny, editors, Proceedings of the 22nd Conference on Application and Theory of Petri Nets, volume 2075 of LNCS, pp. 224–241, Springer 2001.
9. O. Kummer: Introduction to Petri Nets and Reference Nets. Sozionik aktuell, No. 1, 2001. ISSN 1617-2477. Available at http://www.sozionik-aktuell.de.

---

[9] The distinction between weak and strong mobility has been discussed in [1].

10. O. Kummer, F. Wienberg and M. Duvigneau: Reference Net Workshop (Renew). Universität Hamburg 2001. Available at http://www.renew.de.
11. O. Kummer: Referenznetze. Dissertation, Universität Hamburg, 2002.
12. T. Miyamoto and S. Kumagai: A Multi Agent Net Model of Autonomous Distributed Systems. In Proceedings of CESA 96, Symposium on Discrete Events and Manufacturing Systems, pp. 619–623, 1996.
13. J. Odell, H. Van Dyke Parunak and B. Bauer: Extending UML for Agents In G. Wagner, Y. Lesperance and E. Yu, editors, Proceedings of the Agent-Oriented Information Systems (AOIS) Workshop at the 17th National conference on Artificial Intelligence (AAAI), Austin, TX, pp. 3–17, 2000.
14. H. Rölke: Mulan: Modellierung und Simulation von Agenten und Multiagentensystemen mit Referenznetzen. Technical report. Universität Hamburg, Fachbereich Informatik 2002.
15. W. Reisig: Elements of Distributed Algorithms. Springer, Berlin 1998.
16. Unified Modeling Language (UML). Object Management Group (OMG) 2001, Available at http://www.omg.org.
17. R. Valk: Petri nets as token objects: An introduction to elementary object nets. In Jörg Desel and Manuel Silva, editors, Application and Theory of Petri Nets, volume 1420 of LNCS, pp. 1–25. Springer 1998.
18. H. Xu and S.M. Shatz: A Framework for Modeling Agent-Oriented Software. In Proceedings of the 21th International Conference on Distributed Computing Systems (ICDCS-21), Phoenix, Arizona, April 2001.

Re-use of Interaction Protocols
for Agent-Based Control Applications

Stefan Bussmann[1], Nicholas R. Jennings[2], and Michael Wooldridge[3]

[1] DaimlerChrysler AG, Research Information and Communication
Alt-Moabit 96A, 10559 Berlin, Germany
Stefan.Bussmann@daimlerchrysler.com

[2] Dept. of Electronics and Computer Science, University of Southampton
Southampton SO17 1BJ, UK
nrj@ecs.soton.ac.uk

[3] Dept. of Computer Science, University of Liverpool
Liverpool L69 7ZF, UK
M.J.Wooldridge@csc.liv.ac.uk

Abstract. This paper presents a design method for re-using existing interaction protocols in agent-based control applications. In particular, this paper presents a general set of criteria for classifying interaction situations and matching them with existing interaction protocols that are able to resolve the interaction situations. This classification scheme is based solely on criteria derived from the specification of an interaction situation and thus enables a designer to select a suitable interaction protocol for these interaction problems without going through all the interaction protocols available. This design method completes the DACS methodology for agent-oriented analysis and design of control systems.

1 Introduction

The increasing industrial exploitation of agent technology in recent years has highlighted the importance of having agent-oriented software engineering frameworks. Put simply, they are necessary if agent technology is to be widely adopted. To provide such a framework, several agent-oriented methodologies and software engineering techniques have been developed (see e.g. [3,19]). To date, however, most agent-oriented design methodologies proposed have focused on developing an agent-based system from scratch. The methodologies either ignore the large body of agent-oriented techniques already available or leave it to the designer to identify and incorporate those techniques that may be useful in developing the envisioned agent-based system. Both of these situations, however, are undesirable. As with other areas of software [5,15], re-use could significantly improve matters.

To this end, this paper presents a design method for re-using existing interaction protocols. This design method addresses the first and most crucial step in re-use, namely the identification of those interaction protocols that could possibly be used in a design. To perform this identification step, the designer must have a mechanism that enables him to identify a suitable interaction protocol by only specifying his interac-

F. Giunchiglia et al. (Eds.): AOSE 2002, LNCS 2585, pp. 73–87, 2003.
© Springer-Verlag Berlin Heidelberg 2003

tion problem. In particular this needs to be achieved without going explicitly through all the existing interaction techniques and deciding for each one whether it is useful or not. Against this background, this paper presents a classification scheme which is based on criteria solely taken from the specification of an interaction problem and which, as a result, pinpoints to those interaction protocols that could possibly be used in the design. This work is couched in terms of the DACS (design of agent-based control systems) methodology we are developing for analysing and designing agent-based control systems [2].

The remainder of the paper is organised as follows. Section 2 recounts the basic concepts used by the DACS design method. Section 3 presents the main contribution of this paper – the design method for selecting interaction protocols. Section 4 discusses related work. Finally, the last section concludes with an evaluation of the method presented.

2   Overview of DACS Design Methodology

The goal of DACS is to enable an engineer with only limited training in agent technology and no prior experience in agent applications to design an agent-based control system. The engineer is given a description of the control problem to be solved, and then runs through the following three steps in order to design the agent-based system.

1. *Analysis of decision making* – The control decisions that are necessary to operate the target process are identified and analysed.
2. *Identification of agents* – The necessary agents of the control system, their decision responsibilities, and their interaction requirements are identified.
3. *Selection of interaction protocols* – A suitable interaction protocol is chosen for each situation in which the agents need to interact.

The first two steps have already been described in [2]. The third step is the contribution of this paper. The rest of this section describes those concepts developed in the previous work that are necessary to understand the third step.

The method for selecting the interaction protocols builds upon two concepts used to analyse the necessary decision making in step 1: *decision tasks* and *decision dependencies*. A **decision task** specifies a situation at the controlled process in which the controller must make a decision about which action to perform in this situation. A decision task is defined by a *trigger* indicating that the situation has occured; a *decision space* listing the possible alternatives the controller has in this situation; and a set of *(local) constraints and preferences* on the decision space determining which actions are eligible and which are preferred.

Since control decisions can have far-reaching effects, the control decisions may be dependent on each other for finding the best control actions that create an optimal system performance. These **dependencies** are identified and characterised by specifying *non-local constraints and preferences*, i.e., constraints and preferences that involve several decision tasks. Whenever a dependency exists between decision tasks belonging to different agents, these agents need to interact in order to determine the decision alternative that not only satisfies the local, but also the non-local constraints and preferences. To select an existing interaction protocol that is able to perform this interaction is the goal of the design method presented in this paper.

3   Selecting Interaction Protocols

To re-use existing interaction protocols, there must be a design method that enables the designer to select a suitable protocol given the description of a decision dependency between decision tasks. Such a design method must provide a set of criteria such that the interaction protocol which matches a dependency best – according to these criteria – is also the best interaction protocol to resolve the dependency. Given such a set of criteria, the designer only needs to classify a dependency according to these criteria and then search through a library of existing interaction techniques to find the interaction protocol that matches the classification best (see figure 1). In case, this library is computer-based, the search process may even be done automatically.

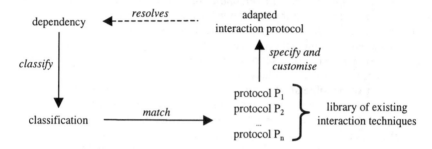

Fig. 1. The process for selecting interaction protocols.

The proposed process for selecting interaction protocols is a *heuristic classification* [4] because the selection mechanism is based on an abstract description of the interaction situation and the protocols. Such an abstraction is necessary if there is no direct matching between problem and solution (see [4] for a discussion). This direct link does not exist because a dependency may be solved by several interaction protocols.

To select an interaction protocol for a given dependency, the designer must consequently perform three steps. The first one is to classify the dependency according to a pre-defined set of criteria (called the **classification scheme** in what follows). The second step of the selection process is to match the classification of the dependency against a library of existing interaction techniques. A **matching procedure** specifies how the matching is performed and how, based on the results of this matching, the interaction protocol best suited to resolve the dependency is identified. To make such a matching possible, the existing interaction protocols must be classified according to the same criteria as the dependency. This process – which needs to be done only once for each interaction protocol – will be called **protocol characterisation** in the following. Once a suitable interaction protocol has been identified, the last step of the selection process is to specify it in terms of the application and, if necessary, to adapt it to the specific requirements of the dependency situation. This final step will be referred to as the **protocol customisation**.

The following subsections describe each aspect of the selection process in detail. The first subsection develops the classification scheme for dependencies. Subsection 3.2 shows how existing interaction protocols must be characterised in order to match the classification scheme and gives two examples of such characterisations. Subsection 3.3 then presents the procedure for matching dependencies to existing protocols, and explains to what extent a chosen protocol can be customised to fit an actual dependency situation in a given application.

3.1   Classification Scheme

The classification scheme is the core mechanism for re-using interaction protocols. To enable efficient re-use, this scheme should classify dependencies such that the interaction protocol which matches the classification of a dependency best is also the best interaction protocol to resolve the dependency. The classification scheme must consequently consist of classification criteria that put dependencies into different classes if they require different (kinds of) interaction protocols. To identify such a set of criteria, it is necessary to look at the requirements a dependency may impose on the interaction process and collect those aspects which differentiate dependencies most with respect to the required interaction process. This is the objective of this subsection.

A dependency consists of a set of decision tasks and a set of non-local constraints and preferences these decision tasks must fulfil (see section 2). Each decision task specifies a set of possible *start situations* in which the decision problem arises; and the decision tasks in combination with the non-local constraints and preferences specify what *goal state* must be achieved in the end. Any interaction protocol supposed to resolve the dependency must be able to reach the goal state from any possible start situation. Start situations and goal state of a dependency thus delineate the functionality of the required interaction protocol. It must be applicable to any start situation and must be able to achieve all aspects of the goal state. Both, start situations and goal state, are therefore analysed below in order to identify classification criteria distinguishing interaction protocols with respect to their applicability.

Start Situation. A start situation of a dependency is basically defined by two aspects: the decision tasks that share a dependency, and the constraints and preferences that restrict their decision making. For the selection of an interaction protocol, both aspects must be classified in application-independent terms. (Application-dependent criteria would limit the universality of the re-use mechanism and are also not appropriate because most interaction protocols are defined in general terms.)

Decision Tasks Involved in the Dependency. The first relevant criterion for the selection of a suitable interaction protocol is certainly the number of decision tasks that need to be co-ordinated. Is there, for instance, a small and fixed number of decision tasks that need to interact, or does the set of decision tasks change over time? Since dependent decision tasks only need to be co-ordinated if they belong to different agents, the first relevant criterion for selecting interaction protocols is therefore the number of agents involved in the dependency.

> **Criterion #1:** *Number of agents involved*
>
> How many agents are involved in the dependency right from the start? May other agents join later?

The possible answers to the above questions are classified according to the requirements they impose on the required interaction process.

fix   The number of agents involved in the dependency is fixed at the beginning of the interaction.

changing   The number of agents involved may change during the interaction, i.e., agents may join the interaction process after it has been started. Agents may join later, for example, because they have been introduced to the control system after the beginning of the interaction.

The second class – *changing* – imposes a stronger requirement on the interaction process than the first class. When the number of agents involved is fixed, the interaction protocol chosen must be able to deal with an arbitrary, but fix number of agents. In the special case that the number of agents involved is fixed and already known at design time, the designer may even choose an interaction protocol that is only able to deal with the number of agents indicated. Some interaction protocols, for instance, are only able to co-ordinate two agents. In case the number of agents is not fixed, but changing, the protocol must additionally be able to integrate new agents into the interaction process after it has been initiated.

Relation of Constraints and Preferences. The other important aspect of the start situation is how the decision tasks involved in the dependency are related to each other. Each agent has its local decision tasks, but is not able to execute them locally because of the non-local constraints and preferences that restrict the local decision making. As a consequence, the agents need to interact. The nature of the restrictions on the local decision making, however, have an influence on the kind of interaction required to deal with these restrictions. Agents that have completely opposing interests will have to interact more than agents that just want to avoid some damaging actions. The second relevant criterion for the selection of a suitable interaction protocol is therefore the relation of local and non-local constraints and preferences.

Criterion #2: *Compatibility of constraints and preferences*
How compatible are the local and non-local constraints and preferences involved in a dependency?

The compatibility is classified according to the kinds of restrictions that create the dependency:

only constraints   There are only constraints. These constraints – by definition – only rule out certain combinations of decision alternatives. Any combination of decision alternatives that is not ruled out is a solution resolving the dependency. Naturally, there may exist no solution satisfying all constraints.

compatible preferences   There exists at least one (local or non-local) preference function on the outcome of the interaction (and possibly additional constraints). In case of more than one preference function, there are solutions that are to the mutual benefit of all agents, i.e., that satisfy all preference functions.

opposing preferences   There are at least two agents that have preferences on the outcome of the interaction and these preferences are opposing, i.e., there is no combination of decision alternatives that maximises all local and non-local preference functions. (Constraints may be present or not.)

Another important aspect of the constraints and preferences linking the decision tasks is to what extent these constraints and preferences are global, i.e., encompass all decision tasks of a dependency. By definition, the non-local constraints and preferences involve at least two decision tasks. However, if there are more than two agents, the non-local constraints and preferences may involve all agents and thus be global, or only link subsets of the agents. This distinction is particularly relevant if there are many agents. In such a case, it may be far easier to co-ordinate small subsets of these agents than to make sure that all agents satisfy a global constraint or maximise a global preference function. Therefore, the start situation is also classified according to the existence of global constraints and preferences.

Criterion #3: *Global constraints and preferences*
> In case there are more than two agents, does there exist a global constraint or preference that involves all decision tasks?

The cases in which there are more than two agents and a global constraint or preference exists, are indicated by *global*. All other cases are defined as ***non-local***.

Goal State. To resolve a dependency, the relevant agents need to choose an action for each decision task such that the local and non-local constraints and preferences are satisfied in the best manner possible. The goal state of a dependency is thus specified by a list of actions – one for each decision task. At least something about this goal state must be unknown at the start in order to represent a decision problem. Thus it will either be unclear which actions are to be taken by each agent or, if the decision spaces include the null action, which agents will be taking an action at all (otherwise the agents do not have a decision task). The interaction protocol to be selected will have to answer whichever question is unanswered at the beginning of the interaction. The first question – which action should be executed – however will be unanswered in most cases, and will therefore hardly distinguish interaction situations. The second question – which agent should commit to an action – on the other hand, may or may not be clear at the beginning. The second question is thus not common to all interaction situations and may consequently be used to distinguish dependencies with respect to the requirements they impose on the interaction protocol. This will be done below (see *role variability*).

The second important aspect of a goal state is how the actual decisions made relate to each other. Not necessarily every decision will equally depend on every other decision involved in the dependency. Consequently, at the end of the interaction not every agent will have to commit itself in front of everybody else to the decisions made (even if they are all dependent on each other). Maybe some agents form a subgroup that is independent in their execution of the rest of the agents involved in the dependency. The number and size of the required joint commitments, however, is relevant to the selection of a suitable interaction protocol. Bilateral joint commitments are easier to achieve than a joint commitment encompassing all agents. The required joint commitments are therefore also analysed below (see *joint commitments*).

The criteria for classifying the joint commitments are presented first because any interaction situation requires joint commitments to be made.

Joint Commitments. In the context of this work, a set of commitments is called a **joint commitment** if the failure to fulfil one of the commitments jeopardises the success of the other commitments. That is, the set of commitments only makes sense if all commitments are fulfilled. If one agent de-commits, all other agents should de-commit, too.

Formally, joint commitments are represented by subsets of the agents involved in a dependency. If one agent of such a subset de-commits, all other agents in this subset should de-commit, too. The joint commitments required by a dependency may thus have quite diverse structures – namely any subset of the power set of the agents is theoretically a possible set of joint commitments. However, to make a comparison of joint commitments feasible and efficient, the classification of the required joint commitments is reduced to two criteria: the number of (independent) joint commitments, and the size of the commitments.

Criterion #4: *Number of joint commitments*

Is the number of joint commitments required in the goal state already known at the beginning of the interaction, or must it be determined by the interaction protocol?

The possible answers to the above question are indicated as follows:

fix   The number of required joint commitments is known at the beginning of the interaction.

variable   The number of required joint commitments must be determined by the interaction protocol.

Criterion #5: *Size of joint commitments*

How many agents are involved in a joint commitment? Do all joint commitments have the same size?

The possible answers to the above question are indicated as follows:

fix   All joint commitments have the same size.

differing The joint commitments may have different size.

variable   The size of the joint commitments must be determined by the interaction protocol.

Role Variability. The goal state is described by a set of agent-action pairs, specifying which agent is executing which action. As discussed above, it may be unclear which of the agents available in the interaction situation will actually perform an action, and thus will be a member of one of the agent-action pairs. To capture this potential uncertainty, the goal state will be characterised with the help of roles [10]. A role describes a specific behaviour without specifying which agent will actually perform this behaviour. In this view, the goal state consists of a set of roles, each specifying an action, and one task of the interaction protocol – apart from identifying these actions – is to assign these roles to agents. To classify this assignment problem for a given dependency, it is necessary to identify which roles are already assigned to agents and which must be assigned during the interaction process.

Criterion #6: *Role assignment*

Is an agent role already assigned to an agent, or must the role assignment be determined by the interaction protocol?

For each role, there are two possible answers: A role is either *fix* or *variable*. The classification of the agent roles can therefore be summarised by stating how many roles are variable (all others then must be fixed). Three cases are distinguished:

none	None of the agent roles are variable.
subset	A subset of the agent roles is variable.
all	All agent roles are variable.

The variability of a role is relevant to the selection of an interaction protocol because a variable role requires that the interaction protocol must not only choose an appropriate action, but must also find an agent to execute it. It is also relevant how many of the agent roles are variable because it is easier to assign some roles than all roles. Who will perform the role assignment if all roles (including the role of assigning the roles) is variable?

Summary. This section has identified six classification criteria that characterise decision dependencies with respect to the interaction process they require. These criteria define 216 possible classifications – namely the product of the possible classifications for each criterion. Due to the diverse aspects covered, these classifications already cover a wide range of different dependency situations. More criteria, however, can be defined and added to the classification scheme if necessary. How many, and in particular which criteria are necessary in order to optimally match interaction situations with interaction protocols ultimately depends on the type of dependencies encountered in an application and on the types of interaction protocols existing. Our experience, however, shows that the criteria presented here provide a sufficient basis for reducing the set of suitable interaction protocols to a small set (which then can be assessed manually).

3.2   Characterising Interaction Protocols

The re-use mechanism proposed in this paper requires that existing interaction protocols are characterised according to the same criteria as the interaction situations (see beginning of this section). Once such a characterisation of the existing interaction protocols is given (and it needs to be done only once for each protocol), the most suitable interaction protocol can be identified by matching the classification of the dependency against a library of existing interaction protocols.

The characterisation of an interaction protocol, though, is not simply a classification according to the scheme presented in the previous subsection. Instead of assigning it to a specific class of dependencies, an interaction protocol should be assigned to all those classes which it can efficiently solve. The task of the characterisation is therefore to analyse the interaction protocol with respect to the classes of dependencies it could possibly address.

As a first step towards a library of existing interaction protocols, a diverse set of protocols has already been characterised. This set includes protocols from consensus formation, bargaining, auction theory (in particular, one-sided and continuous double auctions), negotiation, distributed constraint satisfaction, coalition formation, and distributed planning. Due to space limitations, only two examples of protocol characterisations can be given in this paper. The protocols presented below were chosen because they are characterised quite differently.

The Contract Net Protocol. The contract net protocol (CNP) is a simple, but efficient protocol for assigning tasks to individual nodes in a network [18]. It assumes that one node has a task that needs to be executed and that there are several nodes that are able to execute this task. The node with the task is called the *manager* and the other nodes are (potential) *contractors*. The manager initiates the protocol by announcing the task to the potential contractors, which answer with a bid. The manager compares the bids and chooses the best bid according to its preferences. The node which has sent the best bid then receives an award message and is said to have a contract with the manager about the execution of the task. The other nodes may or may not receive a reject message.

Criterion #1 – Number of agents involved: **fix**

The CNP involves several agents, namely one manager and at least two bidders. The number of bidders must be fixed at the beginning of the interaction because the manager announces the task to be contracted only once to exactly these bidders (of course, the protocol may be changed to accommodate a changing set of bidders).

Criterion #2 – Compatibility of preferences: **compatible**

The constraints and preferences of the different agents must be at least compatible. If the preference were opposing, it would not be possible to find a mutually acceptable compromise with the first bid.

Criterion #3 – Global constraints and preferences   **non-local**

The CNP is not able to handle global preferences because each agent (i.e., manager and contractors) only take into account their local decision preferences.

Criterion #4 – Number of joint commitments: **1**
Criterion #5 – Size of joint commitments: **2**
Criterion #6 – Role assignment: **1/1**

There is only one joint commitment in the goal state, namely that of the manager and the contractor that wins the contract. Obviously, the size of this joint commitment is two and it consists of only two roles. The first role, i.e., that of the manager, is fixed and the other role variable.

The relation of agent roles and joint commitments in the CNP is schematically exemplified in the following figure.

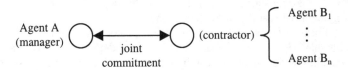

Fig. 2. The decision structure of the CNP.

Partial Global Planning. Partial global planning (PGP) was developed to co-ordinate distributed planners for sensory interpretation, each executing its own local plan for the interpretation of the distributed data [7]. To achieve the co-ordination of the distributed planners efficiently, the agents abstract from their plans and exchange these abstractions. Given the different local plan abstractions, each agent is then able to identify common goals to which the local goals of the agents contribute. Since these common goals may be only partially known to the agents, they are called *partial global goals*. Once a partial global goal has been identified, the local plans can be integrated into partial global plans. PGP in its original description provides two mechanisms to perform this integration: redundant tasks are avoided, and tasks are performed earlier if this facilitates the work of other agents. In contrast to many other interaction protocols, PGP is therefore an on-going mechanism for global co-ordination:

Criterion #1 – Number of agents involved: **changing**

Since the planning process is on-going and intertwined with the execution, agents may join the planning process at any time.

Criterion #2 – Compatibility of preferences: **compatible**

PGP is designed for co-operative agents. There is no mechanism in PGP to reconcile opposing interests.

Criterion #3 – Global constraints and preferences   **global**

During the planning process, the agents construct (partial) global plans and try to optimise the overall system behaviour.

Criterion #4 – Number of joint commitments: **variable**
Criterion #5 – Size of joint commitments: **variable**
Criterion #6 – Role assignment: **all variable**

The number of joint commitments and their size depends on the global goals, i.e., the dependencies, that are identified. Since the local plans may be changed when integrated into the partial global plans, the roles of the agents may change also.

3.3   Matching and Customising Interaction Protocols

Given a library of existing interaction protocols characterised according to the classification scheme, the designer is now able to run through the following steps in order to select a suitable interaction protocol for a given dependency.

1. Collect all decision tasks involved in the dependency.
2. Identify all possible start situations in which this dependency may arise.
3. Perform the classification of the dependency.
4. Given a library of characterised interaction protocols, search for the interaction protocols that best match the classification of the dependency. An interaction protocol matches a dependency best if its classification has the most attributes in common with the classification of the dependency.
5. For each protocol identified, verify whether it is able to reach the goal state from all possible start situations. If this is not the case for a protocol, try to modify the protocol accordingly (see below).
6. Choose the interaction protocol that resolves the dependency best (after the customisation) and specify the (possibly adapted) interaction protocol (e.g., using the specification language presented in [1]).

If all six steps of the above method are successfully completed, the designer has found an interaction protocol that resolves the dependency and has thus solved the design task (concerning the interaction situation). The above method, however, may fail to identify a suitable interaction protocol for a dependency. This may have two reasons:

- It is not possible to resolve the dependency without resolving simultaneously other dependencies the decision tasks are involved in. In such a case, the above method has to be repeated with an enlarged scope. That is, in step one of the method all decision tasks involved in the set of (potentially) relevant dependencies are collected.
- It is possible to resolve the dependency, but there are no suitable interaction protocols in the library available to the designer. In this case, a new interaction protocol must be designed (or the identification of the control agents must be revised in order to arrive at a different set of dependencies).

Customising Interaction Protocols. For each interaction protocol that matches the dependency classification, it must be verified whether this protocol is able to reach the goal state from all possible start situations. An interaction protocol may fail to do so either because it is not applicable to one of the start situations, or because it does not reach the desired goal state. In the latter case, the designer must either redesign the protocol or choose a different protocol. In the former case, it may be possible – either at design or at run time – to transform the actual start situation into one to which the protocol can be applied. Here, two aspects are discussed.

First of all, the agents supposed to initiate the interaction protocol do not receive a trigger, or too many agents initiate the interaction protocol. In both cases, the interaction protocol must be preceded by a phase in which either the triggered agents inform the agents supposed to initiate the interaction protocol, or, in the second case, the agents clarify who should initiate the interaction process (e.g., through a voting process [16]).

Secondly, an agent may not have sufficient knowledge to perform its role in the decision making process. In such a case, the agents may have to gather (or compute) information before they can engage in the actual decision making protocol. As for decision making protocols, there are also a vast number of interaction protocols which are able to gather information in an agent-based system [11].

3.4   Examples

This section gives two examples for matching the classification of a dependency with a suitable interaction protocol. The example dependencies are taken from two real-world control applications at DaimlerChrysler – the first application is already in operation, the second is currently being prototyped.

Choosing a Machine. For the first example, assume that a workpiece must choose a machine to perform the next set of operations. Further assume that an agent is associated with the workpiece and each machine. For choosing the next machine, there is consequently a dependency between the workpiece agent – which wants to choose a machine – and the machine agents – which must accept the workpiece for processing. Finally, assume that there is only one start situation, namely the workpiece agent is looking for a machine. The classification of this dependency is then as follows.

Criterion #1 – Number of agents involved: **fix**

There is a fix number of agents, namely the workpiece agent and all machine agents in the production system that could possibly process the workpiece.

Criterion #2 – Compatibility of preferences: **compatible**
Criterion #3 – Global constraints and preferences   **non-local**

Constraints and preferences are assumed to be compatible because the workpiece agent wants to get processed and the machine agents want to offer processing (however, it may not be that simple in all control applications!). Furthermore, there are no global constraints or preferences; each agent is trying to optimise its performance.

Criterion #4 – Number of joint commitments: 1
Criterion #5 – Size of joint commitments: 2
Criterion #6 – Role assignment: 1/1

The dependency is resolved if the workpiece has identified a machine that is most suitable for processing the workpiece and the machine has agreed to process it. Consequently, the agents are searching for a single joint commitment between two agents. The first role of the joint commitment, the workpiece agent, is obviously fixed, and the second role, that of the machine, is to be determined.

The above classification matches perfectly to the contract net protocol (see section 3.2), even though there exist other protocols, such as voting or auction protocols, that also match well with the above classification. A short analysis, however, shows that the CNP is sufficient to resolve the dependency. There is also no need to customise the CNP. (Due to space limitations, the last step – specifying the interaction protocol is omitted.)

Meeting Deadlines. For the second example, assume that each workpiece in a manufacturing system must meet a deadline for its delivery to the customer. Furthermore assume that each workpiece must run through several machines and that it uses the interaction protocol identified in the previous example to choose the next machine. Since the workpieces may compete for the machines when trying to meet their deadlines, there exists a dependency between all workpieces (and all their decision tasks to choose the next machine) in that the workpieces should resolve these conflicts such that the average tardiness, i.e., the average deadline violation, is minimised. This dependency is classified as follows:

Criterion #1 – Number of agents involved: **changing**

There is a changing set of agents since a new workpiece agent is created every time a new workpiece enters the manufacturing system.

Criterion #2 – Compatibility of preferences: **opposing**
Criterion #3 – Global constraints and preferences   **global**

The workpiece agents may run into conflicts concerning the machine usage that cannot be resolved without one workpiece missing its deadline. The global preference, of course, is to minimise the average tardiness.

Criterion #4 – Number of joint commitments: **variable**
Criterion #5 – Size of joint commitments: **differing**
Criterion #6 – Role assignment: **some variable**

Joint commitments are constantly formed as workpiece agents enter the manufacturing system. In particular, each workpiece agent will engage in several joint commitments with machine agents. The joint commitments, though, may include more than two agents in case several workpiece agents resolve a resource conflict by agreeing on a certain order for using the conflict resource. The size of the commitments is therefore differing. Finally, the roles of the workpiece agents are all fixed, but the roles of the machines are not.

With respect to the existing interaction protocols characterised so far, the above classification matches best with the partial global planning approach which fully matches or subsumes the above classification (see section 3.2). Other interaction protocols, such as the continuous double auction or distributed constraint satisfaction, have less correspondence.

Conceptually, the PGP approach is also able to resolve the above problem of meeting deadlines. Several agents follow their plans to meet a certain deadline by allocating resources and may run into conflicts with other agents. These conflicts must be identified and resolved by the interaction protocol, just as PGP does so for distributed hypothesis formation. Since PGP was designed for distributed hypothesis formation, though, the interaction approach of PGP must be adapted to accommodate the peculiarities of the above problem (the same is true for GPGP as presented in [6]). Firstly, conflicts occur because of an overloaded resource. And secondly, conflicts must be resolved by determining – possibly through negotiation – which workpiece has a higher priority. Strictly speaking, PGP and GPGP thus do not resolve the above dependency because the necessary changes go beyond protocol customisation as defined in the previous subsection. However, with PGP/GPGP a general framework has been identified that provides a basis for developing an adapted interaction protocol.

4   Related Work

The work on interaction-oriented programming has proposed analysis and design methods that use interactions as a basic concept for structuring an agent-based system (see e.g. [8,14]). These approaches put emphasis on the necessary interactions in an agent-based system and use concepts like team modelling or goal decomposition to identify the need for interaction. So far, however, this work has not addressed the aspect of identifying existing interaction protocols able to satisfy this need.

An increasing amount of work has been invested in the development of design patterns for agent-based systems (see e.g. [9,12] for the concepts). In this work, concepts of agent-based systems are specified in a general format in order to allow the re-use of these patterns. The work on design patterns is thus complementary to our work. While design patterns provide the re-usable interaction protocols, our design method explains how to choose the right interaction protocol for the design problem at hand.

Several researchers have developed taxonomies for classifying dependencies (see e.g. [13,17]). But despite their ground-breaking work, these classifications are not sufficient for re-using interaction protocols. Malone and Crowston [13], for instance, only provide a detailed taxonomy for tasks having resource conflicts. Their taxonomy does not cover state or preference conflicts (e.g., two workpieces which need to be assembled into one agreeing on the goal station). Malone and Crowston themselves do not claim to provide a complete taxonomy; for the re-use of interaction protocols, though, a complete taxonomy of interaction protocols is required (even if it is less detailed).

5   Conclusion

This paper has presented a method for re-using existing interaction protocols during the design of agent-based control applications. The main contribution of this work is a set of classification criteria that extracts the general requirements of an interaction situation on the interaction protocol to be used. The classification criteria are easily applied to an interaction situation because they were derived from the general specification of such situations. It is therefore relatively straightforward for a designer following the first two steps of the DACS methodology to perform the classification of each interaction situation. How this is done was shown with the help of two example dependencies from real-world control applications at DaimlerChrysler. Furthermore, the paper has shown – due to the space limitations with only two examples – that the classification scheme puts conceptually different interaction protocols into different classes. The classification scheme thus enables a designer to select a suitable interaction protocol for a given interaction situation and thus to re-use existing interaction protocols he is not familiar with.

This claim has been validated in several real-world control applications – most of which have led to the implementation of a realistic simulation. After the first two applications the method has been revised considerably and the result has been presented here. To complete the evaluation, it is planned to test the complete DACS methodology with engineers designing control systems. Once these tests are successfully completed, the methodology can be released to development teams.

Nevertheless, it is not expected that the design method presented in this paper will remain unaltered after release. First of all, new interaction protocols will be developed in the future and, once characterised, should be added to the protocol library to enlarge the set of protocols that can be re-used. Secondly, new classification criteria may have to be added in the future if the newly developed interaction protocols fall into a single class of the existing classification scheme. Such an extension of the classification scheme could, for example, address further variations of the distributed constraint satisfaction technique. The work presented in this paper, though, has developed the concepts and the basic criteria for re-using existing interaction protocols.

References

1. B. Burmeister, A. Haddadi, K. Sundermeyer: Generic Configurable Cooperation Protocols for Multi-Agent Systems. In C. Castelfranchi, J.-P. Müller (eds.), *From Cognition to Action*, LNAI 957, pp. 157 – 171. Springer-Verlag, 1995.

2. S. Bussmann, N.R. Jennings, M.J. Wooldridge: On the Identification of Agents in the Design of Production Control Systems. In [3], pp. 141 – 162.
3. P. Ciancarini, M.J. Wooldridge (eds.), *Agent-Oriented Software Engineering*, LNCS 1957. Springer-Verlag, 2001.
4. W.J. Clancey: Heuristic Classification. In *Artificial Intelligence*, Vol. 27, pp. 289 – 350, 1985.
5. B. Coulange: *Software Reuse*. Springer-Verlag, 1998.
6. K.S. Decker, V.R. Lesser: Designing a Family of Coordination Algorithms. In *Proc. of the First Int. Conf. on Multi-Agent Systems*, pp. 73 – 80. San Francisco, USA, 1995.
7. E.H. Durfee: Planning in Distributed Artificial Intelligence. In G.M.P. O'Hare, N.R. Jennings (eds.), *Foundations of Distributed Artificial Intelligence*, pp. 231 – 245. John Wiley & Sons, 1996.
8. M.N. Huhns: Interaction-Oriented Programming. In [3], pp. 29 – 44.
9. E.A. Kendall: Role Models: Patterns of Agent Analysis and Design. In *British Telecom Technical Journal*, 1999.
10. E.A. Kendall: Agent Software Engineering with Role Modelling. In [3], pp. 163 – 169.
11. M. Klusch: Information Agent Technology for the Internet: A Survey. In *Journal on Data and Knowledge Engineering*, Vol. 36, No. 3, 2001.
12. J. Lind: Patterns in Agent-Oriented Software Engineering. In this volume.
13. T.W. Malone, K. Crowston: The Interdisciplinary Study of Coordination. In *ACM Computing Surveys*, Vol. 26, No. 1, pp. 87 – 119, 1994.
14. S. Miles, M. Joy, M. Luck: Designing Agent-Oriented Systems by Analysing Agent Interactions. In [3], pp. 171 – 183.
15. H. Mili, F. Mili, A. Mili: Reusing Software: Issues and Research Directions. In *IEEE Trans. on Software Engineering*, Vol. 21, No. 6, pp. 528 – 561, 1995.
16. T.W. Sandholm: Distributed Rational Decision Making. In G. Weiss (ed.), *Multi-Agents Systems*, pp. 201 – 258. MIT Press, 1999.
17. J.S. Sichman, R. Conte, C. Castelfranchi, Y. Demazeau: A Social Reasoning Mechanism Based On Dependence Networks. In *Proc. of the 11ᵗʰ European Conf. on Artificial Intelligence*, pp. 188 – 192. John Wiley & Sons, 1994.
18. R.G. Smith: The contract net protocol: High-level communication and control in distributed problem solving. In *IEEE Transactions on Computers*, Vol. C-29, No. 12, pp. 1104 – 1113, 1980.
19. M.J. Wooldridge, G. Weiß, P. Ciancarini (eds.): *Agent-Oriented Software Engineering II*, LNCS 2222. Springer-Verlag, 2002.

Architecting for Reuse: A Software Framework for Automated Negotiation

Claudio Bartolini[1], Chris Preist[1], and Nicholas R. Jennings[2]

[1] HP Laboratories, Filton Rd, BS34 8QZ, Bristol, UK, +44 117 312 8311
{claudio_bartolini,chris_preist}@hp.com
[2] Dept. of Electronics and Computer Science, University of Southampton, UK
nrj@ecs.soton.ac.uk

Abstract. If agents are to negotiate automatically with one another they must share a negotiation mechanism, specifying what possible actions each party can take at any given time, when negotiation terminates, and what the resulting agreements will be. The current state-of-the-art represents this as a negotiation protocol specifying the flow of messages. However, they omit other aspects of the rules of negotiation (such as obliging a participant to improve on a previous offer), requiring these to be represented implicitly in an agent's design, potentially resulting in compatibility, maintenance and re-usability problems. In this paper, we propose an alternative approach, allowing all of a mechanism to be formal and explicit. We present (i) A taxonomy of declarative rules which can be used to capture a wide variety of negotiation mechanisms in a principled and well-structured way. (ii) A simple interaction protocol, which is able to support any mechanism which can be captured using the declarative rules. (iii) A software framework for negotiation, implemented in JADE [3] that allows agents to effectively participate in negotiations defined using our rule taxonomy and protocol.

1 Motivation

Recently there has been much interest in the role of dynamic negotiation in electronic business transactions. For negotiation to take place between two or more parties, they need to agree on what economists refer to as a *market mechanism* or *negotiation mechanism*. This defines the rules of the "game" which the parties are engaged in and so determines the space of the possible actions that they can take. Within this game, each party adopts a *strategy* which determines exactly which actions they make (in response to actions by other parties or external events) in an effort to maximise their gain. The mechanism must be public and shared by all parties, while an individual's strategy stays private, and is only revealed implicitly through the actions they take. For example, consider a simple market mechanism for an English auction. It is defined by the following rules: (i)The buyers can post bids at any time. (ii) A bid is only valid if it is higher than the currently highest bid. (iii) Termination occurs when no buyer has posted a bid in the last five minutes. (iv) The good is sold to the buyer with the current highest bid at the price bid.

F. Giunchiglia et al. (Eds.): AOSE 2002, LNCS 2585, pp. 88–100, 2003.

The participants in the auction are constrained by these rules, but have a free choice of what action to take within them. A simple strategy for a buyer in such an auction is to set a maximum limit to the price they are willing to pay for the good, and to bid whenever the current highest bid is held by another buyer and is lower than their price limit.

In this paper *we consider mechanisms not strategies.* If a negotiation is to be automated, all agents need a shared understanding of the mechanism. This is done through the specification of a negotiation protocol. The protocol determines the flow of messages between participants, specifying when an agent can send a message, and what messages it can send as valid responses to specified incoming messages. For example, a negotiation protocol for the English auction states that (among other things) that potential buyers send messages specifying their bids to the auctioneer, and receive an accept or reject message in response. When the auction terminates, all participants receive a message informing them of who the winner is, and the winning bid.

Various protocols are used for automated negotiation. They can be one-to-one (such as iterated bargaining [10]), one-to-many or many-to-many (such as auctions [15]). However, most state-of-the-art multi-agent systems are designed with a single negotiation protocol explicitly hard-coded in all agents (usually as finite state machines). This leads to an inflexible environment, only able to accept agents designed for it. An advance on this is provided by standardization activities such as FIPA [6]. FIPA provides formal definitions of several standard negotiation protocols. The FIPA protocol for an English auction, described informally above, is shown in [6].

However, these negotiation protocols only formalise the interactions between the agents involved. They specify the permissable flow of messages, but omit information regarding other aspects of the *rules of negotiation* in a market mechanism. For example, the FIPA English Auction protocol does not specify the criteria for a bid being acceptable (i.e. that it must be greater than the current highest bid) or the conditions under which the auction will terminate (i.e. that no bids have arrived in the last few minutes). Hence, because the multi-agent environment does not make these explicit, the designer of an agent using the protocol must be aware of these negotiation rules and design their agent taking them into account. As a result of this, with the exception of the interaction aspects, the negotiation mechanism is implicit in the design of the multi agent system [8].

From the perspective of good software engineering practice, this approach has several severe disadvantages:

1. Because a negotiation protocol underspecifies a negotiation mechanism, it is not sufficient to merely standardise the protocol. For example, two agents accurately implementing the FIPA English auction protocol may differ in their criteria as to what makes a bid acceptable. One may accept any bid greater than the current highest bid, while another may require the bid to be at least a minimum increment over it. A standard must either make decisions on exactly which negotiation rules apply, or provide a standardised way of agreeing them.

2. The designer of an agent must make themselves aware of the implicit assumptions in any given negotiation protocol, to ensure that their agent behaves appropriately. For this to happen, the designers of a multi-agent system must effectively document these, and ensure that all agent designers comply with them.

3. If the standard specification of a market mechanism is changed, all the agents that comply with it need to be updated to cope with the changes. As the mechanism rules are implicit rather than explicit, unless the agents has been very carefully designed for generality at the beginning, this will be a non-trivial task.

4. Let us assume that a multi-agent system contains several mechanisms which are similar (for example English auctions which have different bid increments or closing conditions). There is no standard way of an agent determining these details and adjusting its behaviour appropriately. This makes reuse of agents between multi-agent systems more difficult.

Given these observations, we propose an alternative to that currently adopted by FIPA. Our approach allows negotiation rules to be explicitly specified and categorised both at the design and at the implementation stage of agent oriented software development. We carry out an analysis of a generic negotiation process, which is able to capture common aspects of a wide variety of types of negotiation[1]. From there we derive: (i) A taxonomy of declarative rules which can be used to capture a wide variety of negotiation mechanisms in a principled and well-structured way. (ii) A simple interaction protocol, which is able to support any mechanism which can be captured using the declarative rules. This approach has the following advantages:

1. The generic negotiation process and rule taxonomy provide valuable conceptual tools for software engineers designing multi-agent systems which involve negotiation mechanisms. Their application will result in the mechanisms being represented in a more modular and explicit way than current approaches.

2. A set of rules together with an interaction protocol will fully specify a negotiation mechanism. Because of this, all information required for the design of agents using the negotiation mechanism is explicit and well-structured. This makes agent design and implementation easier, and reduces the risks of unintentional incorrect behaviour. This also opens the door for future research into creation and analysis of novel market mechanisms through exploration of new combinations of rules.

3. Because the rules specifying the negotiation mechanism are explicitly represented in the system, it is possible for an agent to reason over them to determine its behaviour and strategy. Ideally, an agent would be able to participate effectively in an arbitrary negotiation mechanism specified by any set of rules. This is far beyond current state-of-the-art in negotiation technology. However, there are negotiation algorithms able to participate in

---

[1] We are able to cover most of the bargaining and auctioning protocols that are found in literature. See [2] for details.

several different negotiation mechanisms, and able to adjust their behaviour depending on the details of the mechanism. For example, [4] present an agent algorithm able to simultaneously participate in multiple English, Dutch and Sealed Bid auctions, requiring details of bid increments, closing times and sealed bid winner announcement times to determine its exact behaviour. An agent using such an algorithm could identify auctions of different types by checking the mechanism rules against templates, and could identify parameter values in the rules to determine the mechanism details.

To demonstrate the validity of this approach, in this paper we also describe a software framework for automated negotiation, implemented in JADE [3] that allows agents to effectively participate in negotiations defined using our rule taxonomy and protocol. The software framework can form a highly modular and reusable component in a multi-agent system. It advances the state of the art beyond the negotiation protocol approach because (i) it can be used to implement a wide variety of negotiation mechanisms simply by instantiating it with appropriate sets of rules. (ii) It is easy to maintain and update. If a software engineer determines that a particular negotiation must change its mechanism, all they need do is adjust the rules appropriately. (iii) Agents involved in that negotiation can access the new rules, so at worst can identify that their current behaviour is inappropriate and issue a warning. A more advanced agent would be able to automatically modify their behaviour as necessary, provided the changes to the mechanism were not too great.

2   The Generic Negotiation Framework

In this section, we present an abstraction of the negotiation process, developed from the analysis of many different negotiations, both automated and human. From this, we develop a general protocol for negotiation.

2.1   An Abstract Negotiation Process

The roles involved in the negotiation process are *negotiation participant* and *negotiation host*. In some market mechanisms participants address one another, whereas in others (e.g. auctions), participants send messages to a negotiation host that forwards them to other participants that have the right and interest in seeing them. Our abstraction is that participants always publish their proposals on a common multicast space, the *negotiation locale*, which is managed by the negotiation host. The negotiation locale can be considered as a form of blackboard, with access to write and visibility of information on it mediated by the negotiation host. Visibility rules are associated to proposals so that only the participants that have right to see them can see them. This allows us to see one-to-one and one-to-many negotiation as a particular case of many-to-many[2].

---

[2] This model always requires the participants to trust the negotiation host. Trust consideration are beyond the scope of this paper.

The agent playing the host role may also play a participant role (e.g. in one-to-one negotiation) or may be non-participatory (e.g. the auctioneer in an auction). In some cases, the role of negotiation host may alternate between different entities as the negotiation progresses.

The first action to be taken is for a participant to require *admission* to the negotiation. Admission consists of a simple conversation between the participant and the host where the participant requests admission to a particular negotiation and presents its credentials. Based on the credentials that the participant presents, the negotiation host decides whether to admit the participant to negotiation and informs the participant of the decision. If the participant is admitted, then we move onto the negotiation itself. The admission step is very important because it is when participants are informed of the rules of negotiation.

To be able to negotiate with one another, parties must initially share a *negotiation template*. This specifies the different parameters of the negotiation (e.g. product type, price, supply date etc). Some parameters may be constrained (e.g. product type will almost always be constrained in some way), while others may be completely open (e.g. price). A negotiation locale has a negotiation template associated with it and this defines the object of negotiation within the locale. As part of the admission process to the negotiation, participants must accept the negotiation template. The constraints expressed in the negotiation template remain static as the negotiation proceeds.

The process of *negotiation* is the move from a negotiation template to an acceptable agreement. A single negotiation may involve many parties, resulting in several agreements between different parties and some parties who do not reach agreement. For example, a stock exchange can be viewed as a negotiation where many buyers and sellers meet to trade a given stock. Many agreements are formed between buyers and sellers, and some buyers.

During negotiation, the participants exchange proposals representing the agreements currently acceptable to them. Each proposal will contain constraints over some or all of the parameters expressed in the negotiation template. These proposals are sent to the negotiation host. However, before a proposal is accepted by the locale, it must be valid. To be valid, it must satisfy two criteria:

- It must be a valid restriction of the parameter space defined by the negotiation template. The constraints represent the values of parameters that are currently acceptable. Often, a constraint will consist of a single acceptable value.
- The proposal must be submitted according to the set of rules that govern the way the negotiation takes place. These rules specify (among other things) who can make proposals, when they can be made, and what proposals can be submitted in relation to previous submissions. For example, auctions often have a "bid improvement" rule that requires any new proposal to buy to be for a higher price than previous proposals. Such rules are specified and agreed at the admission stage.

An *agreement* is formed according to the agreement formation rules associated with the negotiation locale. When the proposals in the locale satisfy certain conditions, they are converted by these rules into agreements, and returned to the proposers. The end of a negotiation is determined by termination rules. For example, in an English auction the termination rule would state that the auction finishes when no participant has placed a bid for a certain time, and the agreement formation rule would state that an agreement is formed between the highest bidder and the seller, at the price the bidder has bid.

This abstract process can be specialised to many different negotiation styles. For example, in one-to-one bargaining, participants take turns in exchanging proposals in a previously agreed format. The rules in this case are simple. Any proposal can be made, as long as it is consistent with the negotiation template and made in turn. The negotiation terminates when the same proposal is returned unchanged (which we take as declaration of acceptance) or when one party leaves the negotiation locale. In the former case, an agreement identical to the last proposal is formed. In an English auction, the proposals specify the price of the good, every other parameter being fully instantiated in the negotiation template. Negotiation rules state that every new proposal (bid) will be valid only if it is an improvement over the current best proposal. Termination occurs at a deadline, and the agreement formed will contain the specification of the good as expressed in the negotiation template, at the price specified in the winning bid.

2.2   Definition of the Generic Negotiation Protocol

We begin by describing the admission phase. The protocol requires the participant requesting admission to send an `ACL.PROPOSE`[3] message to the negotiation host. The payload of the message may contain credentials of the participant. The negotiation host replies either with an `ACL.ACCEPT_PROPOSAL` or an `ACL.REJECT_PROPOSAL` message, signifying admission (resp. rejection) of the participant to the negotiation.

After admission, the participants submit proposals by posting them to the negotiation locale. Participants do so by sending an `ACL.PROPOSE` message to the negotiation host. Proposal submission continues until termination is reached, as defined by the termination rules. Termination may occur after agreement formation (as in one-to-one bargaining), before agreement formation (as in a sealed-bid auction) or may be independent (as in a continuous double auction). Each time a participant submits a proposal the negotiation host checks that it is a constrained form of the negotiation template and is syntactically well formed. If the proposal is not valid, it is rejected. The submitter is notified with an `ACL.REJECT_PROPOSAL` message. If the proposal passes this first stage of validation, the negotiation host checks that it satisfies the negotiation rules. These rules define the way in which the negotiation should take place and may include restrictions on when a proposal can be made (e.g. participants must take turns to submit) and semantic requirements on valid proposals (e.g. requirements that a proposal must improve on previous ones). If the proposal passes this second

---

[3] We use FIPA ACL messages to describe the protocol. Other ACLs could equally be used.

validation stage, the current set of proposals and associated data structures are updated accordingly and the submitter and other participants are notified. Who is notified, and the structure of the notification, is defined by the visibility rules and display rules. The submitter is notified through an `ACL.ACCEPT_PROPOSAL` message. Others are notified through `ACL.INFORM` messages.

An agreement formation process can be triggered at any time during negotiation, according to the agreement formation rules. The negotiation host then looks at the current set of proposals to determine whether agreements can be made. Agreements can potentially occur whenever two or more negotiating parties make compatible proposals. If this is the case, agreement formation rules determine exactly which proposals are matched and the final instantiated agreement that will be used.

Agreement rules may state, for example, that the highest priced offer to buy should be matched with the lowest priced offer to sell and that the final agreement will take place at the average price. Often, *tie breaking* agreement rules will be defined that will be used if the main agreement rules can be applied in several ways. For example, earlier posted offers may take priority over later ones. When the agreement formation rules have been applied to determine exactly which agreements are made, the negotiation host notifies the participants with `ACL.INFORM messages.`

Having defined the general protocol for negotiation (for a more complete specification and graphical representation, see [2]), we now show how it can be specialized in a variety of different ways. We do this firstly by presenting a taxonomy of negotiation rules and then (in the context of our prototype implementation) example rules for different negotiation mechanisms.

A Taxonomy of Rules for Negotiation. Our analysis [2] has identified the following categories of negotiation rules:

Rules for admission of participants

Admission rules: Govern admission to negotiation.

Rules for proposal validity

Validity rule: Enforces that any submitted proposal has to be compliant with the negotiation template.

Rules for protocol enforcement

Posting rule: Determines when a participant may post a proposal.

Improvement rule: Specifies, given a set of existing proposals, what new proposals may be posted.

Withdrawal rule: Specifies if and when proposals can be withdrawn, and policies over the expiration time of proposals.

Rules for updating status and informing participants

Update rules: Specifies how the parameters of the negotiation change on occurrence of certain events.

Visibility rule: Specifies which participants can view a given proposal.

Display rule: Specifies if and how the information updater notifies the participants that a proposal has been submitted or an agreement has been made - either by transmitting the proposal unchanged or by transmitting a summary of the situation.

Rules for agreement formation

Agreement formation rules: Determine, given a set of proposals of which at least two are compatible, which agreements should be formed.

Tie-breaking rule: Specific agreement formation rule applied after all others.

Rules for lifecycle of negotiation

Termination rule: Specifies when no more proposals may be posted (e.g. a given time, period of quiescence).

3 Implementation of the Software Framework

In our software framework, the negotiation host functionality is implemented as a responsible agent and a set of subsidiary agents (cmp. [8]). Each sub-agent is responsible for the enforcement of one of the categories of rules described in section 2.2: *Gatekeeper* (admission), *Proposal Validator*, *Protocol Enforcer*, *Information Updater* (updating status and informing participants), *Negotiation Terminator* (lifecycle of negotiation) and *Agreement Maker*. Each sub-agent interacts with other agents, both via direct messaging and by sharing data using a blackboard system. Any agent can join as a negotiation participant, provided it conforms to the generic negotiation protocol described in section 2.

The main task of the negotiation host agents is to evaluate negotiation rules and take actions as a consequence. To do so, they use the blackboard which contains information about the negotiation as a whole (e.g. valid proposals, participants, status of the negotiation). Each of the agents is initialised with the negotiation rules that it is responsible for enforcing. They execute rules either in response to a message or in response to changing data on the blackboard. Full details of the abstract architecture are given in [2].

We have implemented the negotiation framework using the JADE multi-agent platform. JADE [3] is compliant with the FIPA abstract architecture. Agents communicate using messages in the FIPA Agent Communication Language (ACL) [6]. JADE provides tools for inspecting these messages and also provides a library of interaction protocols and generic agent behaviours, which we have used as the basis of our implementation. The negotiation host sub-agents are implemented as rule engines using the Java Expert System Shell (JESS). Following [7], we associate a JESS rule engine with a JADE agent. We implement our negotiation rules in the JESS rule language. The agent's behaviour monitors changes on the blackboard and incoming messages, and executes rules in response to these events. Details on scheduling rules execution are not given here for lack of space. Agents may write information about the negotiation on the blackboard. Proposals are also stored on the blackboard, provided they satisfy the negotiation template. Facts are asserted on the blackboard as JESS assertions. For example, parameters associated with an English auction can be specified in the following way:

```
(negotiation
    (seller-proposal Alice-37)
    (bid-increment 5)
    (termination-window 30min)
    (currently-highest-bid 0))
```

Facts are also asserted about participants and proposal status (valid, active).

3.1   Negotiation Proposals and Templates

The negotiation template is expressed as a collection of JESS facts and predicate constraints[4]. In order to express complex objects, the facts may make reference to JESS templates. In them we declare which fields must appear in every proposal and which are optional. We also define the type of each field and constraints on its value. For example, a negotiation host wishing to conduct auctions of cars could define the parameters as:

```
(deftemplate proposal
    (slot submitter (type STRING))
    (slot role (type STRING))
    (slot automobile (type OBJECT))
    (slot price (type INTEGER)))
```

and constrain the initial parameter space as:

```
(proposal
    (submitter ?S\&:(participant
                    (id ?S)
                    (negotiation-id ?NEG)) ; submitter is a participant
    (role BuyerSeller) ; role defined as either buyer OR seller
    (automobile ?A)      ; must declare an auto
    (price ?P))          ; and a price
```

Negotiation participant agents can send proposals as ACL.PROPOSE messages containing a collection of facts and predicate constraints. The Proposal Validator determines whether the proposal is valid with respect to (i.e. *is subsumed by*) the negotiation template by checking. An example of a proposal that is valid with respect to the template presented above is:

```
(proposal
    (proposal-id Alice-37)   ;ID is generated by the Negotiation Host
    (submitter Alice)
    (role Seller)                ; Alice wishes to sell...
    (automobile
            (make FIAT)          ;.. a FIAT Punto....
            (model Punto))
    (price ?P\&:(>= 3000 ?P)))  ;... for at least 3000.
```

In the next section we give guidelines on how to write negotiation rules for various negotiation mechanisms.

3.2   Negotiation Rules

Agents have standard rule templates, where the rule asserts information in their private fact base. The agent responds to this information, executing appropriate actions and sending messages according to the General Negotiation Protocol. For example, the *display rule* in the Information Updater has the format:

```
(defrule display-rule ; declare the rule name
    (negotiation
        (...)                ; extract and process relevant parameters
    => (assert
            (information-digest (...)))
    ; assert processed parameters to be published in the info digest
```

The *visibility rules* have a similar format, and act as filters on new proposals. They determine which participants can view which parameters of a new proposal.

---

[4] In the next version or the framework[13], we describe negotiation proposals and template in DAML+OIL (see www.daml.org). That allows us to have a more extensible language and make use of shared ontologies (cmp. [12]).

The information they assert is used by the Negotiation Host to mediate the view that different negotiation participants have on the blackboard.

```
(defrule visibility-rule
   (valid-proposal
      (...)                    ; extract and process relevant parameters
      (test (...))             ; test the required condition
   => (assert (visible-proposal (...)))
   ; if valid, assert that the proposal is visible
```

The *termination rule* in the Negotiation Terminator has the format:

```
(defrule termination-rule
      (...)          ; extract and process relevant parameters
      (test (...))         ; test the termination condition
   => (assert (terminate <negotiation-id>)))
   ; if termination condition is met, assert negotiation is terminated
```

Rules in the Protocol Enforcer (both *posting* and *withdrawal*) have a different format. Both when receiving protocols and withdrawal requests, the agent must check whether a series of conditions are all true to determine its action. Because of JESS's cumbersome mechanism to support backward chaining, we implement these rules in the format:

```
(defrule <rule-name>}
   (proposal (proposal-id ?Proposal-id)
      (...))                  ; extract any other relevant parameters
      (test not(...))         ; REQUIRED CONDITION IN A NEGATED FORM!!!
   => (assert (failed <rule-name> ?proposal-id)))
   ; if the condition is NOT met, assert the proposal is NOT valid
```

The Protocol Enforcer has a meta-rule which rejects the proposal if there are any such assertions in the database after the rules have executed, and accepts it otherwise. It executes appropriate actions and sends messages as defined in the General Negotiation Protocol.

Example: Single Item English Auction. Negotiation rules for a single item English auction are presented here as an example to give a flavour of how to write rules. For a more extensive collection of mechanisms see [2].

Assume a Negotiation Host has advertised an agreement template as per section 3.1, and has been contacted by Alice to sell her Fiat Punto via auction. The Host starts a new negotiation, with id auction-37, to sell it. It generates an associated agreement template, which is a specialized version of the one in 3.1, with the automobile slot instantiated with details of her Fiat Punto. The Host asserts facts about the auction on the blackboard.

The negotiation rules which apply to the seller state that they make a single proposal, and then remain silent. In the interests of space, we omit these. The proposal Alice makes is as specified in section 3.3. This confirms the details of the good she is selling, and specifies her reservation price of 3000. Facts about the auction are updated, and now appear as stated in the end of section 3.1.

After this, buyers place bids in the form of proposals that satisfy the buyer proposal validation rules. These are applied by the Protocol Enforcer, and have the format described above (beginning of this section). The conditions are:

[**Posting rule**] This tests that, if a buyer is posting a proposal, then the seller has already posted one.

```
(test (equal ?Role buyer)
      (exists (active-proposal (...) (role seller)))
```

[**Improvement rule**] The price field of the buyer's proposal must be a certain increment above the value of all previously posted buyer proposals. Hence the improvement rule contains the test:

```
(test (> ?Price (+ ?Currently-Highest-Price ?bid-increment)))
```

[**Withdrawal rule**] Auctions do not allow bids to be withdrawn once submitted. Hence, the body of the withdrawal rule (in format specified earlier in this section - *posting* and *withdrawal* rules) contains (test FALSE) and so always fails when executed.

[**Visibility rules**] The seller's initial proposal is visible to all the buyers. However, the field in which the seller constrains the price to be above their reservation price cannot be viewed:

```
(defrule visibility-rule
    (active-proposal(proposal-id ?PID)(role seller))
    (test(TRUE))
        => (assert
            (visible-proposal
                (proposal-id
                    (value ?PID)
                    (visibility all))
                (price
                    (value ?Price)
                    (visibility none))
                (...)))
```

A similarly structured rule states that all active buyer proposals are visible to all participants. Optionally, the identity of a bidder can be maintained private.

[**Display rule**] The currently highest bid price is notified to all participants.

```
(defrule display-rule
(negotiation
    (...)
    (currently-highest-bid ?CHB))
    => (assert
        (information-digest
            (currently-highest-bid ?CHB)))
```

[**Termination rule**] Termination occurs if the auction is inactive for longer than the termination window specified in the negotiation fact base. Hence the rule, in the format specified in the beginning of this section, contains the test:

```
(test (> ?Current-Time (+?Active-Proposal-Time ?Termination-Window))
```

Together with the information asserted in section 3, this results in Alice's auction terminating if it is inactive for 30 minutes.

[**Agreement formation rules**] When negotiation terminates, an agreement is formed between the currently active buyer and the seller. The agreement states that the item specified in the template is sold to the buyer at the price specified in the currently active proposal.

```
(defrule agreement-formation-rule
    (active-proposal
        (proposal-id ?B-PID) (submitter ?BUYER)
        (role buyer) (price ?PRICE))
    (active-proposal
        (proposal-id ?S-PID) (submitter ?SELLER)
        (role seller) (price ?RES-PRICE))
    (test
        (> PRICE RES-PRICE))
    => (assert
        (agreement
            (buyer ?BUYER) (seller ?SELLER) (price ?PRICE))))
```

4   Related Work

Wurman et. al. [14] propose a parametrization of the auction design space. Artikis et. al. [1] propose using deontic constraints to define the contract net protocol. Fontoura et. al. [5] use law-governed interactions [9] to specify policies for Internet auctions. Reeves et. al. [11] present an approach to the negotiation of business contracts that include a translation of the market mechanism into an operational specification for an auction platform.

5   Conclusions

In this paper, we have discussed the shortcomings of the state-of-the-art in representing negotiation mechanisms in agent oriented software engineering. Specifically, we have shown that the protocol approach (adopted by FIPA and many others) results in only part of a mechanism being explicitly formalised and standardised, which can result in significant drawbacks from a software engineering perspective. Alternatively, we propose a modular approach to negotiation mechanisms; a generalised interaction protocol which can be specialised with declarative rules. We provide a taxonomy of such rules, a general framework which implements this approach and give examples of rules for an English auction.

References

1. A. Artikis, J. Pitt, and M. Sergot. Animated specifications of computational societies. In *Proceedings of Conference on Autonomous Agents and Multi-Agent Systems (AAMAS)*, 2002.
2. Claudio Bartolini, Chris Preist, and Nicholas R. Jennings. A generic software framwork for automated negotiation. *HP Technical Report*, TR 2002-2, 2002.
3. Fabio Bellifemmine, Agostino Poggi, and Giovanni Rimassa. Jade - a fipa compliant agent framework. In *4th International Conference on Practical Applications of Intelligent Agents and Multi-Agent Systems*, 1999.
4. Andrew Byde, Chris Preist, and Nicholas R. Jennings. Decision procedures for multiple auctions. In *Proceedings of the 1st Joint International Conference on Autonomous Agents and Multi-Agent Systems, to appear*, 2002.
5. Marcus Fontoura, Mihail Ionescu, and Naftaly Minsky. Law-governed peer-to-peer auctions. In *Proceedings of Eleventh World Wide Web Conference (WWW-2002)*, 2002.
6. Foundation for Physical Agents. Fipa abstract architecture specification, 2000.
7. O. Hoffmann, M. Stumptner, and T Chalabi. A perspective based approach to design. In *Workshop on Planning, Scheduling and Configuration, KI2001*, 2001.
8. N. R. Jennings, T. J. Norman, and P. Faratin. ADEPT: An agent-based approach to business process management. *ACM SIGMOD Record*, 27(4):32–39, 1998.
9. Naftaly H. Minsky and Victoria Ungureanu. Law-governed interaction: a coordination and control mechanism for heterogeneous distributed systems. *ACM Transactions on Software Engineering and Methodology*, 9(3):273–305, 2000.
10. Simon Parsons, Carles Sierra, and Nick Jennings. Agents that reason and negotiate by arguing. *Journal of Logic and Computation*, 8(3):261–292, 1998.

11. Daniel M. Reeves, Michael P. Wellman, and Benjamin N. Grosof. Automated negotiation from declarative contract descriptions. In Jörg P. Müller, Elisabeth Andre, Sandip Sen, and Claude Frasson, editors, *Proceedings of the Fifth International Conference on Autonomous Agents*, pages 51–58, Montreal, Canada, 2001. ACM Press.
12. Valentina Tamma, Michael Wooldridge, and Ian Dickinson. An ontology based approach to automated negotiation. In *Proceedings of Workshop on Agent Mediated Electronic Commerce IV (AMEC-IV)*, 2002.
13. David Trastour, Claudio Bartolini, and Chris Preist. Semantic web support for the business-to-business e-commerce lifecycle. In *Proceedings of Eleventh World Wide Web Conference (WWW-2002)*, 2002.
14. P. Wurman, M. Wellman, and W. Walsh. A parametrization of the auction design space. *Games and Economic Behavior*, 35(1–2):304–338, 2000.
15. Peter R. Wurman, Michael P. Wellman, and William E. Walsh. The Michigan Internet AuctionBot: A configurable auction server for human and software agents. In Katia P. Sycara and Michael Wooldridge, editors, *Proceedings of the 2nd International Conference on Autonomous Agents (Agents'98)*, pages 301–308, New York, 9–13, 1998. ACM Press.

Multi-agent and Software Architectures: A Comparative Case Study

Paolo Giorgini[1], Manuel Kolp[2], and John Mylopoulos[3]

[1] Department of Information and Communication Technology - University of Trento
Via Sommarie 14, I-38100, Trento, Italy
pgiorgini@science.unitn.it
tel.: 39-0461-882052

[2] IAG School of Management- Information Systems Unit - University of Louvain
1 Place des Doyens, B-1348 Louvain-La-Neuve, Belgium
kolp@isys.ucl.ac.be
tel.: 32-10 47 83 95

[3] Department of Computer Science - University of Toronto, 6 King's College Road
M5H 3S5, Toronto, Canada
jm@cs.toronto.edu
tel.: 1-416-978 5180

Abstract. We propose a collection of architectural styles for multi-agent systems motivated by organizational theory and enterprise organization structures. One of the styles is discussed in detail and part of it is formalized using the Formal Tropos specification language. In addition, we conduct a comparative study of organizational and conventional software architectures using a mobile robot control example from the Software Engineering literature.

1   Introduction

We are interested in developing a suitable set of architectural styles for multi-agent systems. Since the fundamental concepts of multi-agent systems are intentional and organizational, rather than implementation-oriented, we turn to organizational theories which study structures as *societies* that emerge from a *design* process.

The purpose of this paper is to present further work on the development of a set of architectural styles for multi-agent systems motivated by and strategic alliances. This paper builds on earlier work reported in [5] by offering some formalization of one of the proposed styles, also a case study comparing organizational with conventional software architectural styles for mobile robot control software.

This research is conducted within the context of *Tropos* [1,8], an agent-oriented software development methodology which is founded on the concepts of *actor* and *goal,* adopted from the *i** [12] modeling framework. Tropos describes in terms of these concepts the organizational environment within which a system will eventually operate, as well as the system itself.

The rest of the paper is organized as follows. Section 2 presents samples of organizational styles that have been identified from organizational theory literature. Section 3 focuses on one of these styles, the structure-in-5, and offers a formalization using the Formal Tropos language. Section 4 presents the mobile robot control case study,

F. Giunchiglia et al. (Eds.): AOSE 2002, LNCS 2585, pp. 101–112, 2003.

identifies relevant software qualities for mobile robots and reports on earlier work that uses conventional architectures. It then applies the organizational styles proposed here and compares these with some conventional architectures with respect to identified qualities. Finally Section 5 summarizes the results of the paper.

2   Organizational Styles

Organizational theory and strategic alliances (e.g., [9]) study alternative styles for (business) organizations. These styles are used to model the coordination of business stakeholders -- individuals, physical or social systems -- to achieve common goals. Each organizational style represents a possible way to structure an organization in order to meet its strategic objectives.

The structure of an organization defines the roles of various intentional components (actors), their responsibilities defined in terms of tasks and goals, and their resources. Moreover, an organizational structure defines how to coordinate the activities of various actors and how they depend on each other.

We propose a macro level catalogue of styles adopting (some of) the abstractions offered by organizational theory for designing multi-agent architectures. In the following we present briefly two of them using $i*$. For other styles, see [5].

An $i*$ strategic dependency model [12] is a graph, where each node represents an actor (an agent, position, or role) and each link between two actors represents a social dependency. Such a dependency can represent the fact that one actor depends on another for a goal to be fulfilled, a task to be performed, or a resource to be made available. The depending actor is called the *depender* and the actor who is depended upon the *dependee*. The object around which the dependency centers (goal, task or resource) is called the *dependum*. The model distinguishes between goals, which are well defined, and softgoals, which do not have a formal definition and are amenable to a different (more qualitative) kind of analysis [2].

For instance, in Figure 1, the *Technostructure, Middle Agency* and *Support* actors depend on the *Apex* for strategic management. Since the goal *Strategic Management* does not have a precise description, it is represented as a softgoal (cloudy shape). The *Middle Agency* depends on the *Technostructure* and *Support* respectively through goal dependencies *Control* and *Logistics* represented as oval-shaped icons. The *Operational Core* is related to the *Technostructure* and *Support* actors through the *Standardize* task dependency and the *Non-operational Service* resource dependency, respectively.

The **structure-in-5** (Figure 1) is a typical organizational style. At the base level, the *Operational Core* takes care of basic tasks — the input, processing, output and direct support procedures — associated with running the organization. At the top lies the *Apex*, composed of executive actors. Below it, sit the *Technostructure, Middle Agency* and *Support* actors, who are in charge of control/standardization, management and logistics, respectively. The *Technostructure* component carries out the tasks of standardizing the behavior of other components, in addition to applying analytical procedures to help the organization adapt to its environment. Actors joining the apex to the operational core make up the *Middle Agency*. The *Support* component assists the operational core for non-operational services that are outside the basic flow of operational tasks and procedures.

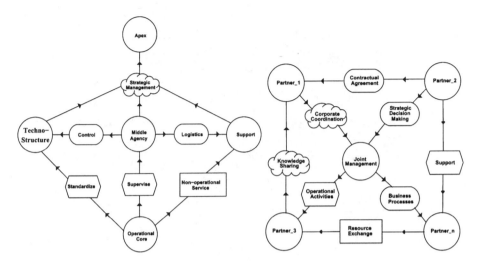

Fig. 1 and 2. Structure-in-5 and Joint Venture

The **joint venture** style (Figure 2) is a more decentralized style that involves an agreement between two or more principal partners to obtain the benefits derived from operating at a larger scale and reusing the experience of the collaboration. Each principal partner can manage and control itself on a local dimension and interact directly with other principal partners to exchange, provide and receive services, data and knowledge. However, strategic operation and coordination is delegated to a *Joint Management* actor, who coordinates tasks and manages the sharing of knowledge and resources.

3   Structure-in-5

In this section we describe in more detail the structure-in-5 style. To specify the structure and formal properties of the style, we use *Formal Tropos* [4] which offers the primitive concepts of *i** augmented with a rich specification language inspired by KAOS [3]. Formal Tropos offers a textual notation for *i** models and allows one to describe dynamic constraints among the different elements of the specification in a first order linear-time temporal logic. Moreover, *Formal Tropos* has a precise semantics which makes Tropos specifications amenable to formal analysis.

Minztberg proposes a basic structure for organizations (for us, organizational styles) based on fives subunits [7], hence its name *structure-in-5* (Figure 1). This decomposition allows one to apply alternative coordination mechanisms (such as mutual adjustment, direct supervision, standardization of skills, outputs and work processes) and design parameters (such as job specialization, behavior formalization, decentralization, unit size, and unit grouping) in order to analyze the different behaviors of the organization.

Basically, this structure defines a hierarchy of roles inside the organization, the responsibilities associated with each subunits, and inter-dependencies among them. Figure 3 shows a more detailed *i** strategic dependency model for this style.

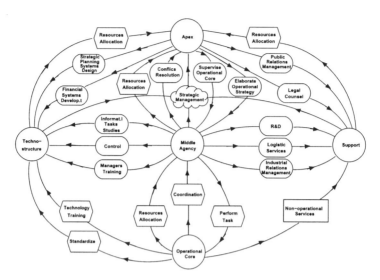

Fig. 3. Structure-in-5 in detail

At the base level one finds the Operational Core where the basic tasks and operations are carried out. Basic tasks include securing inputs for production, also transforming these into outputs. For example, in a manufacturing firm, the purchasing department buys raw materials, while the production department transforms these to products. In addition, outputs need to be distributed and support functions need to be performed (e.g., production machine maintenance, inventory control and the like.) In the following, we focus on the Operational Core specification with respect to the performance of basic tasks. The specification below states that each basic task must be performed within a precise time period that depends on the type of the task. For instance, providing raw materials is a task that must be performed before the production process begins.

Entity BasicTask
 Attribute constant *taskType: TaskType, resourceNeed: Resource, performed: Boolean, timePeriod: Time, output: OutputType*

Entity Resource
 Attribute constant *resourceType:ResourceType*

Actor OperationalCore
 Attribute optional resource: Resource
 Goal PerformBasicTasks
   Mode achieve
   Fulfillment definition
     $\forall task:BasicTask\ (Perform(self,task)\wedge TimePerforming(task)\leq task.time)$

[each basic task in the organization will be performed by the Operational Core within the allotted time period for that type of task]

At the middle level we have three main actors: the Middle Agency, Technostructure, and Support.

The Middle Agency is composed of a chain of middle-line managers with formal authority that join the Strategic Apex to the Operational Core. The managers in the chain are responsible for supervision and coordination of the Operational Core activities, the allocation of the resources to lower levels, and the formulation of tactics consistent with the strategies of the overall organization. For instance, when the strategic apex of the Postal Service decides to realize a project for e-Postal Services, each regional manager, and in turn, each district manager must elaborate the plan as it applies to its geographical area.

In general, the Middle Agency performs all the managerial tasks of the chief executive, but in the context of managing a particular unit. A Middle Agency actor must lead the members of its unit, develop a network of liaison contacts, monitor the environment and its unit's activities, allocate tasks and resources within, negotiate with outsiders, initiate strategic change, and handle exceptions and conflicts. In the following we present a part of the specification for the *PerformTask* dependency between the Middle Agency and Operational Core that concerns the assignment of a task to the Operational Core.

Dependency PerformTask
 Type task
 Mode achieve
 Depender MiddleAgency
 Depndee OperationalCore
 Attribute constant task: BasicTask
 Creation
   condition $\neg task.performed$
   trigger $JustCreated(task)$
 Fulfillment
   condition for depender $task.performed$

[a PerformTask dependency is created when there is a task that has not been performed, and the dependency is fulfilled when the task is performed]

The Technostructure comprises analysts outside the operating work flow, who affect the work of others. They define certain forms of standardization that reduce direct supervision: work process, output, and skills standardization. They are also responsible for training managers of the Middle Agency and operators of the Operational Core. At middle levels, analysts carry out operations research studies of informational tasks, and they design on behalf of the Strategic Apex strategic planning systems and financial systems to control and monitor strategic goals. In the following, we present the specification of the Technostructure with respect to an output standardization goal. In particular, we specify that for each basic task that the Operational Core has to perform, the Technostructure provides a specific output standard to which the task output must conformed to. The output standard depends on the task type and required output properties, such as length, weight, and strength for a machined part, or text length, fonts and document structure for a document.

Actor Technostructure
 Goal StandardizeBasicTasks
   Mode achieve
   Fulfillment definition $\forall task:BasicTask$ $(Standardize(task.output))$
   [for each basic task in the organization, the Technostructure will standardize the output]
 Entity Standard
   Attribute constant *output:OutputType, parameterers : Parameters*

Dependency Standardize
Type task
Mode achieve
Depender OperationalCore
Dependee Technostructure
Attribute constant task :BasicTask
Creation
    condition $\neg\exists standard$: Standard (standard.output=task.output)
    trigger   JustCreated(task)
Fulfillment
    condition for depender
          $\exists$ standard: Standard (standard.output=task.output)

[the Standardize dependency is created when there is no standard for a newly created task, and it is fulfilled when the standard has been created]

The Support is composed of units which specialize in supporting the organization with different services outside its operating work flow. This improves control within the organization and reduces the uncertainty of having to buy services in the open market. The units are self-contained mini-organizations and can support various levels of the structure-in-5 hierarchy: public relations management and legal counsel for the Apex, industrial relations management, logistics, and R&D for the Middle Agency; no-operational services (e.g., cafeteria and mail-room) for the Operational Core.

At the top lies the Apex composed of strategic executive actors responsible for ensuring that the organization serves its mission in an effective way. Their major goals include direct supervision (e.g., allocate resources to the middle level, resolve conflicts within the Middle Agency, and monitor performances), and management of the relations with the environment (e.g., inform influential external actors of organizational activities, develop high-level contact, and negotiating major agreements). They also develop organizational strategies consistent with the interpretation of the environment.

Figure 4 details the Technostructure actor in terms of sub-actors. These include Financial Analysts who develop financial systems for the Apex, also Management and Technology Instructors who train the Middle Agency and Operational Core actors respectively. In addition, there are Technology Analysts that standardize the technology used by the operators and support them in their activities. Work-Study analysts control work process standardization for the Operational Core, while Planning/Control analysts design strategic planning systems for the Apex, control the outputs standardization, and perform quality control for the Middle Agency. Finally, Personnel analysts control skills standardization, and Operations Research analysts carry out operations research studies of informational tasks for the Middle Agency.

4   A Case Study: Architectures for Mobile Robots

Mobile robot control systems must deal with external sensors and actuators. They must respond in time commensurate with the activities of the system in its environment.

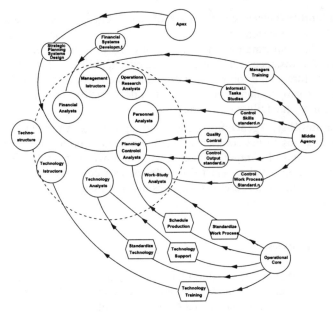

Fig. 4. The Technostructure actor

Consider the following activities [10] an office delivery mobile robot typically has to accomplish: acquiring the input provided by sensors, controlling the motion of its wheels and other moveable part, planning its future path. In addition, a number of factors complicate the tasks: obstacles may block the robot's path, sensor inputs may be imperfect, the robot may run out of power, mechanical limitations may restrict the accuracy with which the robot moves, the robot may manipulate hazardous materials, unpredictable events may leave little time for responding.

4.1   Agent Software Qqualities

With respect to the activities and factors enumerated above, the following agent software qualities can be stated for an office delivery mobile robot's architecture [10].

SQ1 – Coordinativity. Agents must be able to coordinate with other agents to achieve a common purpose or simply their local goals. A mobile robot has to coordinate the actions it deliberately undertakes to achieve its designated objective (e.g., collect a sample of objects) with the reactions forced on it by the environment (e.g., avoid an obstacle).

SQ2 – Predictability. Agents can have a high degree of autonomy in the way they undertake action and communication in their domains. It can be then difficult to predict individual characteristics as part of determining the behavior of the system at large. For a mobile robot, never will all the circumstances of the robot's operation be fully predictable. The architecture must provide the framework in which the robot can act even when faced with incomplete or unreliable information (e.g., contradictory sensor readings).

SQ3 – Failability-Tolerance. A failure of one agent does not necessarily imply a failure of the whole system. The system then needs to check the completeness and the accuracy of data, information and transactions. To prevent system failure, different agents can, for instance, implement replicated capabilities. The architecture must prevent the failure of the robot's operation and its environment. Local problems like reduced power supply, dangerous vapors, or unexpectedly opening doors should not necessarily imply the failure of the mission.

SQ4 – Adaptability. Agents must adapt to modifications in their environment. They may allow changes to the component's communication protocol, dynamic introduction of a new kind of component previously unknown or manipulations of existing agents. Application development for mobile robots frequently requires experimentation and reconfiguration. Moreover, changes in robot assignments may require regular modification.

4.2   Classical Styles

For sample classical solutions, due to lack of space, we only examine three major conventional architectures - the layered architecture [10], control loops [11] and task trees [6] - that have been implemented on mobile robots.

Layered Architecture. According to [10], a classical layered architecture can be viewed as a structure composed of 7 layers. At the lowest level, reside the robot control routines (motors, joints, ...). Levels 2 and 3 deal with the input from the real world. They perform sensor interpretation (the analysis of the data from one sensor) and sensor integration (the combined analysis of different sensor inputs). Level 4 is concerned with maintaining the robot's model of the world.   Level 5 manages the navigation of the robot. The next two levels, 6 and 7, schedule and plan the robot's actions. Dealing with problems and replanning is also part of level 7 responsibilities. The top level provides the user interface and overall supervisory functions.

Control Loop. A controller component initiates the robot actions. Since mobile robots have responsibilities with respect to their operational environment, the controller also monitors the consequences of the robot actions adjusting the future plans based on the return information.

Task Trees. The architecture is based on hierarchies of tasks. Parent tasks initiate child tasks. For instance the task *Gather Object* initiates the tasks *Go to Position*, *Grab Object, Lift Object*, the task *Go to Position* initiates *Move Left* and *Move Forward* and so on. The software designer can define temporal dependencies between pairs of tasks. An example is: "*Grab Object* must complete before *Lift Object* starts." These features permit the specification of selective concurrency.

4.3   Organizational Styles

We are developing organizational architectures for a miniature office delivery robot using the Lego Mindstorms Robotics Invention Systems. Currently, we are testing two architectures working with abstractions reminiscent of those encountered in the layered architecture: the structure-in-5 and the joint-venture.

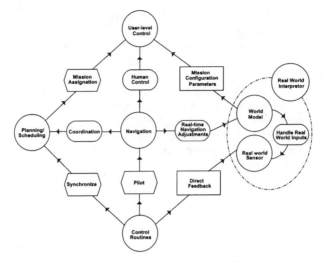

Fig. 5. A structure-in-5 mobile robot architecture.

Structure-in-5. Figure 5 depicts a structure-in-5 robot architecture in *i**. The *control routines* component is the *operational core* managing the robot motors, joints, etc. *Planning/Scheduling* is the *technostructure* component scheduling and planning the robot's actions. The *real world interpreter* is the *support* component composed of two sub-components: *Real world sensor* accepts the raw input from multiple sensors and integrates it into a coherent interpretation while *World Model* is concerned with maintaining the robot's model of the world and monitoring the environment for landmarks. *Navigation* is the *middle agency* component, the central intermediate module managing the navigation of the robot. Finally, the *user-level control* is the human-oriented *strategic apex* providing the user interface and overall supervisory functions.

Joint Venture. The robot architecture is organized around a central joint manager assuming the overall supervisor/coordinator role for the other agent components: a high level path planner, a module that monitors the environment for landmarks, a low level path planner, a motor controller and a perception subsystem that receives sensors data and interprets it. As said in Section 2, each of these agent components can also interact directly with each other.

4.4   Evaluation

In this section, we evaluate each of the five styles – control loop, layered architecture, task trees, structure-in-5 and joint-venture described previously.

Coordinativity. The simplicity of the control loop is a drawback when dealing with complex tasks since it gives no leverage for decomposing the software into more precise cooperative agent components.

The layered architecture style suggests that services and requests are passed between adjacent agent layers. However, information exchange is actually not always straight-forward. Commands and transactions may often need to skip intermediate layers to establish direct communication and coordinate behavior.

A task tree permits a clear-cut separation of action and reaction. It also allows incorporation of concurrent agents in its model that can proceed at the same time. Unfortunately, components have little interaction with each other.

Unlike the previous architectures, the structure-in-5 separates the data (sensor control, interpreted results, world model) from control (motor control, navigation, scheduling, planning and user-level control). The architecture improves coordinativity among components by differentiating both hierarchies – data is implemented by the support component, while control is implemented by the operational core, technostructure, middle agency and strategic apex – as shown in Figure 5.

In the joint venture, each partner component interacts via the joint manager for strategic decisions. Components indicate their interest, and the joint manager returns them such strategic information immediately or mediates the request to some other partner component.

Predictability. The control loop reduces the unpredictable only through iteration. Actions and reactions eliminate possibilities at each turn. Unfortunately, if more subtle steps are needed, the architecture offers no framework for delegating them to separate agent components.

In the layered architecture, the existence of abstraction layers addresses the need for managing unpredictability. What is uncertain at the lowest level become clear with the added knowledge in the higher layers.

The existence of different abstraction levels in the structure-in-5 addresses the need for managing unpredictability. Contrary to the layered architecture, higher levels are more abstract than lower levels: lower levels only involve resources and task dependencies while higher ones propose intentional relationships.

In the joint-venture, the central position and role of the joint manager is a means for resolving conflicts and prevent unpredictability in the robot's world view and sensor data interpretation.

Failability-Tolerance. In the control loop, it is supported in the sense that its simplicity makes duplication of components and behavior easy and reduces the chance of errors creeping into the system.

In the layered architecture, failability-tolerance could be served, when the robot architect strives *not* do something, by incorporating many checks and balances at different levels into the system. Again the drawback is that control commands and transactions may often need to skip intermediate layers to check the system behavior.

In the task trees, exception, wiretapping and monitoring features can be integrated to take into account the needs for integrity, reliability and completeness of data.

In the structure-in-5, checks and control mechanisms can be integrated at different abstractions levels assuming redundancy from different perspectives. Contrary to the layered architecture, checks and controls are not restricted to adjacent layers. Besides, since the structure-in-5 permits to separate the data and control hierarchies, integrity of these two hierarchies can also be verified independently.

The jointure venture, through its joint manager, proposes a central message server/controller. Like in the task trees, exception mechanism, wiretapping supervising or monitoring can be supported by the joint manager to guarantee non-failability, reliability and completeness.

Adaptability. In the control loop, the robot components are separated from each other and can be replaced or added independently. Unfortunately, precise manipulation has to take place inside the components, at a detail level the architecture does not show.

In the layered architecture, the interdependencies between layers prevent the addition of new components or deletion of existing ones. The fragile relationships between the layers can become more difficult to decipher with change.

Task trees, through the use of implicit invocation, make incremental development and replacement of component straightforward: it is often sufficient to register new components, no existing one feels the impact.

The structure-in-5 separates independently each typical component of the robot architecture isolating them from each other and allowing dynamic manipulation. The structure-in-5 is restricted to no more than 5 major components then, as in the control loop, more refined tuning has to take place inside the components.

In the joint venture, manipulation of partner components can be done easily by registering new components to the joint manager. However, since partners can also communicate directly with each other, existing dependencies should be updated as well. The joint manager cannot be removed due to its central position.

Table 1 summarizes the strengths and weaknesses of the five reviewed architectures.

The layered architecture gives precise indications as to the components expected in a robot. The other two classical architectures (control loop and task trees) define no functional components and concentrate on the dynamics. The organizational styles (Structure-in-5 and Joint Venture) focus on how to organize components expected in a robot but also on the intentional and social dependencies governing these components. Exhaustive evaluations are difficult to be established at that point. But, considering preliminary results we can deduce in Table 1, from the discussion in the present section, we can argue that the Structure-in-5 and the Joint-Venture, since they are patterns governed by organizational characteristics, fit better systems and applications that need open and cooperative components like the mobile robot example.

Table 1. Strengths and Weaknesses of Robot Architectures

	Loop	Layers	Task Tree	S-in-5	Joint-Venture
Coordinativity	-	-	+-	++	++
Predictability	+-	+	+-	+	++
Failability-Tolerance	+	+-	+	+	+
Adaptability	+-	+-	+	+	+-

5   Conclusion

We are working towards a collection of architectural styles for multi-agent systems. In this paper we presented in detail one of the organizational styles, the structure-in-5, and conducted a comparative study of some organizational styles and conventional software architectures on a standard case study (the mobile robot control) selected from the Software Engineering literature.

Considering preliminary results established in the paper we can argue that organizational patterns fit better software and applications that need dynamic manipulation and coordination of components since they are driven by organizational characteristics.

We are currently working on formalizing other organizational styles, also applying them to more examples from the literature, for software as well as organizational structures.

References

1. Castro, J., Kolp, M., and Mylopoulos, J. "A Requirements-Driven Development Methodology". In *Proc. of the 13th Int. Conf. on Advanced Information Systems Engineering, CAiSE'01*, Interlaken, Switzerland, June 2001.
2. Chung, L. K., Nixon, B. A., Yu, E. and Mylopoulos, J. *Non-Functional Requirements in Software Engineering*, Kluwer Publishing, 2000.
3. Dardenne, A., van Lamsweerde, A. and Fickas, S. "Goal–directed Requirements Acquisition", *Science of Computer Programming*, 20, 1993, pp. 3-50.
4. Fuxman, A., Pistore M., Mylopoulos, J., and Traverso, P. "Model Checking Early Requirements Specification in Tropos". In *Proc. of the 5th Int. Symposium on Requirements Engineering, RE'01*, Toronto, Canada, Aug. 2001.
5. Kolp, M., Giorgini P., and Mylopoulos J. "An Organizational Perspective on Multi-agent Architectures". *In Proc. of the Eighth International Workshop on Agent Theories, architectures, and languages, ATAL'01*, Seattle, USA, August 1-3, 2001.
6. Lozano-Perez, T., Preface to Autonomous Robot Vehicles. *Cox, L.J. and Wilfong G.T., eds, Springer Verlag*, 1990.
7. Mintzberg, H. Structure in Fives: Designing Effective Organizations, *Prentice-Hall*, 1992.
8. Perini. A, Bresciani, P., Giunchiglia, F., Giorgini, P., Mylopoulos, J., A Knowledge Level Software Engineering Methodology for Agent Oriented Programming. In *Proc. Of the 5th International Conference on Autonomous Agents*, Montreal CA, May 2001, ACM.
9. Scott, W. R. Organizations: Rational, Natural, and Open Systems, *Prentice Hall*, 1998.
10. Shaw, M., and Garlan, D. Software Architecture: Perspectives on an Emerging Discipline, Upper Saddle River, N.J., *Prentice Hall*, 1996.
11. Simmons, R., Goodwin, R., Haigh, K., Koenig, S., and O'Sullivan, J. "A modular architecture for office delivery robots". In *Proc. of the 1st Int. Conf. on Autonomous Agents, Agents '97*, Marina del Rey. CA, Feb 1997, pp.245 - 252.
12. Yu E. Modelling Strategic Relationships for Process Reengineering, *Ph.D. thesis, Department of Computer Science, University of Toronto*, Canada, 1995.

Using UML State Machine Models for More Precise and Flexible JADE Agent Behaviors

Martin L. Griss[1], Steven Fonseca[2], Dick Cowan[1], and Robert Kessler[3]

[1] Software Technology Laboratory
HP Laboratories MS 1137
1501 Page Mill Road, Palo Alto 94304-1126
{martin@griss.com, rm.cowan@verizon.net}
[2] UC Santa Cruz
{fonseca@cse.ucsc.edu}
[3] University of Utah
{Kessler@cs.utah.edu}

Abstract. In order to effectively develop multi-agent systems (MAS) software, a set of models, technologies and tools are needed to support flexible and precise specification and implementation of agent-to-agent conversations, standardized conversation protocols, and corresponding agent behaviors. Experience trying to build complex protocols with the ZEUS and JADE agent toolkits motivated a substantial extension to the JADE agent behavior model. This extension (called SmartAgent) enables more flexible, reusable and precise modeling and implementation of agent behavior. We augment JADE behaviors with uniform message, timing and system events, a multi-level tree of dispatchers that match and route events, and a hierarchical state machine (HSM.) HSM is represented using UML statechart diagrams, and implements a significant subset of UML state machine semantics. Adherence to the UML standard helps bridge object-oriented to agent-oriented programming, and allows us to use industry familiar modeling language and tools such as Rose or Visio. These extensions were tested in a meeting scheduler prototype.

1   Introduction

Systematic agent-oriented engineering techniques must integrate traditional software engineering techniques with multi-agent technology [15, 16] in order to develop robust, industrial strength multi-agent systems. Previous papers [5, 6, 8, 11] describe our experiences building several multi-agent systems using ZEUS [21] and JADE [1].

Recently we have extended the JADE behavior and communication protocol management subsystem [11] to allow richer handling of conversations and behaviors. Our goals are to develop a programming paradigm and implementation that facilitates agent construction through libraries of composable, reusable behavior elements, generated and assembled from input (UML) models. We and others are working in several related areas, including: UML-based modeling for agent systems (AUML [22],

F. Giunchiglia et al. (Eds.): AOSE 2002, LNCS 2585, pp. 113–125, 2003.
© Springer-Verlag Berlin Heidelberg 2003

and others [9, 14, 25]), agent patterns [17, 20], Java-bean based agent component frameworks Gschwind [12], and aspect-oriented programming applied to agents [10, 17].

MAS frameworks such as ZEUS and JADE provide some support for constructing and coordinating sets of behaviors for a particular conversation. However, we found these mechanisms difficult to use when conversations required complex protocols. It was hard to both control the precise order of behavior invocation and flexibly decompose behaviors into coordinating parts that could be updated dynamically.

We chose to use an architecture and implementation supporting hierarchical state machine based (HSM) programming of behavior, augmented with several flexibility enhancing mechanisms (such as events and dispatcher chains). We chose to base our models, tools and implementation as accurately as possible on the UML standard hierarchical state machines [2] in anticipation of developing tools similar to [18]. In [11], we showed a UML interaction diagram of ACL message exchange between three agents in our personal meeting arrangement assistant, and a partial state machine to handle one side of this conversation. In this paper, we show enhancements to the model and automatically generated code for a state machine handling one side of a simplified bidding conversation. Figure 1 is a Visio 2002 statechart diagram of this behavior.

It is this decomposition of agent behavior and conversation management that SmartAgent supports. Section 2 provides a brief review of UML state machines and several agent platforms that support state-based development. Section 3 describes the SmartAgent architecture and design of our event-based, state-oriented extensions to JADE. Section 4 summarizes our experience using these extensions. Section 5 discusses tools and reusability. Section 6 concludes with a summary and next steps.

2   State Machines and MAS Frameworks

State-based programming recognizes that any useful system must respond to the dynamic conditions of its environment. This suits the notion that software agents should autonomously react to their society. State-based programming for agent behavior has been explored to model agent communication and behaviors [22], as well more general reactive systems [13, 23]. JADE offers a lightweight non-hierarchical state machine class with limited functionality while ZEUS provides a more complete non-hierarchical state machine execution subsystem, but the API is not well-designed. The JACKAL conversation engine also uses a state machine model [3, 4].

Since JADE was our chosen platform for our experiments, we will discuss it in detail. When messages arrive, a pool of currently interested behaviors is woken-up and the first ready behavior has an opportunity to process the message. Pattern matching on attributes of the incoming message determines if the action method of this behavior is executed. If the match fails, the current behavior is put back to sleep and matching the next behavior is attempted. Once a behavior accepts a message, the pool of active behaviors are put back to sleep. Explicit reposting of a message is required if the message is to be handled by multiple behaviors. JADE provides a simple state machine, FSMBehaviour that maintains the transitions between states and selects the next state behavior to execute. States are registered, named and stored, and each transition between them is assigned an integer representing its event number. Once the start and finish states are registered, the state machine is ready for execution. When a state behavior finishes, an *onEnd* method returns the event number that determines the one-and-only next transition to fire. If no transitions are associated with the current event number, the default transition is taken, if specified. Note that transitions only serve to link states; they do not encapsulate agent behavior. Dealing with transition event numbers is troublesome.

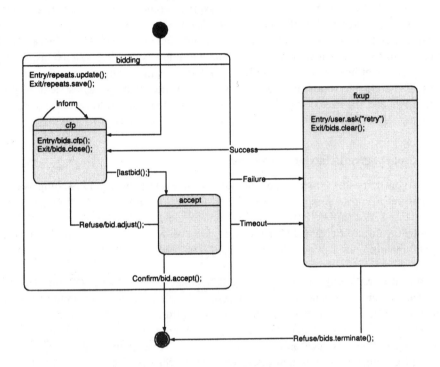

Fig. 1. An example HSM behavior specification as a statechart diagram

The UML state machine [2] evolved from the hierarchical statechart work of Harel [13]. A UML state machine defines states and transitions that connect states. States and machines can be built within other states and machines. This hierarchy of processing elements makes it easier to describe complex conditions and transitions and to handle common default conditions and exceptions. UML state machines are event driven; environment actions come in the form of events that are presented to the state machine, typically driving transitions. Other conditions can also fire transitions and state changes.

3   Design of SmartAgent

Our goal is to provide to the JADE programmer an easy to use set of classes and mechanisms (a conversation manager "kit") to enable the building of robust JADE behaviors. We wanted an explicit representation of the states and transitions, allowing model-based generation, analysis, testing and monitoring tools. We wanted more control over the order of event dispatching, and more powerful event and condition matching. We wanted more flexible and extensible, dynamic addition of activities, transitions, states and complete behaviors, yet still provide precise handling of complex protocols. Finally, we wanted to easily express, combine and reuse core protocol elements and important default and exception handlers.

To this end, we implemented a fairly complete version of the UML hierarchical state machines, augmented with events and flexible dispatching extensions. UML state chart diagrams provide a standard graphical notation with numerous existing tools. The ability to run actions on both states and transitions provides flexibility in expression, and the nested state hierarchy provides a mechanism to factor and inherit common default and exceptional transitions and common behavior fragments.

3.1   SmartAgent Behavior Architecture

SmartAgent consists of three major subsystems: an event fusion and matching system for uniform event handling, an event dispatching system for event routing, grouping and ordering of agent Activities, and hierarchical state machine classes that partition agent behavior into states and transitions. Figure 2 shows a somewhat simplified class structure[1] and Figure 3 shows the event dispatchers and the state machine mechanism.

Event and EventTemplate. Every action that an agent must react to is translated into an event for uniform handling and processing. JADE behaviors and system actions convert received ACL messages, timers and exceptions into events sent into the dispatcher structure (e.g., ControllerBehavior in Figure 3.) These include message events, system events such as ExceptionEvent and TimerEvent, and internal events signaled by other behaviors and activities, such as SuccessEvent and FailureEvent.. We extended JADE's message matching mechanism to allow more complex event matching. An event of a specified type is compared with an **EventTemplate** that defines a function called *matches* that checks to see if the matching criterion is satisfied. For example, a MessageEventTemplate object contains a JADE MessageTemplate that is compared with an incoming JADE ACL message wrapped in a MessageEvent object. EventTemplates allow matching on message arrival, timeouts or other events. Multiple matching checks can be combined using logical connectives. Loose coupling of event handlers is achieved by using the Observer pattern [Gamma et al., 1994] to allow dynamic addition and removal of multiple event listeners, each obtaining a copy of the event. More generally, an Observer-pattern based "software event bus" is used to combine multiple dispatchers and HSM's within an agent.

---

[1] We have removed several classes, interfaces and relationships to simplify explanation.

Dispatching and Controller Mechanism. In [11] we discuss the SmartAgent dispatching mechanism in more detail. A top-level JADE behavior, ControllerBehavior, delivers all received messages as an Event through the dispatch tree, ultimately to some set of Activity. The granularity of an Activity can range from a very simple and short code sequence to another dispatcher or full multi-state state machine. As shown in Figure 2, HSMs, states, and dispatchers all implement Activity, and so (branching) dispatch trees can be built as shown in Figure 3. Dispatchers first determine if the incoming event is for their Activities (via *hasInterest* and *guard*). The *hasInterest* function may use an EventTemplate matcher, while *guard* will check additional requirements (such as testing counters in the agent). If both tests succeed, the dispatcher distributes the event according to its distribution policy (via *eventReceived)*. The dispatch tree allows some control over which Activities will fire, but for more precise control, we use the Hierarchical State Machine.

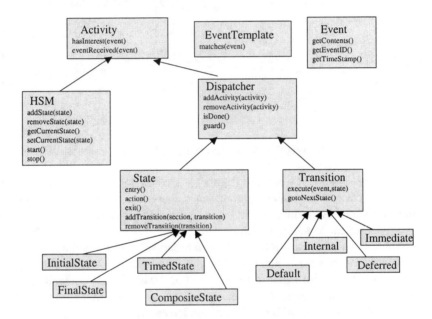

Fig. 2. The simplified HSM architecture[2]

Hierarchical State Machine. In the HSM actions that an agent must perform are further decomposed into states. Incoming events then trigger state transitions. We use three core class hierarchies. First, an HSM class implements the Activity interface. It is the top-level object that receives events from the dispatching subsystem. HSM maintains a current state pointer so when new events are received they can be forwarded to the current state. When transitions are taken, the current state pointer is updated (See Figure 3.)

---

[2] Figure adapted and simplified from that in [Griss et al., 2001].

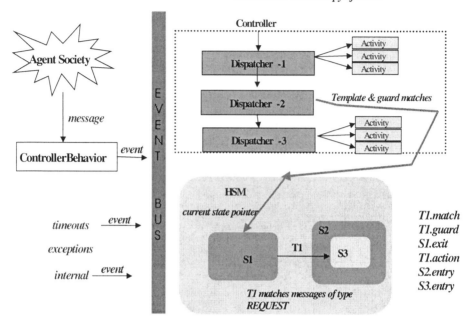

Fig. 3. Event flow from behavior through dispatch tree to an HSM

All states in an HSM descend from a class called State (see Figure 2). State provides the basic functionality that all states share and defines default methods that subclasses might override. For example, the *eventReceived* method is often rewritten and is dependent on the type of the state object.

The normal State class implements *entry*, *action*, and *exit* methods. *Entry* is called each time a new state is entered. The *action* method is invoked when an event is received but does not result in the firing of any transition. By default, *action* runs a set of attached Activities. *Exit* is called before any transition leaves the state. CompositeState extends state, but does not implement *action*. InitialState and FinalState are further simplified. They restrict the kinds of transitions allowed, and do not implement the *entry*, *action*, or *exit* functions. A CompositeState provides the additional capability of encapsulating a collection of nested states. A CompositeState can include its own Initial and Final states. TimedState extends State so that *entry* creates and starts a timer that generates a named timer event after a specified duration has elapsed, and stops and deletes the timer on *exit*. Transitions can trigger on a matching TimerEvent.

States are connected by Transitions, a subclass of Dispatcher. When an event is received by the current state, a check is performed to see if it matches any of the transitions leading to a next state. For a transition to fire, both its event matching and guard must be satisfied. Like state objects, transitions also have an overridable *action* function, which by default runs a list of attached activities.

Internal and deferred transitions do not leave the current state. When an internal transition fires, the HSM continues to remain in the same state, and *entry* and *exit* methods are not run (but the transition Action may run). When a deferred transition fires, the event is placed in the deferred event queue for processing in a later state[3].

Hierarchy in UML state machines provides two inheritance benefits, factoring common entry, exit, actions and tests[4]. First, if an event does not fire a transition of the current state, then the transitions for parent states are recursively checked. This makes it easy to program default agent behavior by having composite states provide default and exceptional transitions to groups of states, allowing inner states to focus only on the main cases. Further, nested states can redefine transitions provided by the parent to override shared defaults. The second benefit is that a chain of entry and exit functions will be run when transitions cross composite state boundaries, and code common to several nested states or all incoming or outgoing transitions can be factored to one place.

For example, Figure 3 shows an incoming ACL message received by the ControllerBehavior, which is sent as a MessageEvent to the Controller. This passes the event through the tree of Dispatchers. Dispatchers that match *hasInterest* and *guard* run their Activities. In this example, the EventTemplate associated with the second Dispatcher matches, and the event is received by a single state machine activity named HSM. Its currentState pointer relays the event to the correct state, in this case S1. S1 searches for a transition that matches the event just received. If transition T1 exists between S2 and S3, where S1 is a top-level state, and S3 is a child of S2, the expected sequence of method invocations is as specified by UML: *S1.exit*, *T1.action*, *S2.entry*, and *S3.entry*. This ensures that *entry* and *exit* code is always run; for example in TimedState this is used to start and stop the timer. First, S1 is exited. Though not shown, the current state pointer of HSM is finally updated to S3. As another example, in Figure 1, *bidding.entry* ensures that that *repeats* is *updated* or *saved* for any of the five transitions taken; transitions *Failure* and *Timeout of* composite state *bidding* are available to both states *cfp* and *accept;* and, *bids.cfp* or *bids.close* could run on one of eight direct, self or inherited transitions.

We have introduced two new types of transitions: immediate and default. Immediate transitions are essentially "triggerless." After a state's entry code is executed, all immediate transitions are evaluated without waiting for an event. When an event arrives, if no transitions fire, we recursively search the parent chain. Default transitions were created when we observed that we often created a parent state enclosing the child state just to hold a single transition to handle any exceptional events. This idiom was so common that we introduced a default transition as a "macro" for this common case.

To summarize, after a transition's *hasInterest* and *guard* return true, the following occurs in this order: 1) The current state's *exit* is run; 2) The transition's *action* is run; 3) The target state's *entry* is run; 4) Guards on any immediate transitions are tested

---

[3] Deferred transitions were only partially implemented.

[4] In principle, at most only a single transition should be viable, including inheritance; in our implementation, this can be optionally checked, but we use nesting to disambiguate.

and the transition fired if appropriate; 5) Any deferred events are now processed, firing transitions if appropriate; 6) The target state then waits for a new event to arrive; regular, deferred and internal transition triggers and guards are checked and then fired if appropriate; 7) If no transitions fire in the previous step, any default transitions are processed; 8) The parent hierarchy is scanned for any matching transition; and 9)If no transition fires, the event is discarded, the state's action is evaluated, and processing continues back at Step 5.

3.2   Experience Using SmartAgent

As we developed and evaluated the integrated model, we used two experimental vehicles. One was an extensive set of sample state machines. The other was a re-implementation of our personal assistant and meeting assistant system. We used table-driven event and meeting request senders for debugging, exhaustive testing of corner cases, exploring new features, improving the robustness of the meeting system and assessing the benefits of explicit state-based programming. [11].

The meeting system was originally written using a state-like model (with case statements over integer states,) so adapting it for the HSM was relatively straightforward. The original conversation models were informally sketched as state machines (such as in Figure 1), so formalizing states, transitions, templates, guards, and actions was fairly direct. Mapping from the UML statechart diagrams into code was immediate. In [11] we show how meeting handler code written the old way was transformed.

The original JADE code has many switch statements both for state processing and for message handling. State changes occurred by changing the state variable to the value of an integer constant. In the new code states are defined directly by instantiating class State or a subclass, such as TimedState, or CompositeState. Likewise, Transitions are also explicitly instantiated classes, and are explicitly attached to source and target States at time of creation. The code is easier to read, and tools are able to directly generate and analyze the network structure of the state machine. Listing 1 shows the one-to-one correspondence between elements in Figure 1 and lines of Java code.

We have built about a dozen state machines to handle various parts of the personal assistant system, and a loosely coupled internal agent architecture, in which a rich set of internal events is exchanged between HSM's [19]. It is clear to us that using this model is far superior to using the model that is provided by the base JADE system. We can construct more robust, more complicated state-based interactions in less time and with less hand-written code.

4   Drawing and Generation Tools

The UML statechart diagram (Figure 1) was drawn using Visio 2002. When we first started using an early HSM, we hand drew the state machines on paper or a white board. We then hand coded from these diagrams. As the protocols became more complex, we wanted a tool to draw the HSM and to enhance as we developed short-hand notations and extensions. We experimented with several tools, including Rational Rose, ArgoUML and the UML stencils in Visio. After some irritation at the restrictions imposed by the other tools, we quickly developed our own stencils in Visio (we had done this before for other diagrammatic languages), with custom properties used for the attributes. This allows us to use color to indicate important states and transitions, and easy cut-and-paste of diagrams into slides and documents.

After building several state machines from Visio diagrams, we realized how valuable the diagram was. We ended up constantly referencing back to the diagram during implementation and debugging to help "understand" what was happening in the state machine. However, we realized that it was a tedious and error-prone process to make sure that the initial implementation exactly reflected the states and transitions described in a diagram. With that motivation, we then implemented a simple code generation facility, written as a Visual Basic addin in Visio. It currently generates Java and can handle some notational extensions, such as converting trigger expressions, such as *Inform* into calls on support routines *M.Inform()*. This creates an EventTemplate to match an *Inform* performative. (See Listing 1.) It will be easy to also generate XML and RDF, needed for other projects in our group. In the future, we plan to investigate round-trip engineering and the possibility of using the visualization of the diagrams to help in debugging the state machine execution.

5   Reuse and Extensibility

The SmartAgent implemention of HSM and Dispatcher has taken great care to use the standard extensibility mechanisms of Java, namely Interfaces, Abstract classes, Adapter classes, and class inheritance. For example, the HSM uses ordinary public Java classes to represent states and transitions of various kinds. This means that individual states or transitions, and even groups of states and transitions, can be reused or extended, either in-line using the *new State() {...};* construction (such as lines 10-13 in Listing 1), or by defining a new class that extends or implements some other class or interface.

We defined a new Subgraph class that extends CompositeState to support constructing reusable clusters of States and Transitions that can be instantiated in several places in a larger state machine[5]. We added a new Subgraph icon to the Visio stencil to show the use of a subgraph (shown in Figure 4); the generator code also needed small extensions. This subgraph can export selected internal states (using *public State getA()* etc.), shown as the A and B "ports" on the subgraph icon in Figure 4, so that transitions from outside the subgraph can be easily "wired in" to sources or target states in the subgraph, using code such as shown in Listing 2.

---

[5] This is different from referencing or embedding a complete HSM, since transitions can occur directly to and from States in the subgraph.

```
1 public class Example extends HSM {
2  public Example(SmartAgentAdapter anAgent,String name) {
3   super(anAgent, name);
4   Composite bidding = new Composite("bidding",this) {
5     public void entry () {
6       super.entry();
7       repeats.update();
8     } };
9   State accept = new State("accept",bidding);
10  State cfp = new State("cfp",bidding) {
11    public void entry () { bids.cfp();  }
12    public void exit ()   { bids.close();  }
13  };
14  State fixup = new State("fixup",this) {
15    public void entry () { user.ask("retry");  }
16    public void exit ()   { bids.clear();  }
17  };
18  InitialState initial=new InitialState("initial",this);
19  FinalState finish=new FinalState("finish",this);
20  Transition Tran0 =new Transition("Tran0",null,initial,cfp);
21  Transition Tran1 =new Transition("Tran1",null,cfp,accept){
22    public boolean guard (Event e) { return lastbid();  }
23  };
24  Transition Tran2 =new Transition("Tran2",M.Failure(),bidding,fixup);
25  Transition Tran3 =new Transition("Tran3",M.Confirm(),accept,finish){
26    public void action (Event e, State s) {  bid.accept();  }
27  };
28  Transition Tran4 =new Transition("Tran4",M.Timeout(),bidding,fixup);
29  Transition Tran5 =new Transition("Tran5",M.Refuse(),fixup,finish){
30    public void action (Event e, State s) {  bids.terminate();  }
31  };
32  Transition Tran6 =new Transition("Tran6",M.Success(),fixup,cfp);
33  Transition Tran7 =new Transition("Tran7",M.Inform(),cfp,cfp);
34  Transition Tran8 =new Transition("Tran8",M.Refuse(),accept,cfp){
35    public void action (Event e, State s) { bid.adjust();  }
36  } };
37 }
```

Listing 1 – A segment of the generated HSM code for state machine in Figure 1

```
Subgraph sg1=new Subgraph("sg1", this);
Subgraph sg2=new Subgraph("sg2",this);
Transition t1=new Transition("t1",M.Request(), sg1.getB(),sg2.getA());
```

Listing 2 – Using and wiring subgraph

6   Summary, Conclusions and Future Work

Our enhanced state machine based JADE agent behavior model allows more precise control over robust agent behavioral issues such as timeouts, default and exception handling, and order of behavior execution. In addition, we have increased the flexibility and adaptability of our system. Our model integrates events, activities, event dispatching and hierarchical state machines to overcome the difficulties we encountered in our previous experiments with ZEUS and JADE. Visio 2002 tools make it easy to quickly draw new behaviors, and generate compatible JADE code. Key to this integration was:

- Event fusion, which converts all messages, exceptions, timeouts and other systems events into a common event hierarchy that can be matched and dispatched uniformly by rules, dispatchers and state machines.

- Event invoked activities, with a simple Activity interface that can be implemented by most other elements (simple expressions, rule modules, JADE behaviors and state machines).

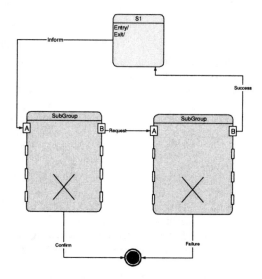

Fig. 4. Repeated use of a pre-wired subgraph

It is very easy to add default handlers. Timed states handle those situations where a target agent fails to respond, and state/transition hierarchy cleanly separates the "main" flow of the conversation and its exception handling.

While we tried to follow the UML state chart semantics very closely, we made some modifications, interpretations, and extensions to better suit a natural, precise yet compatible extension to JADE. Close compatibility with UML yields a rich, yet understandable system. The significant changes and extensions include:

- Dynamic addition of dispatchers, states, transitions and activities
- Immediate and default transitions
- Dynamic inheritance of transitions in the state hierarchy
- Embedded HSM, remote invocation of HSM, HSM subgraph reuse

To better support the factoring of more complex state machines, we expect to complete the implementation of deferred transitions, and of concurrent states, with fork and join states.

Acknowledgements

Special thanks to David Bell for earlier work that helped motivate and define the scope of this work, and to Reed Letsinger for critique and feedback as we developed these extensions.

References

1. F. Bellifemine, A. Poggi & G. Rimassi, "JADE: A FIPA-Compliant agent framework", Proc. Practical Applications of Intelligent Agents and Multi-Agents, April 1999, pg 97-108 (See http://sharon.cselt.it/projects/jade)
2. G. Booch, J. Rumbaug & I. Jacobson, The Unified Modeling Language User Guide, Addison-Wesley, 1999
3. RS. Cost, T. Finin, Y. Labrou, X. Luan, Y. Peng, I. Soboroff, J. Mayfield & A. Boughannam, "Jackal: A Java-Based Tool for Agent Development." Working Notes of the Workshop on Tools for Developing Agents (AAAI '98) (AAAI Technical Report).
4. RS. Cost, T. Finin, Y. Labrou, X. Luan, Y. Peng, I. Soboroff, J. Mayfield & A. Boughannam, An Agent-based Infrastructure for Enterprise Integration, ASA/MA, October, 1999, p. 219-33
5. SP Fonseca, ML. Griss, & R. Letsinger, Evaluation of the ZEUS MAS Framework, Hewlett-Packard Laboratories, Technical Report, HPL-2001-154
6. Steven P. Fonseca, Martin L. Griss, Reed Letsinger, An Agent Mediated E-Commerce Environment for the Mobile Shopper, Hewlett-Packard Laboratories, Technical Report, HPL-2001-157
7. E. Gamma, R Helm, R Johnson & J Vlissides, "Design patterns," Addison-Wesley, 1995.
8. ML Griss & R Letsinger, Games at Work - Agent-Mediated E-Commerce Simulation, Workshop, Autonomous Agents 2000, Barcelona, Spain, June 2000. (Also HP Laboratories Technical Report, HPL-2000-52.)
9. ML. Griss, "My Agent Will Call Your Agent," Software Development Magazine, February. (See also "My Agent Will Call Your Agent ... But Will It Respond?" Hewlett-Packard Laboratories, Tech Report, TR-HPL-1999-159).
10. ML. Griss, Implementing Product-Line Features By Composing Component Aspects, Proc. First International Software Product-Line Conference, Denver, CO., Aug 2000
11. M. Griss, S. Fonseca, D. Cowan and R. Kessler, SmartAgent: Extending the JADE Agent Behavior Model, Proceedings of SCI SEMAS Workshop, Orlando, Florida, July 2002 (to appear).
12. T Gschwind, M Ferudin, & S Pleisch, ADK - Building Mobile Agents for Network and Systems Management from Reusable Components, ASA/MA. Los Alamitos, IEEE.
13. D Harel and M Politi, Modeling Reactive Systems with Statecharts, McGraw Hill, 1998
14. Huget, Marc-Philippe, Extending Agent UML Protocol Diagrams, Third International Workshop on Agent-Oriented Software Engineering, AAMAS, July 2002, p. 111-122

15. NR. Jennings, and MR. Wooldridge, Agent Technology, Springer.
16. NR. Jennings, On Agent-Based Software Engineering, Artificial Intelligence, March, 2000, vol. 117, no. 2, p. 277-96
17. EA. Kendall, Role Model Designs and Implementations with Aspect-oriented Programming, Proc. Of OOPSLA 99, Oct, Denver, ACM SIGPLAN, p. 353-369
18. Koning, Jean-Luc and Romero-Hernandez, Ivan, Generating Machine Processable Representations of Textual Representations of AUML, Third International Workshop on Agent-Oriented Software Engineering, AAMAS, July 2002, p. 39-50
19. R Letsinger,. Three Architectural Principles for the Design of Personalisable Agents, HP Labs Tech Report, HPL-2001-300, December 2001
20. Lind, Jurgen, Patterns in Agent-Oriented Software Engineering, Third International Workshop on Agent-Oriented Software Engineering, AAMAS, July 2002, p. 1-12
21. H. Nwana, D. Nduma, L. Lee, J. Collis, "ZEUS: a toolkit for building distributed multi-agent systems", in Artificial Intelligence Journal, Vol. 13, No. 1, 1999, pp. 129-186. (See http://www.labs.bt.com/projects/agents/zeus/).
22. J Odell, H. VD Parunak & B Bauer, Extending UML for Agents, AOIS Workshop at AAAI 2000, www.auml.org. Also see http://www.jamesodell.com/publications.html
23. M Samek & P Montgomery, State-Oriented Programming, Embedded Systems Engineering, August, 2000, p. 21-43.
24. Wagner, Gerd, A UML Profile for External AOR Models, Third International Workshop on Agent-Oriented Software Engineering, AAMAS, July 2002, p. 99-110

Generating Machine Processable Representations of Textual Representations of AUML

Jean-Luc Koning and Ivan Romero-Hernandez

CoSy-Inpg, 50 rue Laffemas, BP 54, 26902 Valence cedex 9, France
Jean-Luc.Koning@esisar.inpg.fr,Ivan.Romero@imag.fr
http://www-leibniz.imag.fr/CoSy

Abstract. Odell et al have proposed an agent modeling language (AUML), which extends some UML artifacts to cope with the special requirements of multiagent systems, especially *interaction*. In this paper, we introduce a textual notation for the AUML modeling specification and show how one could translate it in order to generate both an extended finite state machine and a specification that can be directly processed by a model-checker.

1 Introduction

Agent developers are increasingly interested in methodologies supporting the specific characteristics of multiagent systems [1]. In order to accomplish this, there are two kinds of approaches: semi-formal and formal. Semi-formal approaches propose standard notations and even specification languages, but are looking for a more pragmatic developing cycle, where the notation and methodological processes are adjusted to the peculiarities of multiagent systems, but any exhaustive verification is obviated. The formal methodologies look for an unambiguous specification and a stronger validation, using an agent modeling language and focusing the verification process, at a cost of a (likely) longer developing cycle.

Nowadays agent modeling languages are more or less sophisticated variations of modeling languages for parallel systems. These languages are usually focused on one of two possible system aspects: either processing or data. Some authors suggest that a third aspect should be taken into consideration: dynamic behavior, as agents themselves are *active*, in contrast with objects or reactive modules.

Currently no language or methodology cover every aspect of system development. This lack of complete system covering poses serious problems to formal language promoters, and must be solved in order for the industry to widely accept formal languages for system modeling.

UML defines a set of conventions and notation artifacts based on many precedent object oriented notations, but emphasizing on simplicity, graphical intuitiveness and relative independence of the methodology used by system developers. In its current definition, UML supports static and dynamic models,

F. Giunchiglia et al. (Eds.): AOSE 2002, LNCS 2585, pp. 126–137, 2003.

use cases, implementation models and defines a semi-formal notation to improve the specification of semantic properties of the system, the object constraint language [2]. As it is implied by its name, the *Unified Modeling Language* is not a methodology by itself, but a suggested notation to be used within the framework of a methodology.

Odell et al [3, 4] have proposed an agent modeling language (AUML), which extends some UML artifacts to cope with the requirements of agent-oriented analysis and design, specially *interaction*. The AUML proposal divides the interaction protocol specification to three closely related layers. The *Overall protocol representation layer* deals with the creation of a general view of the protocol. It makes use of the package notation and extends it to represent the existence of interactions among related agents (roles) instead of simple class conglomerates linked semantically, as in UML. The *interaction among agents representation layer* extends UML sequence diagrams in making them more expressive, thus allowing a richer notation for object lifeline branching and communication. The *agent's internal processing representation layer* makes use of UML activity diagram and state-charts to enable a further understanding of the agent's internal behavior.

In this paper, we introduce a textual notation of AUML modeling specification and show how one could translate it in order to generate both an extended finite state machine and a specification that can be directly processed by the SPIN model-checker [5].

SPIN is a tool for analyzing the logical consistency of distributed systems, which is based on the automata theory and on-the-fly verification techniques. It also can be used as simulator to exhaustively check for system assertions, deadlocks, etc. PROMELA is a C-like process modeling language for SPIN. It provides all the necessary concepts that we need to implement AUML sequence diagrams specifications of interaction protocols including message sending and receiving primitives, parallel and asynchronous composition or concurrent processes, and communication channels.

2   A Case Study: The FishMarket Bidding Protocol

The FishMarket Electronic Auction House is a protocol first proposed and formalized by Carles Sierra in [6]. Because of its characteristics, FishMarket is quite a natural application for multiagent systems. This protocol is based in the real auction process inside a traditional fish market, the *Lonja de Blanes* market in Spain.

FishMarket is intended as an open system, where buyers with different strategies can enter and compete with one another in a system fair enough for all parties, and where it is possible to get a good approximation of the best price-earnings ratio for both buyers and sellers.

Given its moderate complexity, real applicability and previous extensive modeling, FishMarket is an interesting "real life" case study. We will focus here on a single part of FishMarket: the Auction scene.

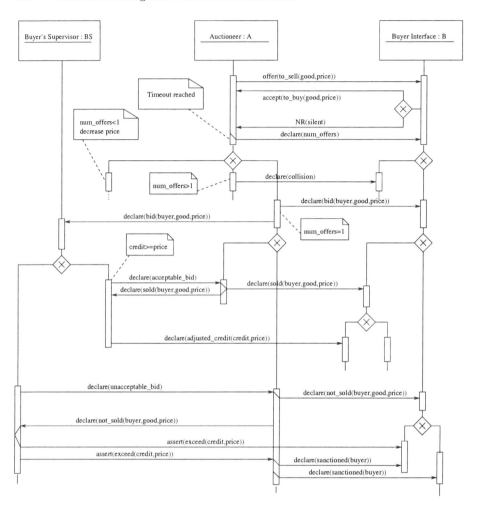

Fig. 1. Main sequence diagram for the Auction scene.

Figure 1 shows a AUML sequence diagram for the whole auction scene. This diagram focuses on the interaction between *roles*. It expresses all the interactions that any entity, belonging to a specified role, could receive or generate.

First, following the temporal ordering, the Auctioneer sends a broadcast message `offer(to-sell(good, price))`, shown here with a stick-headed arrow. The buyer begins its internal processing and eventually answers with an `accept(to-buy(good, price))` message, or stays silent. As the buyer either answers or not, we use the AUML notation for that kind of eventuality: a crossed diamond box with two branches.

When the bidding window expires—an internal event represented with a labeled UML comment box—the Auctioneer sends a `declare(num-offers)` message. Once the Auctioneer has notified the buyers the number of bids, the Auctioneer's program flow divides in three execution branches, and this is stated in the diagram using the exclusive-or diamond box below Auctioneer's time line:

1. Left execution branch: When $num_{\text{offers}} < 1$ the Auctioneer decreases the *price* variable and resumes its execution from the beginning. To our knowledge, there is no AUML notation to represent iteration. Therefore, this eventuality must be stated explicitly in natural language.

2. Center execution branch: When $num_{\text{offers}} > 1$ the Auctioneer declares a collision, increases the *price* variable and resumes its execution from the beginning. One more time, the lack of explicit graphical notation for iteration yields to stating it in natural language.

3. Right execution branch: When $num_{\text{offers}} = 1$ the Auctioneer declares that a single bid has been stated and declares it as a broadcast message to every buyer *and* to the Buyers' Supervisor agent, which begins then its internal processing. Be $B = \{buyer_1, buyer_2, ..., buyer_n\}$ the set of buyers active in the Auction, and $credit(b) : B \longmapsto \Re$ the credit function. Once the Supervisor agent knows the buyer's identity $buyer_i \in B$ and the good *price* variable, two execution branches are possible:

   (a) When $credit(buyer_i) \geq price$, the Buyers' Supervisor declares to the Auctioneer that the bid is acceptable, using a `declare(acceptable_bid)` speech act. After receiving the Supervisor's approval, the Auctioneer declares the good as sold, and broadcasts a `declare(sold(good, price, buyer_i))` message. After receiving confirmation from the Auctioneer, the Buyers' Supervisor adjusts $buyer_i$ credit, doing $credit(buyer_i) = credit(buyer_i) - price$, and notifies $buyer_i$ his/her new credit status. Next, the Auctioneer finishes the auction process and begins the next process: Buyers' and Sellers' settlement, which are not considered here.

   (b) When $credit(buyer_i) < price$, the Buyers' Supervisor agent declares to the Auctioneer that the bid is unacceptable, using a `declare(unacceptable_bid)` speech act. Once a Supervisor's denial has been received, the Auctioneer declares the good as not sold, broadcasting a `declare(not-sold(good, price, buyer_i))` message to every buyer and Supervisor. Next the Supervisor asserts $buyer_i$ and the Auctioneer that the credit is insufficient, showing to $buyer_i$ its credit. When $buyer_i$ knows his/her credit, the Auctioneer declares $buyer_i$ as sanctioned. Next, the Auctioneer proceeds to restart the bidding round.

3   Automatic Translation: The ATOS Approach

3.1   Model-Checking AUML Sequence Diagrams

AUML [7] sequence diagrams are an extension of their UML counterparts, designed to allow the representation of agent interactions over time. As our interest is centered on interaction protocol specification and validation, the extended notation of AUML sequence diagrams represent a natural choice for our efforts.

Wei et al [8] define a translation process from AUML sequence diagrams to a formal specification expressed on the PROMELA language [9]. Their algorithm is designed to take a sequence diagram specification, and to generate an extended finite state machine (EFSM) where transitions are activated on input or guard triggering, and generate an output. They also propose another algorithm which, once the EFSM is generated, translate it to a final PROMELA specification, acceptable by the free and widely used formal verificator SPIN.

Unfortunately their interest was focused on AUML improvement, and they left the implementation of their translator as a open issue. So, we took the task of implementing an analogous translator in order to accelerate our own efforts looking for improvements on the interaction protocol validation process. The result of this efforts is the ATOS system.

3.2   General Overview of ATOS

The ATOS [1] system presented here, takes as input an AUML sequence diagram specification conveyed with an *ad hoc* syntax in one or several text files and translates it into a single PROMELA specification. In this paper, we introduce and use a slightly modified subset of the ITU-T Z.120 standard [10]. Once the final specification is created, it must be tested using SPIN, as ATOS does not verify system properties like liveness or security but only creates a syntactically valid result. The approach is intended to be minimalistic, and best-effort. Despite the incompleteness of the chosen approach, the software is helpful to demonstrate the applicability of AUML on industrial agent-oriented CASE tools.

Figure 2 shows the general structure of the system. There are two main interfaces, the first one links ATOS to the AUML specification generator, which could be a simple text editor, or yet another specific purpose system (which is now being developed in parallel), capable to generate an input specification for ATOS from a graphic user interface. The description of that specification generator is beyond the scope of this paper.

3.3   Input Language

The basic element of a AUML sequence diagram is the *Communication Act*, e.g., an entity sending or receiving a message to/from another. For ATOS, a communication act is a tuple $E = (CA_{type}, A, B, C)$, where $CA_{type} = \{in, out\}$ is the set of all communication act types supported by ATOS, A and B are sets of labels representing the source and destination agents of this communication act; and $C = (I, E, O)$ is another tuple, where I is an input symbol to receive, E a logical expression (guard) and O an output symbol to send whenever the messages specified on I have arrived and E is true. These input and output symbols are, in fact, translated to mtype defined labels in the final specification.

Next we show the different kinds of Communication Acts proposed by AUML that ATOS can handle, and their equivalency on tuples:

---

[1] ATOS is an acronym for **A**UML **to** PROMELA/SPIN.

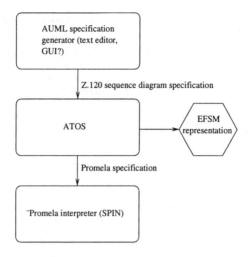

Fig. 2. ATOS system general scheme.

- Message sending:
  $(out, \{src\}, \{tgt\}, (\emptyset, true, msg_{out}))$
  in this case, the input message set to *void* (not waiting for messages) and the guard expression evaluated as *true*, enable immediately the occurrence of this output event.
- Message receiving:
  $(in, \{src\}, \{tgt\}, (msg_{in}, true, \emptyset))$.
- Message sending triggered by internal events:
  $(out, \{src\}, \{tgt\}, (\emptyset, P, msg_{out}))$.
- Message sending triggered by input (causality):
  $(out, \{src\}, \{tgt\}, (msg_{in}, true, msg_{out}))$.
- XOR message sending:
  $(out, \{src\}, \{tgt_1\}, (\emptyset, true, msg_{out_1}))!..!$
  $(out, \{src\}, \{tgt_k\}, (\emptyset, true, msg_{out_k}))$.
- OR message sending:
  $(out, \{src\}, \{tgt_1\}, (\emptyset, true, msg_{out_1})) + ..+$
  $(out, \{src\}, \{tgt_k\}, (\emptyset, true, msg_{out_k}))$.
- AND message sending:
  $(out, \{src\}, \{tgt_1\}, (\emptyset, true, msg_{out_1})) \&..\&$
  $(out, \{src\}, \{tgt_k\}, (\emptyset, true, msg_{out_k}))$.
- Multicast message:
  $(out, \{src\}, \{tgt_1, tgt_2, ..., tgt_k\}, (\emptyset, true, msg_{out}))$.

AUML proposes four different artifacts to represent flow control inside an agent, all of which are available on ATOS:

- Sequential composition: $E_1 \rightarrow E_2$, E_1 happens before E_2.
- XOR choice: $E_1!E_2$, either E_1 or E_2 will be executed but not both.

- OR choice: $E_1 + E_2$, either E_1 and E_2 happen in parallel, or E_1 happens but not E_2, or E_1 do not happen but E_2 does.
- AND choice (parallelism): $E_1 \& E_2$, both E_1 and E_2 happen.

3.4   Visual to Textual Description Mapping

While visual modeling is actually better for human understanding, CASE tools need a mapping that takes a visual scheme as input, and generates a machine readable description on the output. For ATOS, this mapping can straightfor-wardly be automatized, but unfortunately for time reasons no AUML graphic editor has been implemented yet.

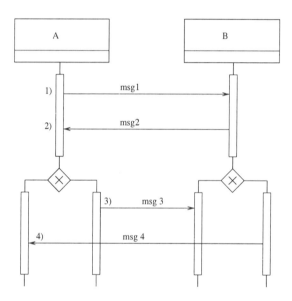

Fig. 3. A sample sequence diagram.

Figure 3 shows an example of AUML sequence diagram. The first communi-cation act is a message sending: *msg1* from A to B (1), the second a response: *msg2* from B to A (2), and so on. The diamond boxes are AUML notation for an inclusive XOR thread execution, so either communication acts (3) or (4) happen but not both. Using the mapping specified above, the communication acts from agent A's perspective would be

```
(out,A,B,(null,true,msg 1)) -> (in,B,A,(msg 2, true, null)) ->
((out,A,B,(null,true,msg 3)) ! (in,B,A,(msg 4,true,null)))
```

and from agent B's perspective it would be

```
(in,A,B,(msg 1,true,null)) -> (out,B,A,(msg 2, true, null)) ->
((in,A,B,(msg 3,true,null)) ! (out,B,A,(null,true,msg 4)))
```

Wei et al [8] proposed to use a Z.120-like syntax to represent communication acts, and currently ATOS uses it. The syntax for this notation is actually irrelevant, in fact Z.120 was chosen for simplicity, and can be substituted by another structured markup, XML for instance.

3.5   Processing

The input specification processing encompasses six relevant parts:

1. Generate an internal representation: the parser takes one of the input files and generates a symbol tree where atomic communication acts are leafs and flow control operators are branches linking them.
2. Eliminate all OR choices: the parser looks recursively for OR operators ("+") on the tree, and replaces them with expressions containing XOR and sequential composition operators only, using the next equivalence $(A + B = (A \rightarrow B)!(B \rightarrow A)!A!B)$, this generates a new intermediary specification.
3. Eliminate all AND choices: the parser generates a new symbol tree from the last intermediary specification, and looks recursively for AND operators ("&") on it. It replaces them with expressions containing XOR and sequential composition operators only, using the next equivalence $(A\&B = (A \rightarrow B)!(B \rightarrow A))$ (interleaving). A second intermediary specification is generated.
4. Generate the EFSM. The system takes the last intermediary specification (without any AND-OR choices), generates another tree from it, and creates the EFSM.
5. PROMELA code generation. The FSM for the specified agent is translated to PROMELA code (into a single process), every transition is mapped to an atomic output or input through a channel, the current state is included as a guard in order to assure a sequenced execution.
6. Repeat all previous steps for every input specification. Once every input specification has been processed, join all generated PROMELA code in a single specification file, adding accessory statements in order to make it executable by the interpreter (channel declarations, mtype label declarations extracted from message symbols and a main process synthesis).

Every intermediate specification is observationally equivalent to the last one, and expressed on the same syntax, thus are readable by ATOS itself . Only a final OR and AND free specification can be translated to EFSM, given the impossibility to model effective parallelism on SPIN.

It is worth noting that ATOS does not exhaustively verify the system's properties, this system is a translator, not a validator. Such a task is delegated over a much more powerful system: SPIN. However, ATOS neither accepts nor generates syntactically or semantically incorrect specifications.

The ATOS system follows an "as is" policy regarding translation of input specifications, allowing the developer to change either the input specification (the visual model), the final PROMELA specification and even the intermediate specifications.

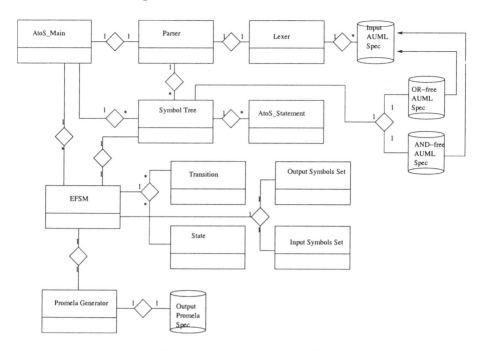

Fig. 4. Class diagram for ATOS.

4   The ATOS System

Figure 4 shows the class structure of the ATOS system, using the UML notation.

- The class ATOS *Main* displays a minimal user interface and coordinates the functioning of all other classes. This class has a single object of *Parser* class that builds the *Symbol Tree* object associated with any file *AUML Input Specification*. This is stated graphically in the diagram with a "1 to many" relationship between *Parser* and *Symbol Tree*.
- *Symbol Tree* contains many objects of the class ATOS *Statement*, these objects represent atomic statements. There are of two kinds : communication acts and flow control operators, which are defined previously in section 3.3.
  - The *Symbol Tree* object stores communication acts as leafs and execution operators in non leaf nodes.
  - *Symbol Tree* is able to rewrite the entire specification, eliminating every occurrence of both parallel composition operators ('+' and '&'), replacing them by an interleaved equivalent using only XOR and sequential composition operators. The "one to one" relationship linking *Symbol Tree* with two intermediary specification files, states the fact that ATOS eliminates one type of parallel operator at a time. Both intermediary output specifications are readable by the *Parser* object as input specifications, in figure 4. That capability is represented by arrows going from each intermediate specification to the input specification.

- Every *EFSM* object has a single object of class *SymbolTree* associated, but not every *Symbol Tree* has an *EFSM,* given the impossibility to represent adequately actual parallelism on SPIN, thus a *Symbol Tree* object containing parallel operators ('+' or '&') can not be translated into an *EFSM* object. In order to eliminate these operators from the initial input specification, we use the intermediary specification generation feature of *Symbol Tree.*

  By convention, *EFSM* objects generate the finite state machine: every communication act (input or output) is assigned to a transition, sequential composition operators create linear transition paths and XOR operators create non deterministic choices.

- Every *EFSM* object is associated with another object of class PROMELA *Generator.* This class takes the FSM and writes a PROMELA representation for it.

Taking the sample AUML sequence diagram in figure 3, the EFSM class generates the following textual representation for *Agent A*:

```
FSM for A is
state A_init : ( A_init -> A_OUTPUT_msg1_2 , ( [] / / [msg1] )) ,

state A_OUTPUT_msg1_2 : ( A_OUTPUT_msg1_2 -> A_INPUT_msg2_3 ,
                          ( [msg2] / / [] )) ,


state A_INPUT_msg2_3 : ( A_INPUT_msg2_3 -> A_OUTPUT_msg3_4 ,
            ( [] / / [msg3] )) , ( A_INPUT_msg2_3 -> A_INPUT_msg4_5 ,
                          ( [msg4] / / [] )) ,

state A_OUTPUT_msg3_4 :

state A_INPUT_msg4_5 :
```

The notation denotes every state followed by its corresponding transitions. Transitions are expressed as three statements separated by slash symbols. State names are generated by concatenating agent's name, communication act type (in or out) and exchanged message names. The first state in the example is *A_init,* this state has only one transition, going from itself to state A_OUTPUT_msg_1_2 and sending a *msg_1* message. Final states like *A_OUTPUT_msg3_4* or *A_INPUT_msg4_5* do not have any transition.

Once the EFSM has been generated, we obtain an equivalent PROMELA code fragment representing the same *Agent A*:

```
mtype = {msg_1, msg_2, msg_3, msg_4} ;        /* Messages */

chan B_A [1] of {int};                        /* Channels */

proctype A ()
{                                             /* System states */
```

```
#define A_init            10
#define A_OUTPUT_msg1_2 11
#define A_INPUT_msg2_3   12
#define A_OUTPUT_msg3_4 13
#define A_INPUT_msg4_5   14

int state;                       /* State pointer for this process */

state = A_init;                  /* State initialization */

do                               /* Transitions */
::if
  ::state == A_init            -> atomic{B_A!msg1;state = A_OUTPUT_msg1_2}
  ::state == A_OUTPUT_msg1_2 -> atomic{B_A?msg2;state = A_INPUT_msg2_3}
  ::state == A_INPUT_msg2_3  -> atomic{B_A!msg3;state = A_OUTPUT_msg3_4}
  ::state == A_INPUT_msg2_3  -> atomic{B_A?msg4;state = A_INPUT_msg4_5}
  ::state == A_OUTPUT_msg3_4 -> break;
  ::state == A_INPUT_msg4_5  -> break;
  fi
od
}
```

State control is done using a pointer variable (integer) named *state*, whose value changes following the execution path. It is worth noting that every duo input-output operation and state change, is inside a PROMELA *atomic* statement, this is done in order to eliminate some usual concurrency problems that yield execution inconsistencies: an *atomic* clause tells SPIN to serialize the execution of anything inside it.

5   Concluding Remarks

Following the translation process exposed on section 3.3 and applying it to the sequence diagram shown on figure 1, we were able to obtain a set of three input sub-specifications, one for each agent involved in the Auction scene. Each input specification was processed with the ATOS system, obtaining a final PROMELA/SPIN specification expressing the system behavior. However, as ATOS creates a single PROMELA process per input specification, e.g., ATOS assumes the communication acts to be from a single entity to another single entity, the role-oriented scheme shown in figure 1 must be transformed in order to actually simulate an acceptable system behavior.

In the FishMarket auction case, it implies the generation of multiple analogous copies of the Buyer agent specification, every one with exactly the same behavior, but with a different name in order to represent accurately the one-to-many abstract relationship between the Auctioneer agent and the Buyers, thus the number of input specifications increases.

So far, ATOS' current implementation supports *static* specifications only, those where the structure is established at the beginning and stays the same until the end, while PROMELA itself supports dynamic process instantiation and run-time communication channel creation. The language proposed to represent AUML sequence diagrams cannot express models with a dynamically changing structure (new module instantiation, channel creation) because AUML sequence diagrams do not provide any symbolic artifacts to express such eventualities. They are conceived more as a tool concerned with *interactions* among objects (or agents) and less as an artifact describing *system structure* changes through time. As our proposed language is specifically designed to express sequence diagrams, it has at its best, an expressiveness equivalent to them.

Despite the one-to-one mapping between visual notation and textual representation, excessive statement verbosity makes it hard to avoid syntactic or mnemonically induced semantical errors. Our current notation introduces too much symbols for a single communication act. Unfortunately such verbosity can hardly be avoided, as communication acts usually contain long message names and complex guards. That propensity to spurious errors on the input specification could be a severe disadvantage, and suggests the necessity to automate the now handmade process of input specification generation. However, once a first syntactically correct specification has been obtained, the development of a formal model becomes notoriously accelerated.

References

1. Wooldridge, M., Jennings, N.R., Kinny, D.: The gaia methodology for agent-oriented analysis and design. Journal of Autonomous Agents and Multi-Agent Systems **3** (2000) 285–312
2. OMG: Unified Modeling Language Specification. Object Management Group, 250 First Avenue, Needham, MA 02494 USA. 1.4 edn. (2001)
3. Bauer, B., Muller, J., Odell, J.: Agent UML: A formalism for specifying multiagent interaction. In Ciancarini, Wooldridge, eds.: International journal of software engineering and knowledge engineering. Volume 11. Springer, Berlin (2001) 91–103
4. Odell, J., Van Dyke Parunak, H., Bauer, B.: Extending UML for agents. In Wagner, G., Lesperance, Y., Yu, E., eds.: Agent-Oriented Information Systems Workshop, Austin, Texas, ICue Publishing (2000)
5. Holzmann, G.J.: Design and Validation of Computer Protocols. Prentice-Hall (1991)
6. Rodríguez, J.A., Noriega, P., Sierra, C., Padget, J.: Fm96.5 a java-based electronic auction house. On Line Publication (1997) main reference for Fish Market.
7. Odell, J., Van Dyke Parunak, H., Bauer, B.: Representing agent interaction protocols in uml. In Ciancarini, P., Wooldridge, M., eds.: Proceedings of First International Workshop on Agent-Oriented Software Engineering, Limerick, Ireland, Springer-Verlag (2000)
8. Wei, J., Cheung, S.C., Wang, X.: Towards a methodology for formal design and analysis of agent interaction protocols : An investigation in electronic commerce. In: International Software Engineering Symposium (ISES-2001), Wuhan. (2001)
9. Holzmann, G.J.: The model checker SPIN. IEEE Transactions on Software Engineering **23** (1997) 279–295
10. ITU-TS: ITU-TS Recommendation Z.120: Message Sequence Chart 1996 (MSC96). Technical report, ITU-TS, Geneva (1996)

A UML Profile for External Agent-Object-Relationship (AOR) Models

Gerd Wagner

Eindhoven University of Technology, Faculty of Technology Management
G.Wagner@tm.tue.nl
http://tmitwww.tm.tue.nl/staff/gwagner

Abstract. We present a UML profile for an agent-oriented modeling approach called *Agent-Object-Relationship (AOR)* modeling, where an entity is either an agent, an event, an action, a claim, a commitment, or an ordinary object, and where special relationships between agents and events, actions, claims and commitments supplement the fundamental association, aggregation/composition and generalization relationships of UML class models.

1 Introduction

In [Wag02], we have proposed an agent-oriented modeling language for the analysis and design of organizational information systems, called *Agent-Object-Relationship* modeling language (AORML) . In the AORML, an entity is either an agent, an event, an action, a claim, a commitment, or an ordinary object. Special relationships between agents and events, actions, claims and commitments supplement the fundamental association, generalization and aggregation relationships of UML class models. AORML can be viewed as an extension of the Unified Modeling Language (UML). We believe that AORML, by virtue of its agent-oriented categorization of different classes, allows more adequate models of organizations and organizational information systems than plain UML.

Casting the AOR metamodel as a UML profile allows AOR models to be notated using standard UML notation. This means that most UML tools (specifically the ones that support the extension mechanisms of UML, such as stereotypes and tagged values) can be used to define AOR models. Standard practice for defining UML profiles has been adopted. A mapping of AOR metamodel classes to their base UML classes, with accompanying stereotypes, tagged values and constraints is presented. An implementation of this mapping can be used, for example, to generate XMI metadata conforming to the AOR metamodel from models notated using the UML profile. Specialized AOR tools will more likely directly use the AOR metamodel rather than the UML profile as a basis for storing and manipulating models.

There are two basic types of AOR models: external and internal ones. An *external AOR model* adopts the perspective of an external observer who is observing the (prototypical) agents and their interactions in the problem domain under

F. Giunchiglia et al. (Eds.): AOSE 2002, LNCS 2585, pp. 138–149, 2003.

consideration. In an *internal AOR model*, we adopt the internal (first-person) view of a particular agent to be modeled. This distinction suggests the following system development path: in the analysis phase, draw up an external AOR model of the domain under consideration including one or more focus agents (this yields a domain model); in the design phase, for each focus agent, transform the external AOR model into an internal one according to the agent's perspective (this is called "internalization", resulting in a functional design model); then, refine the internal AOR model of each focus agent into an implementation model for the target language (such as SQL or Java). A complete internal AOR model is a formal specification of a high-level state transition system, where perception, reaction and commitment/claim handling provide the basic transition types.

The UML does not support the concept of an agent as a first class citizen. In the UML, there is a certain ambiguity with respect to the agent concept. Human and artificial agents, if they are 'users' of a system, are called *actors* being involved in *use cases* but remaining external to the system model, while software agents within the boundaries of the system are called 'active objects'. In the UML, the customers and the employees of a company would have to be modeled as 'objects' in the same way as rental cars and bank accounts, while in the AOR approach they would be modeled as institutional or human agents to be represented in the system of that company (which itself could be modeled as an artificial agent).

In AOR modeling, only agents can communicate, perceive, act, make commitments and satisfy claims. Objects do not communicate, cannot perceive anything, are unable to act, and do not have any commitments or claims.

2   AOR Models

While plain UML supports the design of *object-oriented* information systems realized with the help of relational and object-relational database technology, AORML is to support the high-level design of *agent-oriented* information systems. An *AOR information system model* consists of a number of external AOR models being (business) domain analysis models or *computation-independent business models*, as they are called in the Model-Driven Architecture (MDA) of the OMG, and a number of internal AOR models including (*platform-independent* and *platform-specific*) design models and implementation models, as shown in Figure 1.

In an **External AOR Model**, we adopt the view of an external observer who is observing the (prototypical) agents and their interactions in the problem domain under consideration. Typically, an external AOR model has a *focus*, that is an agent, or a group of agents, for which we would like to develop a state and behavior model.

An **Internal AOR Model** depicts *the world* as it may be represented in the mental state of the focus agent. If the focus agent is an organization, the internal AOR model represents its view of *the world*, and may be used to design its information system.

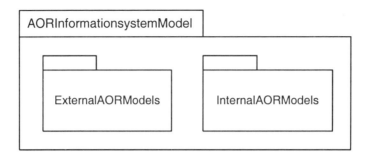

Fig. 1. An AORModel consists of an ExternalAORModel (corresponding to a domain analysis model) and an InternalAORModel (corresponding to a design model).

Thus, AOR modeling suggests the following development path for organizational information systems:

1. In analysis, develop a (computation-independent) domain model of an organization (or a group of organizations) and its (or their) environment from the perspective of an external observer of the scenario in the form of an external AOR model. In addition, use some requirements engineering method to capture and analyze the system requirements as defined by the customers of the system, and turn them into a complete and consistent requirements specification.
2. Transform the external AOR domain model into a (platform-independent) internal AOR design model for the focus agent for that an information system is to be developed (typically an organization or an organizational unit). If there are several focus agents, and for each of them an information system is to be developed, this step can be iterated. Refine these internal design models by taking the requirements specification into consideration, adding design artifacts as needed.
3. Refine the internal AOR design models obtained in the previous step into platform-specific design models, such as database design models (logical database schemas), e.g. for object-relational (SQL-99) database management systems, or into sets of corresponding logical data structure definitions in a target language such as Java.
4. Refine the platform-specific design models into implementation models (such as physical database schemas) by taking performance and storage management issues, as well as the specific features of the target language (such as SQL-99 or Java), into consideration.
5. Generate the target language code.

Step 2 (mapping to platform-independent design) and step 3 (mapping to platform-specific design) are described in [Wag02].

The meta-concepts of AOR modeling that are common to both Internal and External AOR modeling are listed as UML *stereotypes* in Table 1.

Table 1. A summary of the stereotypes that are common to both Internal and External AOR modeling. *Restricted generalization* means that whenever a generalization relationship involves a class of that stereotype as either subclass or superclass, the other class involved must also be of that stereotype.

Stereotype	Base Class	Parent	Constraints
AORModel	Model	NA	
Agent	Class	NA	Restricted generalization.
BiologicalAgent	Class	Agent	Restricted generalization.
HumanAgent	Class	BiologicalAgent	Restricted generalization.
ArtificialAgent	Class	Agent	Restricted generalization.
SoftwareAgent	Class	ArtificialAgent	Restricted generalization.
Robot	Class	ArtificialAgent	Restricted generalization.
EmbeddedSystem	Class	ArtificialAgent	Restricted generalization.
InstitutionalAgent	Class	Agent	Restricted generalization.
Organization	Class	InstitutionalAgent	Restricted generalization.
OrganizationalUnit	Class	InstitutionalAgent	Restricted generalization.
Object	Class	NA	Restricted generalization.

2.1   Object Types

Object types, such as `Book` or `SalesOrder`, are visualized as plain rectangles like classes in standard UML class diagrams.

2.2   Agent Types

We distinguish between *artificial* agents, *human* agents and *institutional* agents[1]. Examples of human agent types are Person, Employee, Student, Nurse, or Patient. Examples of institutional agents are organizations, such as a bank or a hospital, or organizational units. An institutional agent consists of a number of internal agents that perceive events and perform actions on behalf of it, by playing certain *roles*.

In certain application domains, there may also be artificial Agent Types, such as software agents (e.g., involved in electronic commerce transactions), embedded systems (such as automated teller machines), or robots. For instance, in an automated contract negotiation or in an automated purchase decision, a legal entity may be represented by an artificial agent. Typically, an artificial agent is owned, and is run, by a legal entity that is responsible for its actions.

In AOR diagrams, an agent class is visualized as a rectangle with rounded corners. Icons indicating a single human, a group, or a robot may be used for visualizing the distinction between human, institutional and artificial agent.

Agents may be related to other entities by means of ordinary domain relationships (associations). In addition to the designated relationships *generalization* and *composition* of ER/OO modeling, there are further designated relationships relating agents with events, actions and commitments. They are discussed below.

---

[1] Notice that we do not distinguish between 'agents' and 'actors'. Both terms denote the same concept. By default, we use the term 'agent'.

2.3   External and Internal Agents

With respect to an institutional agent, one has to distinguish between external and internal agents. Internal agents, by virtue of their contractual status (or ownership status, in the case of artificial internal agents), have certain rights and duties, and assume a certain position within the subordination hierarchy of the institution they belong to. In the case of a hospital, examples of human internal agents are doctors and nurses; examples of artificial internal agents are communication-enabled information systems and agentified embedded systems, such as patient monitoring systems.

2.4   Commitments and Claims

Representing and processing commitments and claims in information systems explicitly helps to achieve coherent behavior in (semi-)automated interaction processes. In [Sin99], the social dimension of coherent behavior is emphasized, and commitments are treated as ternary relationships between two agents and a 'context group' they both belong to. For simplicity, we treat commitments as binary relationships between two agents.

Commitments to perform certain actions, or to see to it that certain conditions hold, typically arise from certain communication acts. For instance, sending a sales quotation to a customer commits the vendor to reserve adequate stocks of the quoted item for some time. Likewise, acknowledging a sales order implies the creation of a commitment to deliver the ordered items on or before the specified delivery date.

Obviously, a commitment of a_1 (the debtor) towards a_2 (the creditor) to do the action α is mirrored as a claim of a_2 against a_1 to create the action event α.

3   External AOR Models

In the external-observer-view adopted in external AOR models, *the world* (i.e. the application domain) consists of various types of

1. *agents*,
2. communicative and non-communicative *action events*,
3. *non-action events*,
4. *commitments/claims* between two agent types,
5. ordinary *objects*,
6. various *designated relationships*, such as *sends* and *does*,
7. ordinary *associations*.

In the view of an external observer, actions are also events, and commitments are also claims, exactly like two sides of the same coin. Therefore, an external AOR model contains, besides the agent and object types of interest, the action event classes and commitment/claim classes that are needed to describe the interaction between the focus agent(s) and the other types of agents.

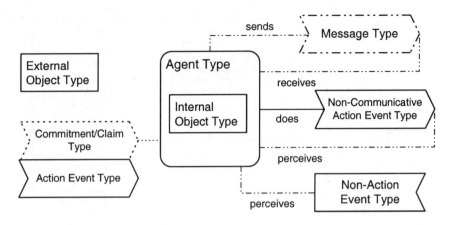

Fig. 2. The core elements of External AOR modeling.

Object types, in an external AOR model, belong to one or several agents (or agent types). They define containers for beliefs. If an object class belongs exclusively to one agent or agent class (in the sense of a private belief type), the corresponding rectangle is drawn inside this agent (type) rectangle. If an object class represents beliefs that are shared among two or more agents (or agent types), the object class rectangle is drawn outside the respective agent (type) rectangles.

An external AOR model does not include any design or implementation artifacts (it is *computation-independent*, in the terminology of OMG's MDA). It rather represents a conceptual analysis view of the problem domain and may also contain elements which are merely descriptive and not executable by a computer program (as required for enterprise modeling).

An external AOR model may comprise one or more of the following diagrams:

Agent Diagrams depicting the agent types of the domain, certain relevant object types, and the relationships among them (an example is shown in Figure 3).

Interaction Frame Diagrams depicting the action event classes and commitment/claim classes that determine the possible interactions between two agent types (or instances).

Interaction Sequence Diagrams depicting proto-typical instances of interaction processes.

Interaction Pattern Diagrams focusing on general interaction patterns expressed by means of a set of reaction rules defining an interaction process type.

The agent diagrams, interaction frame diagrams and interaction pattern diagrams of a model may be merged into a single all-encompassing *External AOR Diagram (EAORD)*. Interaction sequence diagrams are normally not included in such an EAORD, since they depict instances only, and are not at the type level.

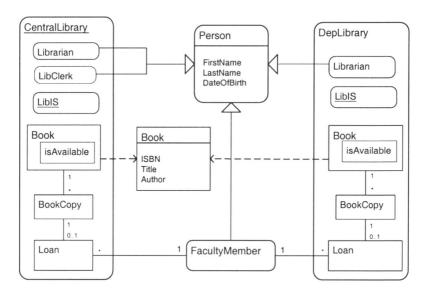

Fig. 3. An AOR agent diagram for the university libraries domain. The central library and the department libraries are institutional agents, having librarians as human internal agents and a library information system as an artificial internal agent. Also, `FacultyMember` is an agent class in this domain. Important object types are `Book`, `BookCopy` and `Loan`, that is, libraries have beliefs about their books, their book copies, and their loans. The subclass `Book.isAvailable` is formed by all books that satisfy the status predicate `isAvailable`, that is, for which there is at least one book copy available.

Each agent has beliefs about its internal agents, about its objects, and about all external agents and shared objects that are related to it.

3.1   Actions Are Events but not All Events Are Actions

In the external observer perspective, all actions of agents are at the same time also events that may be perceived by other agents. The other way around, there are many events that are created by the corresponding actions of agents. However, there are also events which are not created by actions (e.g., temporal events, or events created by natural forces). Consequently, we make a distinction between *action events* and *non-action events*.

In an External AOR Diagram, an action event type is graphically rendered by a special arrow rectangle where one side is an incoming arrow linked to the agent (or agent class) that performs this type of action, and the other side is an outgoing arrow linked to the agent (or agent class) that perceives this type of event. Communicative action event rectangles have a dot-dashed line. In the case of a non-action event, the corresponding event rectangle does not have an outgoing arrow (see Figure 4).

Table 2. A tabular definition of the stereotypes of external AOR modeling. *No aggregation* means that classes of that stereotype must not participate in any aggregation.

Stereotype	Base Class	Parent	Constraints
Event	Class	NA	Restricted generalization. No aggregation.
Action Event	Class	Event	Restricted generalization. No aggregation.
Communicative Action Event	Class	Action Event	Restricted generalization. No aggregation.
Non-Communicative Action Event	Class	Action Event	Restricted generalization. No aggregation.
NonActionEvent	Class	Event	Restricted generalization. No aggregation.
CommitmentClaim	Class	NA	Restricted generalization. No aggregation.
does	Association	NA	The domain class must be an agent type and the range class must be a non-communicative action event type. Multiplicity is one-to-many.
perceives	Association	NA	The domain class must be an agent type and the range class must be a non-communicative action event type or a non-action event type. Multiplicity is one-to-many.
sends	Association	NA	The domain class must be an agent type and the range class must be a communicative action event type. Multiplicity is one-to-many.
receives	Association	NA	The domain class must be an agent type and the range class must be a communicative action event type. Multiplicity is one-to-many.
hasClaim	Association	NA	The domain class must be an agent type and the range class must be a commitment/claim type. Multiplicity is one-to-many.
hasCommitment	Association	NA	The domain class must be an agent type and the range class must be a commitment/claim type. Multiplicity is one-to-many.

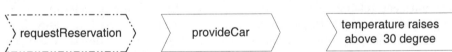

Fig. 4. A communicative action event, a non-communicative action event, and a non-action event.

3.2   Commitments/Claims

In external AOR modeling, a *commitment* of agent a_1 towards agent a_2 to perform an action of a certain type (such as a commitment to deliver an item) can also be viewed as a *claim* of a_2 against a_1 that an action event of that type will happen. Commitments/claims are conceptually coupled with the type of action event they refer to (such as *deliverItem* action events). This is graphically

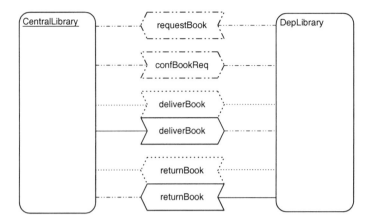

Fig. 5. The interaction frame between the central library and the department libraries: a department library may request a book from the central library; when such a book request has been confirmed by the central library, then there is a commitment to deliver the requested book (visualized by the dashed-line *deliverBook* arrow rectangle); normally, such a commitment leads to a corresponding action (visualized by the solid-line *deliverBook* arrow rectangle); after a book has been delivered, there is a commitment to return it in due time.

rendered by an arrow rectangle with a dotted line on top of the action event rectangle it refers to, as depicted in Figure 2.

3.3   Interaction Frame Diagrams

In an external AOR model, there are four types of designated relationships (association stereotypes) between agents and action events: sends and receives are associations that relate an agent with communicative action events, while does and perceives are associations that relate an agent with non-communicative action events. In addition, there are two types of associations between agents and commitments/claims: hasCommitment and hasClaim. These association stereotypes are visualized with particular connector types as depicted in Figure 5.

An *interaction frame diagram*, in an external AOR model, describes the possible interactions between two (types of) agents. It consists of various types of

1. communicative action events,
2. non-communicative action events,
3. commitments/claims (coupled with the corresponding types of action events), and
4. non-action events.

An example of an interaction frame diagram is shown in Figure 5.

3.4   Interaction Sequence Diagrams

An interaction sequence diagram depicts (some part of) an instance of an interaction process. An *interaction process* is a sequence of action events and

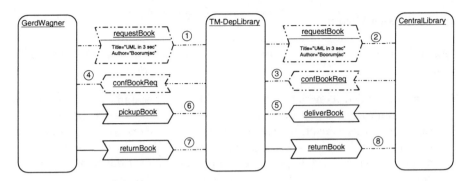

Fig. 6. A social interaction process involving three agents. It is an option to display the object types referred to in the arguments of messages and action events within the agents that have to deal with them.

non-action events, performed and perceived by agents, and following a set of rules (or protocol) that specifies the type of the interaction process. Agents may interact with their inanimate environment, or they may interact with each other. A *social interaction process* is a temporally ordered, coherent set of action events and non-action events, involving at least one communicative action event, performed and perceived by agents, and following a set of rules, or protocol, that is governed by norms, and that specifies the type of the interaction process[2]. An example of a social interaction process is shown in Figure 6. Social norms imply, for instance, that after having confirmed a book request, the library is committed to deliver the requested book.

We consider a business process as a special kind of a *social interaction process*. Unlike physical or chemical processes, social interaction processes are based on communication acts that may create commitments and are governed by norms. We distinguish between an interaction process type and a concrete interaction process (instance), while in the literature the term 'business process' is ambiguously used both at the type and the instance level. Social interaction process types are modeled in *Interaction Pattern Diagrams* with the help of *reaction rules* (see [TW01,Wag02]).

4   Internal AOR Models

In an *internal* AOR model, we adopt the internal view of a particular agent to be modeled. In this first-person-view, *the world* (i.e. the application domain) consists of various types of other *agents, actions, commitments, events, claims*, ordinary *objects*, various *designated relationships*, such as *isSentTo* and *isPerceivedBy*, and ordinary *associations*.

For space reasons, we cannot present the UML profile for internal AOR models here.

---

[2] Notice that we did not choose *activities* as the basic elements of a process. While an *action* happens at a time instant (i.e., it is immediate), an *activity* is being performed during a time interval (i.e., it has duration), and may consist of a sequence of actions.

5 Related Work

Some predefined UML 'stereotypes' come quite close to some of the AOR meta-concepts:

Signals are defined as a class stereotype. They correspond to some degree to a communicative action event (or message) type in external AOR models. For activity diagrams, there are two signal symbols: one for sent signals, and one for received signals, corresponding to the AOR distinction between communication acts (outgoing messages) and communication events (incoming messages). Strangely, the receipt of a signal is treated as an action that may follow any activity (which seems to denote the special action type *wait for signal*).

Active objects are another example of a class stereotype. An active object is an object that "owns a thread and can initiate control activity" (cited from the OMG Unified Modeling Language Specification). Thus, active objects are rather an implementation, and not a domain, modeling concept. In a certain sense, they form a superclass of software agents, but they do not reflect the AOR distinction between agent and object.

The UML Profile for Business Modeling. included in the UML 1.4 standard defines the class stereotypes 'worker' and 'entity'. A ≪Worker≫ is "an abstraction of a human that acts within the system", so this concept seems to correspond to the AOR concept of an internal human agent. All other (passive) business objects are called ≪Entity≫. The UML Profile for Business Modeling seems to be a rather ad-hoc proposal for making a distinction between active and passive 'business objects' and for resolving some of the conceptual difficulties arising from the UML definition of an ≪Actor≫.

The Eriksson-Penker Business Extensions. In [EP99], Eriksson and Penker propose an approach to business modeling with UML based on four primary concepts: resources, processes, goals, and rules. In this proposal, there is no specific treatment of agents. They are subsumed, together with "material, information, and products" under the concept of *resources*. This unfortunate subsumption of human agents under the traditional 'resource' metaphor prevents a proper treatment of many agent-related concepts such as commitments, authorization, and communication/interaction.

5.1 Agent UML

In [OvDPB00], an agent-oriented extension of UML, called *Agent UML (AUML)*, mainly concerning sequence diagrams and activity diagrams, has been proposed. However, UML class diagrams are not modified, and no distinction between agents and objects is made in AUML.

6   Conclusion

We have shown that the AOR modeling language can be viewed as a UML profile. In fact, we need to define two profiles, one for external and one for internal AOR models. It is, however, difficult to express the AOR behavior modeling construct of *reaction rules* since these rules are not expressible as UML 'stereotypes'. So, we can only cast the AOR state modeling fragment as a UML profile. The inclusion of reaction rules for AOR behavior modeling is not supported by the UML extension mechanisms.

References

[EP99]   H.E. Eriksson and M. Penker. *Business Modeling with UML: Business Patterns at Work.* John Wiley & Sons, 1999.

[OvDPB00] J. Odell, H. van Dyke Parunak, and B. Bauer. Extending UML for agents. In G. Wagner, Y. Lesperance, and E. Yu, editors, *Proc. of the 2nd Int. Workshop on Agent-Oriented Information Systems*, Berlin, 2000. iCue Publishing.

[Sin99]   M.P. Singh. An ontology for commitments in multiagent systems. *Artificial Intelligence and Law*, 7:97–113, 1999.

[TW01]   K. Taveter and G. Wagner. Agent-oriented enterprise modeling based on business rules. In *Proc. of 20th Int. Conf. on Conceptual Modeling (ER2001)*, pages 527–540, Yokohama, Japan, November 2001. Springer-Verlag. LNCS 2224.

[Wag02]   G. Wagner. The Agent-Object-Relationship metamodel: Towards a unified conceptual view of state and behavior. Technical report, Eindhoven Univ. of Technology, Fac. of Technology Management, Available from `http://AOR.rezearch.info`, May 2002. To appear in *Information Systems*.

Extending Agent UML Sequence Diagrams

Marc-Philippe Huget

Agent ART Group
University of Liverpool
LIVERPOOL L69 7ZF
United Kingdom
M.P.Huget@csc.liv.ac.uk

Abstract. Agents in multiagent systems need to interact in order to exchange information, cooperate or coordinate. This interaction is frequently done through interaction protocols based on distributed system communication protocols. Communication protocols are not directly used due to many differences between agents and objects or processes such as autonomy and interaction [23] [28]. Designers use formal description techniques to represent their protocols. These formal description techniques are either those coming from distributed systems or those specifically tailored to agents. In the last category, Agent UML [24] is certainly one of the most known. This paper presents Agent UML sequence diagrams and addresses several new stereotypes.

1 Introduction

Interaction is a key component in multiagent systems. It helps agents to complete their tasks either by exchange of information, cooperation or coordination. Interaction in multiagent systems is frequently performed through protocols. These protocols are based on distributed system communication protocols. Several formal description techniques are available to represent interaction protocols such as finite state machines [14], Petri nets [7], the language Z [10], the language LOTOS [20], the language SDL [19] or temporal logic [13]. The main drawback of these formal description techniques is to not consider agent specific features such as autonomy or decision making. A new class of (semi-) formal description techniques appeared to tackle this point. Such formal description techniques are FLBC [9], COOL [2] or AgenTalk [21] to name a few. A particular graphical modeling language has emerged recently based on work done in object-oriented software engineering. This graphical language is Agent UML [24]. Agent UML is an extension of UML [6] to tackle differences between agents and objects.

Agent UML particularly addresses agent representation through class diagrams [3] [15] and protocols through sequence diagrams (also called protocol diagrams) [25] [5]. Agent UML sequence diagrams were initially one of the most used diagrams because they were adopted by FIPA to express agent interaction protocols [11].

This paper focuses on Agent UML sequence diagrams and some new stereotypes. At this time, current version of sequence diagrams are unable to cover

F. Giunchiglia et al. (Eds.): AOSE 2002, LNCS 2585, pp. 150–161, 2003.

all the needs in multiagent systems. For instance, it is impossible to represent the notion of time on these diagrams. Moreover, broadcast and techniques to improve the reliability of protocols are absent.

The paper is organized as follows. Section 2 presents the current version of Agent UML sequence diagrams. The presentation is inspired from the paper [4] which is the reference on sequence diagrams. Section 3 presents the new proposed stereotypes. Then, the example of the English Auction is given in Section 4 to exemplify some of the new stereotypes. Section 5 concludes this paper and presents future work.

2   Agent UML Sequence Diagrams

Sequence diagrams are defined as follows in UML: *"A diagram that shows object interactions arranged in time sequence. In particular, it shows the objects participating in the interaction and the sequence of messages exchanged. Unlike a collaboration diagram, a sequence diagram includes time sequences but does not include object relationships."*. In the context of multiagent systems, agents are employed instead of objects in the previous definition.

Several notions are encompassed in sequence diagrams: agents or agents' roles, messages, constraints on messages and the sequence of messages. All these notions are explained in this section.

Agents and Agents' Roles

A role is a specific set of behaviors, properties, interfaces and service descriptions which allow to distinguish a particular role from another one.

A protocol can be defined at the level of concrete agent instances or for a set of agents satisfying a distinguished role and/or class. An agent satisfying a distinguished agent role and class is called *agent of a given agent role* and *class*, respectively. The general form of describing agent roles in Agent UML is:

instance-1...instance-n / role-1...role-m : class

denoting a distinguished set of agent instances *instance-1...instance-n* satisfying the agent roles *role-1...role-m* with n, m $\geq$ 0 and *class* it belongs to. Instances, roles or class can be omitted, in the case that the instances are omitted, the roles and class are not underlined.

Agents are rendered on sequence diagrams as a box and a text defined as follows: instance "/" role ":" class. For instance, for auction protocols, one could have Smith/Auctioneer. Figure 1 presents the roles of *Initiator* and *Participant*.

Lifelines and Threads of Control

The agent lifeline in sequence diagrams defines the time period during which an agent exists, represented by vertical dashed lines. When a lifeline is created for a role, this role becomes active for the protocol. This lifeline is present as long as the role has actions in the protocol. Lifelines can be splitted or merged when

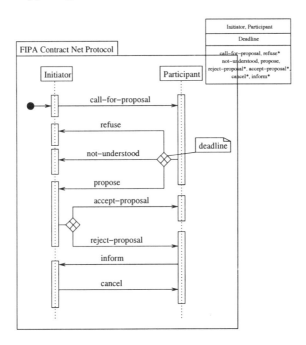

Fig. 1. Contract Net Protocol

several alternatives are available in the protocol or several paths are merged in one. It is, for instance, the case on Figure 1. Lifelines are splitted on the answer of the *Participant* which could be *not-understood*, *propose* or *refuse*. Lifelines are anchored to role boxes.

Added to lifelines, there are threads of interaction —UML uses the term *focus of control*. The thread of interaction shows the period during which an agent role is performing some tasks as a reaction to an incoming message. It only represents the duration of the action, but not the control relationship between the sender of the message and its receiver. A thread of interaction is rendered as a tall thin rectangle superposed on lifelines. If a metric is defined for the time axis, the thread of interaction corresponds exactly to the time needed to perform actions triggered by the incoming messages.

Connectors

The lifelines may be splitted in order to demonstrate two kinds of behaviors: parallelism and decisions. Three connectors are supplied for these features. The connector AND is rendered as a thick vertical line. It means that messages have to be sent concurrently. The connectors OR is rendered as a diamond and XOR is rendered as a diamond and a cross within. They mean that a decision between several messages has to be done. When considering the connector OR, zero or several messages is chosen: a subset of the set {*CA-1, CA-2, CA-3*}. In the case of several messages are taken, the messages are sent in parallel. The connector

XOR also represents a decision but in this case, one and only one message is chosen, it is either *CA-1* or *CA-2* or *CA-3*.

Various Notions

Several other notions are present on sequence diagrams:

Conditions: The connectors OR and XOR are examples where a decision is done on next messages. An usual solution to tackle this non determinism is to use conditions. As a consequence, a message can be sent if and only if the conditions attached to this message are satisfied. Conditions on sequence diagrams are rendered as a textual string nested by curly braces as shown on Figure 9 for the *request(price)* message. The textual string can be written as a free format text or as an OCL (*Object Constraint Language*) expression [26]. Conditions are written just before the message on sequence diagrams as shown on Figure 9.

Multiplicity: Sequence diagrams represent agents either by their instances or by their role in the protocol. When using roles, it is interesting to know the number of agents involved in both the sender role and the receiver role. The cardinality for sender and receiver roles are given by the multiplicity. It is for instance the case on Figure 9 for the *propose* message where n *AuctionParticipants* send a *propose* to the *Auctioneer*.

Type of message: Normally, messages are sent asynchronously. It is also possible to send messages synchronously. Normally, messages are drawn horizontally. This indicates the duration required to send the message is "atomic", i.e. it is brief compared to the granularity of the interaction and that nothing else "happen" during the message transmission. If the messages require some time to arrive, for instance for mobile communication, during which something else can occur.

Comments: It is possible to insert some comments on diagrams. Comments are inserted as notes.

Nested and interleaved protocols: Since protocols are reusable, it is possible to link protocols together. Two solutions are available in Agent UML sequence diagrams: nested protocols and interleaved protocols. Nested protocols correspond to protocols within another protocols. This case is used when one needs to repeat several times a protocol. Nested protocols continue while conditions hold.

Interleaved protocols correspond to protocols which are called during the execution of a second protocol. Bauer et al. give the example of an auction participant who requests some information about her/his bank account [5].

3   A Proposal of New Stereotypes

Agent UML is proposed to tackle differences between agents and objects but it remains several needs not provided such as the notion of time or a better reliability in interactions. The following list of features is a first proposal to this purpose:

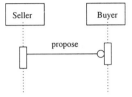

Fig. 2. Broadcast in sequence diagrams

1. broadcast
2. synchronization
3. triggering actions
4. exception handling
5. time management
6. atomic transactions
7. message sending until receiver acknowledges receipt

All these features are explained in detail in this section. We also describe how they are included as stereotypes in Agent UML.

Broadcast

The term *broadcast* means messages is sent to an undetermined set of agents. The sender is unable to give the list of agents since this message is sent to agents on the network. We do not mistake the broadcast mechanism to the multicast one. Indeed, in multicast, agents are specified by the sender (even if the number of agents is important) and this mechanism is already present in Agent UML sequence diagrams. Designers have just to insert the number of agents on the arrow. The broadcast is rendered as an arrow where the arrowhead is a circle (see Figure 2). Broadcast can also be applied to a structure such as groups, hierarchies or communities. In this case, the message is only sent to this structure and spread within the structure. The name of the structure is adorned close to the arrowhead.

The broadcast could be used when the manager of the task in the Contract Net protocol [8] announces the task. A second example is when the auctioneer informs agents that the auction begins or when it proposes a new item to sell. Another example is when agents are looking for services as Jini does it [1].

Synchronization

One example of synchronization is when agents in Sian's protocol [27] have to decide if one assumption is true, false or if the assumption needs to be modified. The synchronization allows agents to define a meeting point during interaction. All agents have to reach this point if agents want to follow the interaction. The synchronization is represented by an arrow where the arrowhead is crossed out by a vertical line (see Figure 3). The synchronization is realized on the message which labels this arrow.

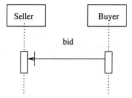

Fig. 3. Synchronization in sequence diagrams

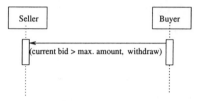

Fig. 4. Triggering actions in sequence diagrams

Triggering Actions

The triggering action management presents some similarity with exception management since in both cases, they represent situations which are not the normal path in the interaction. However, a difference exists between exceptions and triggering actions. In the former, we represent abnormal situations and in the latter, situations occurring which need to send a particular message or to do some specific actions. One example of triggering actions is during an ascending price auction when an agent sends a proposal which is lower than the current price. In this case, the auctioneer warns the agent of this error by sending a message. It is not an exception since this message does not endanger the auction.

Triggering actions are rendered as a textual string inside parentheses. This string is located under arrows as shown on Figure 4. Usually, the textual string corresponds to conditions written as a free-format text or as an OCL expression [26]. Triggering actions are fired when conditions become true.

The triggering actions could be applied to the Supply Chain Management when the agent workers do not finish their tasks at time. Then, a message can be sent to the dispatcher agent informing of this situation to reschedule the delivery [16].

Exception Management

As far as we know, the notion of exception is barely used neither in interaction protocols nor in communication protocols. We can only quote Moore's proposal [22]. In our opinion, the notion of exception in protocols are important since it allows designers to get rid of abnormal situations coming from either an improper use of protocols or when system performance slows down.

The notion of exception refers to a behavior which is not the expected behavior. It is for example the case when an agent answers in the interaction with

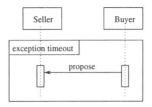

Fig. 5. Exceptions in sequence diagrams

a performative which does not belong to the list of allowed performatives for this state of interaction. The receiver can fire an exception and send a *not-understood* message to the sender.

A second use case is when the system performance drops and answer time increases. It might be interesting to insert an exception dealing with the delay between two messages. If the delay between two messages is greater than the allowed delay, an exception can be fired. Exceptions allow interactions to stop which can otherwise not terminate. It is, for instance, the case if the receiver of the previous message is disconnected or the network is down.

Figure 5 gives how exceptions are represented in sequence diagrams. Designers use a package where the package name is the keyword *exception* and the exception written textually.

An example of exception in the Supply Chain Management is when the client agent cancels the order which is negotiated at this moment. This cancellation stops definitively the protocol for placing an order.

Time Management

The current proposal in sequence diagrams for representing delay and deadlines is to describe deadlines with a note on arrows, for instance, the example of the comment *deadline* on the Contract Net protocol when receiving the proposals (see Figure 1). Our proposal is to insert the time management at two levels:

1. An application domain of multiagent systems and interaction protocols is electronic commerce and negotiation. It could be interesting to have a deadline on the whole interaction, for instance, when the interaction is stalled because an agent is disconnected or the network is down. A second case is when the negotiation is no longer progressing. The use of exception allows negotiations to stop which will otherwise not finish.
   This deadline is inserted at the beginning of the sequence diagram above the agents' roles since it is applied to the whole interaction. This deadline is given by the keyword *time* and a delay which is the allowed delay for the interaction (see Figure 6a).
2. It is necessary to give some delay between two messages as Agent UML proposes it with comments. This time, we give the delay inside parentheses under the arrow and preceded by the keyword "d:" (see Figure 6b).

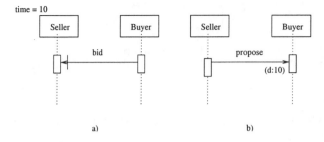

Fig. 6. Time management in sequence diagrams

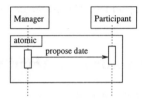

Fig. 7. Atomic transactions in sequence diagrams

Time management and exceptions seem to be a convenient way to deal with overrunning delays. In this case, agents can trigger an exception and do something in consequence.

Atomic Transactions

The atomicity of transactions is a term used in information systems. It means that a set of actions is linked and if one of them fails, other actions have to be cancelled. For instance, the following situation must be forbidden: the financial transactions (credit and debit) are done but the delivery fails or the opposite.

The insertion of the atomicity in sequence diagrams is done by inserting all the messages in a package (see Figure 7). All the messages must be sent properly and if one of them fails, the other messages must be canceled. One example is for meeting scheduling. If one person can not receive the message, the sender has to cancel the other ones. The cancellation is performed by a new message sent to the receivers of this message.

Sending Messages until Delivery

Networks are not perfectly reliable and messages can be lost and as a consequence not delivered to agents. The meaning of this new feature is to send the message until the receiving agents send an acknowledgment message. This feature is represented by an arrow where the arrowhead is a plain circle (see Figure 8). This feature needs agents use some acknowledgment process like the hand-shaking protocol.

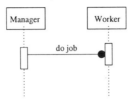

Fig. 8. Sending messages until delivery in sequence diagrams

This feature is interesting when we consider the domain of workflow. The acknowledgment could correspond to the performance of the action associated to this message.

4   One Example of Protocol in Agent UML

We take the example of the English Auction [12] to exemplify the use of sequence diagrams and some new stereotypes. In English Auctions, an agent (the Auctioneer) wants to sell an item, it informs agents (or just a part of them who could be interested in it) (the Auction Participants) that a new auction begins. The Auctioneer informs the Auction Participants how much the item is. Then, the auction participants inform the Auctioneer whether they accept the bid. If the Auctioneer has more than two Auction Participants who accept the bid, it selects the one who sent first the agreement and informs it that it wins this round. It informs other Auction Participants who sent an offer that their bids are rejected. The auction is ongoing till it remains only one auction participant who accepts the bid.

When the Auctioneer closes the auction, it compares the current price for this item with the reserved price. If the current price is greater than the reserved price, the item is won by the last agent who accepts the bid. Auction Participants are informed that the auction is closed.

The protocol in Agent UML is shown on Figure 9.

The proposed protocol presents some differences with the ones proposed by FIPA [12] and Bauer et al. [4].

The first message is sent to all agents on the network by broadcast whereas FIPA's approach and Bauer's approach consider to send it only to a set of agents represented by n on the protocol. This situation is repeated once for the second message which details the item and the price. The deadline for the bidding is given on arrows. Bauer et al. propose to insert this deadline as a comment. Then, auction participants can answer either by a *not understood*[1] message or by a *propose* message. If auction participants send a *propose* message, they inform the auctioneer they accept the bid. When the deadline is passed (given by d^2(current

---

[1] FIPA defines in its specifications that all FIPA agents have to be able to send the message *not understood* if they do not understand the content of the message or the message.

[2] The function d means the difference between the two parameters.

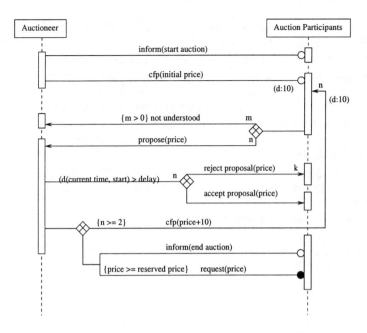

Fig. 9. The English Auction Protocol in Agent UML

time, start) > delay), the Auctioneer informs the Auction Participants if they
have won this round (by a *accept proposal* message) or if they have lost this round
(by a *reject proposal* message). The winner is the auction participant which sent
first the acceptance of the bid. If the auctioneer has more than two agents which
accept the price, it proposes once again the item at a higher price.

If the auctioneer has only one agent, it closes the auction and informs all the
auction participants. If the current price is greater than the reserved price, it
informs the last auction participant who accepts the bid that it wins the item.
We use the stereotype *sending until delivery* for this message.

The main differences with the two other versions are that we use the broadcast, deadlines, triggering actions and conditions on the end of the auction. Bauer
et al's model is more complete than the one from FIPA.

5   Conclusion

In this paper, we present a semi-formal modeling language for describing interaction protocols called Agent UML which is an extension of UML. The advantage
of such a language is that it is graphical and is based on a language which is well-
known to programmers and companies. Programmers will have less difficulty to
pass to Agent UML since they are used to developing with UML.

Interaction protocols are described through sequence diagrams in Agent
UML. Agents can be described either by their identity or by their role in this

interaction. The sequence of messages is given by the lifelines which represent the different paths in the interaction.

Our work in the domain of reliability, electronic commerce in multiagent systems and Supply Chain Management gives us some features which are not present in the current version of Agent UML such as: broadcast, synchronization, triggering actions, exception, deadline, atomic transactions and sending messages until acknowledgment. This paper shows how to represent protocols using these features in Agent UML. All these features will be submitted for an insertion into the Agent UML specification.

A second work is to extend Agent UML sequence diagrams with mobility and security features. Interaction between agents on mobile devices affect the way to interact.

As soon as these features will be accepted by Agent UML community, we can insert them in our Agent UML exchange format language [17] and in our model checking process [18]. Finally, most of these features would be used in our Supply Chain Management [16].

References

1. Jini, Sun. http://www.sun.com/jini.
2. M. Barbuceanu and M. S. Fox. COOL : A language for describing coordination in multiagent system. In *First International Conference on Multi-Agent Systems (ICMAS-95)*, pages 17–24, San Francisco, USA, June 1995. AAAI Press.
3. B. Bauer. UML class diagrams revisited in the context of agent-based systems. In M. Wooldridge, P. Ciancarini, and G. Weiss, editors, *Proceedings of Agent-Oriented Software Engineering (AOSE 01)*, number 2222 in LNCS, pages 1–8, Montreal, Canada, May 2001. Springer-Verlag.
4. B. Bauer, J. Müller, and J. Odell. Agent UML: A formalism for specifying multi-agent interaction. In P. Ciancarini and M. J. Wooldridge, editors, *Agent-Oriented Software Engineering (AOSE-00)*, 2000.
5. B. Bauer, J. P. Müller, and J. Odell. An extension of UML by protocols for multia-gent interaction. In *International Conference on MultiAgent Systems (ICMAS'00)*, pages 207–214, Boston, Massachussetts, july, 10-12 2000.
6. G. Booch, J. Rumbaugh, and I. Jacobson. *The Unified Modeling Language User Guide*. Addison-Wesley, Reading, Massachusetts, USA, 1999.
7. R. S. Cost, Y. Chen, T. Finin, Y. Labrou, and Y. Peng. Modeling agent conver-sation with colored Petri nets. In J. Bradshaw, editor, *Autonomous Agents'99, Special Workshop on Conversation Policies*, May 1999.
8. R. Davis and R. G. Smith. Negotiation as a metaphor for distributed problem-solving. *Artificial Intelligence*, 20:63–109, 1983.
9. F. Dignum. FLBC: From messages to protocols. In F. Dignum and C. Sierra, editors, *European Perspective on Agent Mediated Electronic Commerce*. Springer Verlag, 2000.
10. M. d'Inverno and M. Luck. Formalising the contract net as a goal-directed system. In W. V. de Velde and J. Perram, editors, *Agents Breaking Away, MAAMAW 96*, number 1038 in Lecture Notes in Artificial Intelligence, pages 72–85. Springer-Verlag, 1996.

11. FIPA. Fipa interaction protocol library specification. Technical Report XC00025, FIPA, 2000.
12. FIPA. *Specification*. Foundation for Intelligent Physical Agents, http://www.fipa.org/repository/fipa2000.html, 2000.
13. M. Fisher and M. Wooldridge. Specifying and executing protocols for cooperative action. In *International Working Conference on Cooperating Knowledge-Based Systems (CKBS-94)*, Keele, 1994.
14. A. Haddadi. *Communication and Cooperation in Agent Systems: A Pragmatic Theory*, volume 1056 of *Lecture Notes in Computer Science*. Springer Verlag, 1996.
15. M.-P. Huget. Agent UML class diagrams revisited. In B. Bauer, K. Fischer, J. Muller, and B. Rumpe, editors, *Proceedings of Agent Technology and Software Engineering (AgeS)*, Erfurt, Germany, October 2002.
16. M.-P. Huget. An application of agent UML to supply chain management. Technical Report ULCS-02-015, Department of Computer Science, University of Liverpool, 2002.
17. M.-P. Huget. A language for exchanging Agent UML protocol diagrams. Technical Report ULCS-02-009, Department of Computer Science, University of Liverpool, 2002.
18. M.-P. Huget. Model checking Agent UML protocol diagrams. Technical Report ULCS-02-012, Department of Computer Science, University of Liverpool, 2002.
19. C. Iglesias, M. Garrijo, J. Gonzales, and J. Velasco. Design of multi-agent system using mas-commonkads. In Springer-Verlag, editor, *Proceedings of ATAL 98, Workshop on Agent Theories, Architectures, and Languages*, volume LNAI 1555, pages 163–176, Paris, France, July 1998.
20. J.-L. Koning. Algorithms for translating interaction protocols into a formal description. In K. Ito, editor, *IEEE International Conference on Systems, Man, and Cybernetics Conference (SMC-99)*, Tokyo, Japan, October 1999.
21. K. Kuwabara, T. Ishida, and N. Osato. AgenTalk: Describing multiagent coordination protocols with inheritance. In *Seventh IEEE International Conference on Tools with Artificial Intelligence*, pages 460–465, Herndon, Virginia, November 1995.
22. S. A. Moore. On conversation policies and the need for exceptions. In *Autonomous Agents'99 Special Workshop on Conversation Policies*, 1999.
23. J. Odell. Objects and agents compared. *Journal of Object Computing*, 1(1), May 2002.
24. J. Odell, H. V. D. Parunak, and B. Bauer. Extending UML for agents. In G. Wagner, Y. Lesperance, and E. Yu, editors, *Proceedings of the Agent-Oriented Information Systems Workshop at the 17th National conference on Artificial Intelligence*, Austin, Texas, july, 30 2000. ICue Publishing.
25. J. Odell, H. V. D. Parunak, and B. Bauer. Representing agent interaction protocols in UML. In P. Ciancarini and M. Wooldridge, editors, *Proceedings of First International Workshop on Agent-Oriented Software Engineering*, Limerick, Ireland, june, 10 2000. Springer-Verlag.
26. OMG. UML 1.4. Technical report, OMG, 2001.
27. S. S. Sian. Adaptation based on cooperative learning in multi-agent systems. In Y. Demazeau and J.-P. Müller, editors, *Decentralized AI*, volume II, pages 257–272, Amsterdam, The Netherlands, 1991. Elsevier Science Publishers B.V.
28. M. Wooldridge. *An Introduction to Multiagent Systems*. John Wiley and Sons, April 2002.

The Tropos Software Development Methodology: Processes, Models and Diagrams

Fausto Giunchiglia[1], John Mylopoulos[2], and Anna Perini[3]

[1] Department of Information and Communication Technology, University of Trento
via Sommarive, 14, I-38050 Povo, Italy
fausto@dit.unitn.it
[2] Department of Computer Science, University of Toronto
M5S 3H5, Toronto, Ontario, Canada
jm@cs.toronto.edu
[3] ITC-Irst, Via Sommarive, 18, I-38050 Trento-Povo, Italy
perini@irst.itc.it
phone +39 0461 314 330

Abstract. *Tropos* is a novel agent-oriented software development methodology founded on two key features: *(i)* the notions of agent, goal, plan and various other knowledge level concepts are fundamental primitives used uniformly throughout the software development process; and *(ii)* a crucial role is assigned to requirements analysis and specification when the system-to-be is analyzed with respect to its intended environment. This paper describes the basic concepts on which Tropos is founded and the types of models one builds out of them. We also specify the analysis process through which design flows from external to system actors through a goal analysis and delegation. In addition, we provide an abstract syntax for Tropos diagrams and other linguistic constructs.

1 Introduction

New application areas such as eBusiness, application service provision and peer-to-peer computing call for software systems which have open, evolving architectures, operate robustly and exploit resources available in their environment. To build such systems, software engineers are discovering the importance of mechanisms for communication, negotiation, and coordination between software components. We expect that many will be turning to multi-agent system technologies and methodologies for guidance and support in building the software systems of the future.

We are developing a comprehensive software engineering methodology, named *Tropos*, for multi-agent systems.

In a nutshell, the two key features of Tropos are: *(i)* the use of knowledge level [13] concepts, such as agent, goal, plan and other through all phases of software development, and *(ii)* a pivotal role assigned to requirements analysis when the environment and the system-to-be is analyzed.

The phases covered by the proposed methodology are as follows.

Early Requirements: during this phase the relevant stakeholders are identified, along with their respective objectives; stakeholders are represented as actors, while their objectives are represented as goals;

F. Giunchiglia et al. (Eds.): AOSE 2002, LNCS 2585, pp. 162–173, 2003.

Late Requirements: the system-to-be is introduced as another actor and is related to stakeholder actors in terms of actor dependencies; these indicate the obligations of the system toward its environment, also what the system can expect from actors in its environment;

Architectural Design: more system actors are introduced and they are assigned subgoals or subtasks of the goals and tasks assigned to the system;

Detailed Design: system actors are defined in further detail, including specifications of communication and coordination protocols;

Implementation: during this phase, the Tropos specification, produced during detailed design, is transformed into a skeleton for the implementation. This is done through a mapping from the Tropos constructs to those of an agent programming platform such as JACK [2]; code is added to the skeleton using the programming language supported by the programming platform.

The Tropos methodology has been motivated and illustrated with several case studies, see for instance [16, 17, 8]. The purpose of this paper is to provide additional detail on the methodology. Examples from the case study presented in [16], will be used to illustrate. The rest of the paper is structured as follows. Section 2 presents the Tropos primitive knowledge level concepts used for building the different types of models, and illustrates them with examples. Section 3 describes the analysis process that guides model evolution through different development phases. The Tropos modeling language is then defined in Section 4 in terms of UML diagrams, while related work is discussed in Section 5. Conclusions and directions for further research are presented in Section 6.

2   Concepts and Models

The Tropos conceptual models and diagrams are developed as instances of the following intentional and social concepts: actor, goal, dependency, plan, resource, capability, and belief. Below we discuss each one in turn.

Actor. The notion of actor models an entity that has strategic goals and intentionality. An actor represents a *physical agent* (e.g., a person, an animal, a car), or a *software agent* as well as a *role* or a *position*. A *role* is an abstract characterization of the behavior of an actor within some specialized context, while a *position* represents a set of roles, typically played by one agent. An agent can occupy a position, while a position is said to cover a role. Notice that the notion of actor in Tropos is a generalization of the classical AI notion of software agent.

Goal. A goal represents the strategic interests of actors. Our framework distinguishes between hard goals and softgoals, the latter having no clear-cut definition and/or criteria as to whether they are satisfied. Softgoals are useful for modeling software qualities [3], such as security, performance and maintainability.

Dependency. A dependency between two actors indicates that one actor depends on another in order to attain some goal, execute some plan, or deliver a resource. The former actor is called the *depender*, while the latter is called the *dependee*. The object (goal, plan resource) around which the dependency centers is called *dependum*. By depending on other actors, an actor is able to achieve goals that it would otherwise be unable to achieve on its own, or not as easily, or not as well. At the same time, the depender becomes vulnerable. If the dependee fails to deliver the dependum the depender would be adversely affected in its ability to achieve its goals.

Plan. A plan represents a way of satisfying a goal.

Resource. A resource represents a physical or an informational entity that one actor wants and another can deliver.

Capability. A capability represents the ability of an actor to define, choose and execute a plan to fulfill a goal, given a particular operating environment.

Belief. Beliefs are used to represent each actor's knowledge of the world.

Notice how the notions of belief, goal (or desire), and plan (or intention) are the key concepts of the BDI framework. The notion of dependency, instead, is quite interesting and novel, and it turns out to be very important when modeling the intentional inter-dependencies between actors

These concepts can be used to build different types of models throughout the development process. We illustrate these with examples extracted from a substantial software system developed for the government of Trentino (Provincia Autonoma di Trento, or PAT), and partially described in [16]. The system (which we will call throughout the *eCulture system*) is a web-based broker of cultural information and services for the province of Trentino, including information obtained from museums, exhibitions, and other cultural organizations and events to be used by a variety of users, including Trentino citizens and visitors.

We consider, in turn, examples of actor, dependency, goal and plan models. Other types of models are not discussed here for lack of space; see [18] for more examples.

2.1 Actor and Dependency Models

Actor and dependency models result from the analysis of social and system actors, as well as of their goals and dependencies for goal achievement. These types of models are built in the early requirements phase when we focus on characterizing the application domain stakeholders, their intentions and the dependencies that interleave them. Actor and dependency models are graphically represented through *actor diagrams* in which actors are depicted as circles, their goals as ovals and their softgoal as cloud shapes. The network of dependency relationships among actors are depicted as two arrowed lines connected by a graphical symbol varying according to the dependum: a goal, a plan or a resource. Figure 1 shows the *actor diagram* for the eCulture domain as resulting from a first early requirement analysis. In particular, the actor Citizen is associated with a single relevant goal: get cultural information, while the actor Visitor has an associated softgoal enjoy visit. Along similar lines, the actor PAT wants to increase internet use for Trentino citizens, while the actor Museum wants to provide cultural services.

Actor models are extended during the late requirements phase by adding the system-to-be as another actor, along with its inter-dependencies with social actors. For example, in Figure 2 the actor PAT delegates a set of goals to the eCulture System actor through goal dependencies namely, provide eCultural services, which is a goal that contributes to the main goal of PAT increase internet use and softgoals such as extensible eCulture System, flexible eCulture System, usable eCulture System, and use internet technology.

Actor models at the architectural design level provide a more detailed account of the system-to-be actor and its internal structure[1]. This structure is specified in terms

---

[1] See also [7] for a discussion of the modeling activities during architectural design.

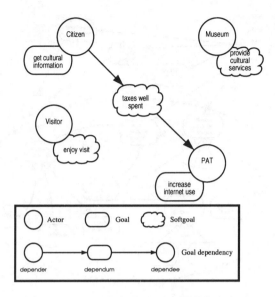

Fig. 1. Actor diagram of the stakeholders of the eCulture System.

of subsystem actors, interconnected through data and control flows that are modeled as dependencies. This model provides the basis for capability modeling, an activity that will start later on during the architectural design phase, along with the mapping of system actors to software agents.

2.2 Goal and Plan Models

Goal and plan models allow the designer to analyze goals and plans from the perspective of a specific actor by using three basic reasoning techniques: *means-end analysis*, *contribution analysis*, and *AND/OR decomposition*. For goals, means-end analysis proceeds by refining a goal into subgoals in order to identify plans, resources and softgoals that provide means for achieving the goal (the end). Contribution analysis allows the designer to point out goals that can contribute positively or negatively in reaching the goal being analyzed. In a sense, contribution analysis can be considered as a special case of means-end analysis, where means are always goals. AND/OR decomposition allows for a combination of AND and OR decompositions of a root goal into sub-goals, thereby refining a goal structure.

Goal models are first developed during early requirements using initially-identified actors and their goals. Figure 3, shows portions of the goal model for PAT, relative to the goals that Citizen has delegated to PAT through an earlier goal analysis. Goal and plan models are depicted through *goal diagrams* that represent the perspective of a specific actor as a balloon that contains graphs whose nodes are goals (ovals) and /or plans (hexagonal shape) and whose arcs represents the different types of relationships that can be identified between its nodes. In Figure 3, the goals increase internet use and eCulture System available are both well served (through a contribution relationship) by the goal build eCulture System. Within an actor balloon, softgoal analysis is also

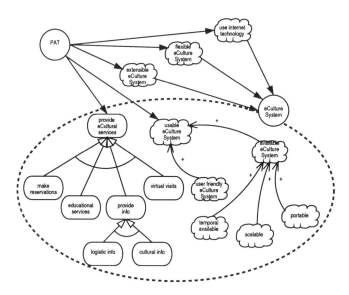

Fig. 2. An actor diagram including PAT and eCulture System and a goal diagram of the eCulture System.

performed identifying positive or negative contributions from other goals. The softgoal taxes well spent gets positive contributions from the softgoal good services, and the goal build eCulture System.

Goal models play an analogous role in identifying (and justifying) actor dependencies during late requirements and architectural design. Figure 2 shows a goal diagram for the eCulture System, developed during late requirements analysis. In the example we concentrate on the goal provide eCultural services and the softgoal usable eCulture System. The goal provide eCultural services is AND-decomposed into four subgoals make reservations, provide info, educational services and virtual visits. The goal (provide info) is further decomposed into (the provision of) logistic info, concerning timetables and visiting information for museums and cultural info. Virtual visits are services that allow Citizen to pay a virtual visit to a city of the past (e.g., Rome during Cæsar's time!). Educational services include presentation of historical and cultural material at different levels of detail (e.g., at a high school or undergraduate university level) as well as on-line evaluation of the student's grasp of this material. Make reservations allows Citizen to make reservations for particular cultural events, such as concerts, exhibitions, and guided museum visits.

3   The Development Process

In this section we focus on the generic design process through which these models are constructed. The process is basically one of analyzing goals on behalf of different actors, and is described in terms of a non deterministic concurrent algorithm, including a completeness criterion. Note that this process is carried out by *software engineers* (rather than software agents) at *design-time* (rather than run-time).

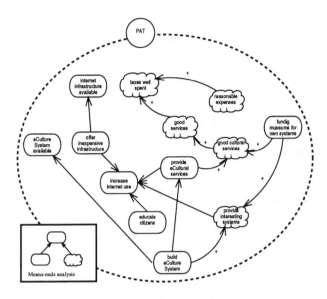

Fig. 3. Goal diagram for PAT.

Intuitively, the process begins with a number of actors, each with a list of associated root goals (possibly including softgoals). Each root goal is analyzed from the perspective of its respective actor, and as subgoals are generated, they are delegated to other actors, or the actor takes on the responsibility of dealing with them him/her/itself. This analysis is carried out concurrently with respect to each root goal. Sometimes the process requires the introduction of new actors which are delegated goals and/or tasks. The process is complete when all goals have been dealt with to the satisfaction of the actors who want them (or the designers thereof.)

Assume that *actorList* includes a finite set of actors, also that the list of goals for *actor* is stored in *goalList(actor)*. In addition, we assume that *agenda(actor)* includes the list of goals *actor* has undertaken to achieve personally (with no help from other actors), along with the plan that has been selected for each goal. Initially, *agenda(actor)* is empty. *dependencyList* includes a list of dependencies among actors, while *capabilityList(actor)* includes $< goal, plan >$ pairs indicating the means by which the actor can achieve particular goals. Finally, *goalGraph* stores a representation of the goal graph that has been generated so far by the design process. Initially, *goalGraph* contains all root goals of all initial actors with no links among them. We will treat all of the above as global variables which are accessed and/or updated by the procedures presented below. For each procedure, we use as parameters those variables used within the procedure.

The procedure *rootGoalAnalysis* conducts concurrent goal analysis for every root goal. Initially, root goal analysis is conducted for all initial goals associated with actors in *actorList*. Later on, more root goals are created as goals are delegated to existing or new actors. Note that the **concurrent for** statement spawns a concurrent call to *goalAnalysis* for every element of the list *rootGoalList*. Moreover, more calls to *goalAnalysis* are spawn as more root goals are added to *rootGoalList*. **concurrent for** is assumed to terminates when all its threads do. The predicate *satisfied* checks whether all root goals in *goalGraph* are satisfied. This predicate is computed in terms of a label propagation algorithm such as the one described in [12]. Its details are beyond the scope of this paper. *rootGoalAnalysis* succeeds if there is a set of non-deterministic selections within the concurrent executions of *goalAnalysis* procedures which leads to the satisfaction of all root goals.

global $actorList, goalList, agenda, dependencyList, capabilityList, goalGraph$;
procedure $rootGoalAnalysis(actorList, goalList, goalGraph)$
  begin
    $rootGoalList =$ **nil**;
    for $actor$ **in** $actorList$ **do**
      for $rootGoal$ **in** $goalList(actor)$ **do**
        $rootGoalList = add(rootGoal, rootGoalList)$;
        $rootGoal.actor = actor$;
      end ;
    end ;
  end ;
  concurrent for
    $rootGoal$ **in** $rootGoalList$ **do**
    $goalAnalysis(rootGoal, actorList)$
  end concurrent for ;
  if $not[satisfied(rootGoalList, goalGraph)]$ **then** $fail$;
end procedure

The procedure *goalAnalysis* conducts concurrent goal analysis for every subgoal of a given root goal. Initially, the root goal is placed in *pendingList*. Then, **concurrent for** selects concurrently goals from *pendingList* and for each decides non-deterministically whether it will be expanded, adopted as a personal goal, delegated to an existing or new actor, or whether the goal will be treated as unsatisfiable (*'denied'*). When a goal is expanded, more subgoals are added to *pendingList* and *goalGraph* is augmented to include the new goals and their relationships to their parent goal. Note that the selection of an actor to delegate a goal is also non-deterministic, and so is the creation of a new actor. The three non-deterministic operations in *goalAnalysis* are highlighted with italic-bold font. These are the points where the designers of the software system will use their creative in designing the system-to-be. Finally, we have to specify two of the sub-procedures used in *goalAnalysis*. For the lack of space, we leave these and others to the imagination of the reader. During early requirements, this process analyzes initially-identified goals of external actors ("stakeholders"). At some point (late requirements), the system-to-be is introduced as another actor and is delegated some of the subgoals that have been generated from this analysis. During architectural design, more system actors are introduced and are delegated subgoals to system-assigned goals. Apart from generating goals and actors in order to fulfill initially-specified goals of external stakeholders, the development process includes specification steps during each phase which consist of further specifying each node of a model such as those shown in Figure 3. Specifications are given in a formal language (*Formal Tropos*) described in detail in [6].

These specifications add constraints, invariants, pre- and post-conditions which capture more of the semantics of the subject domain.

procedure $goalAnalysis(rootGoal, actorList)$
  $pendingList = add(rootGoal, \textbf{nil})$;
  concurrent for $goal$ **in** $pendingList$ **do**
    $decision = \textbf{\textit{decideGoal}}(goal)$
    case of $decision$
    $expand$:
      begin
        $newGoalList = expandGoal(goal, goalGraph)$;
        for $newGoal$ **in** $newGoalList$ **do**
          $newGoal.actor = goal.actor$;
          $add(newGoal, pendingList)$;
        end ;
      end ;
    $solve$: $acceptGoal(goal, agenda(goal.actor))$;
    $delegate$:
      begin
        $actor = \textbf{\textit{selectActor}}(actorList)$;
        $delegateGoal(goal, actor, rootGoalList, dependencyList)$;
      end ;
    $newActor$:
      begin
        $actor = \textbf{\textit{newActor}}(goal)$;
        $actorList = add(actor, actorList)$;
        $delegateGoal(goal, actor, rootGoalList, dependencyList)$;
      end ;
    $fail$: $goal.label =' denied'$;
    end case of ;
  end concurrent for ;
end procedure

4   The Tropos Modeling Language

The modeling language is at the core of the Tropos methodology. The abstract syntax of the language is defined in this section in terms of a UML metamodel.

Following standard approaches [14], the metamodel has been organized in four levels, as shown in Table 1. The four-layer architecture makes the Tropos language extensible in the sense that new constructs can be added. Semantics for the language is handled in [6] and won't be discussed here.

The **meta-metamodel** level provides the basis for metamodel extensions. In particular, the meta-metamodel contains language primitives that allows for the inclusions of constructs such as those proposed in [6]. The **metamodel** level provides constructs for modeling knowledge level entities and concepts. The **domain** model level contains

Table 1. The four level architecture of the Tropos metamodel.

Level	Description	Examples
meta metamodel	Basic language structural elements	Attribute, Entity
metamodel	Knowledge level notions	Actor, Goal, Dependency
domain	Application domain entities	PAT, Citizen, Museum
instance	Domain model instances	Mary: instance of Citizen

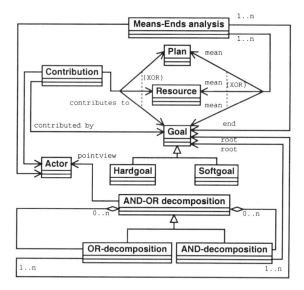

Fig. 4. The goal concept specified by an UML class diagram.

a representation of entities and concepts of a specific application domain, built as instances of the metamodel level constructs. So, for instance, the examples used in section 2 illustrate portions of the eCulture domain model. The **instance** model level contains instances of the domain model. We focus below only the metamodels for goals[2].

The concept of goal is represented by the class Goal in the UML class diagram depicted in Figure 4. The distinction between hard and softgoals is captured through a specialization of Goal into subclasses Hardgoal and Softgoal respectively.

Goals can be analyzed, from the point of view of an actor, performing means-end analysis, contribution analysis and AND/OR decomposition (listed in order of strength). Let us consider these in turn.

---

[2] The metamodels concerning the other concepts are defined analogously with the partial description reported here. A complete description of the Tropos language metamodel can be found in [18].

Means-ends analysis is a ternary relationship defined among an Actor, whose point of view is represented in the analysis, a goal (the end), and a Plan, Resource or Goal (the means). Means-end analysis is a weak form of analysis, consisting of a discovery of goals, plans or resources that can provide means for reaching a goal. Means-end analysis is used in the model shown in Figure 3, where the goals educate citizens and provide eCultural services, as well as the softgoal provide interesting systems are means for achieving the goal increase internet use.

Contribution analysis is a ternary relationship between an Actor, whose point of view is represented, and two goals. Contribution analysis strives to identify goals that can contribute positively or negatively towards the fulfillment of a goal (see association relationship labelled contributes to in Figure 4). A contribution can be annotated with a qualitative metric, as used in [3], denoted by $+, ++, -, --$. In particular, if the goal g1 contributes positively to the goal g2, with metric $++$ then if g1 is satisfied, so is g2. Analogously if the plan p contributes positively to the goal g, with metric $++$, this says that p fulfills g. A $+$ label for a goal or plan contribution represents a partial, positive contribution to the goal being analyzed. With labels $--$, and $-$ we have the dual situation representing a sufficient or partial negative contribution towards the fulfillment of a goal. Examples of contribution analysis are shown in Figure 3. For instance the goal funding museums for own systems contributes positively to both the softgoals provide interesting systems and good cultural services, and the latter softgoal contributes positively to the softgoal good services.

AND-OR decomposition is also a ternary relationship which defines an AND- or OR-decomposition of a root goal into subgoals. The particular case where the root goal g1 is decomposed into a single subgoal g2, is equivalent to a $++$ contribution from g2 to g1.

5   Related Work

As indicated in the introduction, the most important feature of the Tropos methodology is that it aspires to span the overall software development process, from early requirements to implementation. This is represented in Figure 5 which shows the relative coverage of Tropos as well as i* [20], KAOS[4], GAIA [19], Prometheus [15], AAII [11], MaSE [5], and AUML [1].

While Tropos covers the full range of software development phases, it is at the same time well-integrated with other existing work. Thus, for early and late requirements analysis, it takes advantage of work done in the Requirements Engineering community, and in particular of Eric Yu's i* methodology [20]. It is interesting to note that much of the Tropos methodology can be combined with non-agent (e.g., object-oriented or imperative) software development paradigms. For example, one may want to use Tropos for early development phases and then use UML for later phases. At the same time, work on AUML (see also [9, 10]) allows us to exploit existing UML techniques during (our version of) agent-oriented software development. As indicated in Figure 5, our idea is to adopt AUML for the detailed design phase. An example of how this can be done is given in [16].

The metamodel presented in Section 4 has been developed in the same spirit as the UML metamodel for class diagrams. A comparison between UML class diagrams and the

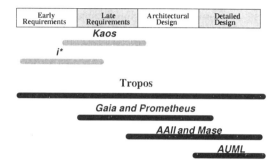

Fig. 5. Comparison of Tropos with other software development methodologies.

diagrams presented in Section 4 emphasizes the distinct representational and ontological levels used for class diagrams and actor diagrams (the former being at the software level, the latter at the knowledge level). This contrast also defines the key difference between object-oriented and agent-oriented development methodologies. Agents (and actor diagrams) cannot be thought as a specialization of objects (and class diagrams), as argued in previous papers. The difference is rather the result of an ontological and representational shift.

6   Conclusion

This paper provides a detailed account of Tropos, an agent oriented software development methodology which spans the software development process from early requirements to implementation for agent oriented software. The paper presents and discusses (in part) the five phases supported by Tropos, the development process within each phase, the models created through this process, and the diagrams used to describe these models.

Throughout, we have emphasized the uniform use of a small set of knowledge level notions during all phases of software development. We have also provided an iterative, actor and goal based, refinement algorithm which characterizes the refinement process during each phase. This refinement process, of course, is instantiated differently during each phase.

Acknowledgments

We thank all the Tropos Project people working in Trento and in Toronto.

References

1. B. Bauer, J. P. Müller, and J. Odell. Agent UML: A formalism for specifying multiagent software systems. *Int. Journal of Software Engineering and Knowledge Engineering*, 11(3):207–230, 2001.
2. P. Busetta, R. Rönnquist, A. Hodgson, and A. Lucas. JACK Intelligent Agents - Components for Intelligent Agents in Java. Technical Report TR9901, AOS, January 1999.

3. L. K. Chung, B. A. Nixon, E. Yu, and J. Mylopoulos. *Non-Functional Requirements in Software Engineering.* Kluwer Publishing, 2000.
4. A. Dardenne, A. van Lamsweerde, and S. Fickas. Goal-directed requirements acquisition. *Science of Computer Programming*, 20(1–2):3–50, 1993.
5. S. A. Deloach. Analysis and Design using MaSE and agentTool. In *12th Midwest Artificial Intelligence and Cognitive Science Conference (MAICS 2001)*, Miami University, Oxford, Ohio, March 31 - April 1 2001.
6. A. Fuxman, M. Pistore, J. Mylopoulos, and P. Traverso. Model Checking Early Requirements Specifications in Tropos. In *Proceedings Fifth IEEE International Symposium on Requirements Engineering (RE01)*, pages 174–181, Toronto, Canada, August 2001.
7. P. Giorgini, M. Kolp, and J. Mylopoulus. Multi-Agent and Software Architectures: A comparative case study. In *this book*.
8. F. Giunchiglia, A. Perini, and F. Sannicolò. Knowledge level software engineering. In J.-J.C. Meyer and M. Tambe, editors, *Intelligent Agents VIII*, LNCS 2333, pages 6–20, Seattle, WA, USA, August 2001. Springer-Verlag.
9. Martin L. Griss, Steven Fonseca, Dick Cowan, and Robert Kessler. Using UML State Machine Models for More Precise and Flexible JADE Agent Behaviors. In *this book*.
10. Marc-Philippe Huget. Extending Agent UML Protocol Diagrams. In *this book*.
11. D. Kinny, M. Georgeff, and A. Rao. A methodology and modelling technique for systems of BDI agents. In J.W. Perram W. Van de Velde, editor, *Agents Breaking Away, 7th European Workshop on Modelling Autonomous Agents in a Multi-Agent World*, volume 1038 of *Lecture Notes in Computer Science*, pages 56–71. Springer-Verlag, 1996.
12. J. Mylopoulos, L. K. Chung, and B. A. Nixon. Representing and using non-functional requirements: A process-oriented approach. *IEEE Transactions on Software Engineering*, June 1992.
13. A. Newell. The Knowledge Level. *Artificial Intelligence*, 18:87–127, 1982.
14. OMG. *OMG Unified Modeling Language Specification*, version 1.3, alpha edition, 1999.
15. Lin Padgham and Michael Winikoff. Prometheus: A Methodology for Developing Intelligent Agents. In *this book*.
16. A. Perini, P. Bresciani, F. Giunchiglia, P. Giorgini, and J. Mylopoulos. A Knowledge Level Software Engineering Methodology for Agent Oriented Programming. In *Proceedings of the Fifth International Conference on Autonomous Agents*, pages 648–655, Montreal CA, May 2001.
17. A. Perini, A. Susi, and F. Giunchiglia. Coordination specification in Multi-Agent Systems. From requirements to architecture with the Tropos methodology. In *14th International Conference on Software Engineering and Knowledge Engineering (SEKE'2002)*, Ischia, Italy, July 2002. ACM Press.
18. F. Sannicolò, A. Perini, and F. Giunchiglia. The Tropos modeling language. A User Guide. Technical Report 0204-13, ITC-irst, January 2002.
19. M. Wooldridge, N. R. Jennings, and D. Kinny. The Gaia methodology for agent-oriented analysis and design. *Journal of Autonomous Agents and Multi-Agent Systems*, 3(3), 2000.
20. E. Yu. *Modelling Strategic Relationships for Process Reengineering.* PhD thesis, University of Toronto, Department of Computer Science, University of Toronto, 1995.

Prometheus: A Methodology
for Developing Intelligent Agents

Lin Padgham and Michael Winikoff

RMIT University, GPO Box 2476V, Melbourne, Australia
{linpa,winikoff}@cs.rmit.edu.au
http://www.cs.rmit.edu.au
Phone: +61 3 9925 2348

Abstract. As agents gain acceptance as a technology there is a growing need for practical methods for developing agent applications. This paper presents the *Prometheus* methodology, which has been developed over several years in collaboration with Agent Oriented Software. The methodology has been taught at industry workshops and university courses. It has proven effective in assisting developers to design, document, and build agent systems. Prometheus differs from existing methodologies in that it is a detailed and complete (start to end) methodology for developing intelligent agents which has evolved out of industrial and pedagogical experience. This paper describes the process and the products of the methodology illustrated by a running example.

1 Introduction

As agents are gaining acceptance as a technology and are being used, there is a growing need for practical methods for developing agent applications. This paper presents the *Prometheus*[1] methodology for developing intelligent agent systems.

The methodology has been developed over the last several years in collaboration with Agent Oriented Software[2] (AOS). Our goal in developing Prometheus was to have a process with associated deliverables which can be taught to industry practitioners and undergraduate students who do not have a background in agents and which they can use to develop intelligent agent systems. To this end Prometheus is *detailed* and *complete* in the sense of covering all activities required in developing intelligent agent systems.

Our claim is that Prometheus is developed in sufficient detail to be used by a non-expert. Prometheus has been taught to an undergraduate class of (third year) students who successfully designed and implemented agent systems using JACK. A second year student over the summer vacation was given a description of the methodology and a description of an agent application (in the area of Holonic Manufacturing). With only (intentionally) limited support, the student was able to design and implement an agent system to perform Holonic Manufacturing using a simulator of a manufacturing cell.

---

[1] Prometheus was the wisest Titan. His name means "forethought" and he was able to foretell the future. Prometheus is known as the protector and benefactor of man. He gave mankind a number of gifts including fire. (*http://www.greekmythology.com/*)

[2] *http://www.agent-software.com*

F. Guinchiglia et al. (Eds.): AOSE 2002, LNCS 2585, pp. 174–185, 2003.

Unfortunately space limitations preclude a detailed comparison with the many existing methodologies. We simply note that Prometheus differs from existing methodologies [1–5, 7–16, 18, 19, 23–25, 27] in that it:

- Supports the development of *intelligent* agents which use goals, beliefs, plans, and events. By contrast, many other methodologies treat agents as "simple software processes that interact with each other to meet an overall system goal" [6].
- Provides "start-to-end" support (from specification to detailed design and implementation) and a *detailed process*, along with design artifacts constructed and steps for deriving artifacts.
- Evolved out of practical industrial and pedagogical experience, and has been used by both industrial practitioners and by undergraduate students. By contrast, many other methodologies have been used only by their creators and often only on small (and unimplemented) examples.
- Provides hierarchical structuring mechanisms which allow design to be performed at multiple levels of abstraction. Such mechanisms are crucial to the practicality of the methodology on large designs.
- Uses an iterative process over software engineering phases rather than a linear "waterfall" model. Although the phases are described in a sequential fashion in this paper, the intention is *not* to perform them purely in sequence. Rather, one repeats the whole process with a changing focus. While the first iteration will be almost entirely activities associated with the system specification phase, subsequent iterations will involve a mixture of activities from different phases and will shift the activities mix more and more towards the later phases.
- Provides (automatable) cross checking of design artifacts. Like [17], we believe that automated consistency checking is vital for the practicality of a methodology.

Of the properties above, perhaps the most contentious is the first: many existing methodologies intentionally do not support intelligent agents, rather, they aim for generality and treat agents as black boxes. We believe that in this case, generality needs to be sacrificed in favour of usefulness. By specifically supporting the development of BDI-like agents we are able to provide detailed processes and deliverables which are useful to developers. Of course, this makes Prometheus less useful to those developing non-BDI-like agents. However, note that the initial stages of the methodology *are* appropriate for the design of any kind of multi agent system.

Although none of these properties is unique in isolation, their combination is, to the best of our knowledge, unique. We believe that these properties are all essential for a practical methodology that is usable by non-experts and accordingly the design of Prometheus was guided by these properties. Although Prometheus' contribution is the combination of these properties, this combination was achieved through careful design of the methodology. It is not possible to easily construct a methodology which has the above properties by combining methodologies that have some of them. For example, given a methodology that provides automated support but does not support intelligent agents and another methodology that supports intelligent agents but not provide automated cross-checking; it is not at all obvious how a hybrid methodology could be created that supports both features.

The *Prometheus* methodology consists of three phases. The *system specification phase* focuses on identifying the basic functionalities of the system, along with inputs (percepts), outputs (actions) and any important shared data sources. The *architectural design phase* uses the outputs from the previous phase to determine which agents the system will contain and how they will interact. The *detailed design phase* looks at the internals of each agent and how it will accomplish its tasks within the overall system.

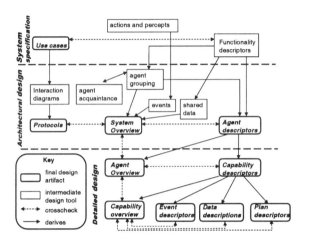

The rest of this paper describes the methodology using a running example: an online bookstore that assists customers in finding and choosing books, manages deliveries, stock, customer and supplier information, and does selective advertising based on interests. It is, of course, not possible to describe a methodology in detail in 12 pages. However, we hope that an understanding of its structure and some sense of its phases, deliverables, activities, and depth of detail can be gained.

2   System Specification

Agent systems are typically situated in a changing and dynamic environment, which can be affected, though not totally controlled by the agent system. One of the earliest questions which must be answered is how the agent system is going to interact with this environment. In line with [22] we call incoming information from the environment "percepts", and the mechanisms for affecting the environment "actions".

As discussed in [26] it is important to distinguish between percepts and events: an event is a significant occurrence for the agent system, whereas a percept is raw data available to the agent system. Often percepts can require processing in order to identify events that an agent can react to. For example, if a soccer playing robot's camera shows a ball where it is expected to be then this percept is not significant. However, if the ball is seen where it is not expected then this *is* significant.

Actions may also be complex, requiring significant design and development outside the realm of the reasoning system. This is especially true when manipulation of physical effectors is involved. We shall not address percept processing and actions any further in this paper. Both can be done within the agent system (either in specific agents, or distributed) or outside of the agent part of the system. If done within the agent part of the system then the Prometheus methodology can be applied, otherwise existing methodologies can be used.

The online bookstore has the percepts of customers visiting the website, selecting items, placing orders (using forms), and receiving email from customers, delivery services and book suppliers. Actions are bank transactions, sending email, and placing delivery orders.

In parallel with discovering or specifying (which of these will depend on the situation) the percepts and actions the developer must start to describe what it is the agent system should do in a broader sense - the functionalities[3] of the system. For example, in order to define the book store we may need to define functionalities such as *"the book store will provide a personalised interface to customers"* and *"the book store will maintain its stock"*. These functionalities start to give an understanding of the system - some sense of its purpose.

It is important in defining functionalities that they be kept as narrow as possible, dealing with a single aspect or goal of the system. If functionalities are too broad they are likely to be less adequately specified leading to potential misunderstanding.

In defining a functionality it is important to also define the information that is required, and the information produced by it. The functionality descriptor produced contains a **name**, a short natural language **description**, a list of **actions**, a list of relevant **percepts**, **data used** and **produced** and a brief description of **interactions** with other functionalities. For example, the following describes the *welcomer* functionality in the online bookstore.

Welcomer: provides a customised response to the user when they log into the site.
Actions: provide link to status of existing orders, welcome by name, welcome as new user, query enjoyment of recent purchases, indicate special offers relevant to interests.
Percepts: Customer accesses site.
Data access: Reads customer information, special offers, and customer interactions data. Writes customer interactions data.
Interactions: No interactions with other functionalities.

While functionalities focus on particular aspects of the system, *use case scenarios* give a more holistic view of the system. The basic idea is borrowed from object oriented design. However, the use case scenarios are given slightly more structure.

The central part of a use case scenario in Prometheus is the sequence of steps describing an example of the system in operation. Each step is annotated with the name of the functionality responsible, as well as information used or produced. These annotations allow cross checking for consistency with the functionality descriptors.

The use case templates which we use contain an **identification number**, a brief natural language **overview**, an optional field called **context** which indicates when this scenario would happen, or the start point of the scenario, the **scenario** itself which is a sequence of steps, a summary of all the **information** used in the various steps, and a list of small **variations**. Because a scenario captures only one particular sequence of steps it

---

[3] A number of methodologies call these "roles". We prefer to avoid overloading the term since it has a similar, but non-identical, meaning in the context of teams of agents.

can be useful to indicate small variations with a brief description. Any major variations should be a separate use case scenario.

3 Architectural Design

The major decision to be made during the architectural design is which agents should exist. We assign functionalities to agents by analysing the artifacts of the previous phase to suggest possible assignments of functionalities to agents. These are then evaluated according to the traditional software engineering criteria of coherence and coupling.

The process of identifying agents by grouping functionalities involves analysing the reasons for and against groupings of particular functionalities. If functionalities use the same data it is an indication for grouping them, as is significant interaction between them. Reasons against groupings may be clearly unrelated functionality or existence on different hardware platforms. More generally, we seek to have agents which have strong coherence and loose coupling.

It can be useful at this stage to draw a matrix having all functionalities on one axis and the properties or relationships on the other axis. Specific properties and relationships that are useful in deriving groupings of functionalities are whether two functionalities are *related*, whether they are *clearly unrelated*, the *data used*[4] and *data produced* as well as *information received* from other functionalities and data that is *written by two (or more) functionalities*. The last two columns can be derived from the information in the previous columns.

In order to evaluate a potential grouping for coupling we use an agent acquaintance diagram. This diagram simply links each agent with each other agent with which it interacts. A design with fewer linkages is less highly coupled and therefore preferable. The design for the book store depicted below (on the right) is reasonable, since it indicates low coupling. A design which produced an acquaintance diagram where each agent was linked to every other agent would be highly undesirable. Note that Prometheus uses a consistent notation to depict agents, events, plans, capabilities, etc. This notation is summarised below, on the left.

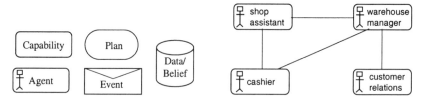

A simple heuristic for assessing coherence is whether an agent has a simple descriptive name which encompasses all the functionalities without any conjunctions ("and"). For example, the shop assistant agent combines the functionalities of visit manager, client welcomer, query processor, pro-active helper, and customer DB manager; yet it has a simple descriptive name.

Once a decision has been made as to which agents the system should contain it is possible to start working out and describing some of the necessary information about

---

[4] Both *read* (in the case of data stores) and *received* (in the case of events and messages).

agents. The high level information about each agent is contained in the form of an agent descriptor, similar to functionality descriptors. Questions which need to be resolved about agents at this stage include: How many agents of this type will there be (singleton, a set number, or multiple based on dynamics of the system, e.g. one sales assistant agent per customer)? What is the lifetime of the agent? If they are created or destroyed during system operation (other than at start-up and shut-down), what triggers this? Agent initialisation - what needs to be done? Agent demise - what needs to be done? What data does this agent need to keep track of? What events will this agent react to?

Agent descriptors contain the above information plus the **name** and **description** of the agent, a brief description of ways in which it **interacts** with other agents and a list of the **functionalities** which are incorporated within this agent. For example consider the following agent descriptor:

Name: Shop assistant agent

Description: greets customer, follows through site, assists with finding books

Cardinality: 1/customer. Instantiated on customer arrival at site

Functionalities included: visit manager, client welcomer, query processor, pro-active helper, customer DB manager.

Reads data: user profile, client orders

Writes data: user profile

Interacts with: cashier (to pay for purchase); warehouse manager (to get price, availability and to hand over order for shipping)

Consistency checking should be done to ensure that agent descriptors are consistent with the set of functionality descriptors which have been incorporated within the agent. Particular items to check are the information, and the agent interactions. If a functionality is listed as interacting with another functionality, then this should translate into an agent interaction, unless the two functionalities are incorporated within the same agent.

At this stage of the design it is important to identify what **events** (i.e. significant occurrences) will be generated as a result of information from the environment (the percepts), either directly or after processing. These are the things the agents will notice, which will cause them to react in some way. A decision must be made as to which agents will react to which events.

In order to accomplish the various aims of the system agents will also send messages to each other. These must also be identified at this stage. It is also necessary to identify what information fields will be carried in these messages, as this forms the interface definition between the agents.

If the implementation platform does not provide specialised message types, these must be specified precisely at this stage to enable modularity in the development of the detailed design for the individual agents.

Shared data objects (if any) must also be identified at this stage. A good design will minimise these, but there may be situations where it is reasonable to have shared data objects. If multiple agents will be writing to shared data objects this will require significant additional care for synchronisation (as agents operate concurrently with each other). Often what at first appears to be a shared data object can be reconceptualised as a data source managed by a single agent, with information provided to other agents as they need it. Alternatively each agent may have its own version of the information, without there being any need for a single centralised data object. Data objects should be specified using traditional object oriented techniques.

The **system overview diagram** ties together the agents, events and shared data objects. It is arguably the single most important artifact of the entire design process, although of course it cannot really be understood fully in isolation. By viewing this diagram we obtain a general understanding of how the system as a whole will function. Messages between agents can include a reply, although this is not shown explicitly on the diagram.

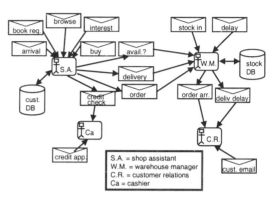

Looking further at agent descriptors provides any additional detail needed to understand the high level functioning of the system.

The final aspect of the architectural design is to specify fully the **interaction** between agents. Interaction diagrams are used as an initial tool for doing this, while fully specified interaction protocols are the final design artifact.

Interaction diagrams are borrowed directly from object oriented design, showing interaction between agents rather than objects. One of the main processes for developing interaction diagrams is to take the use cases developed in the specification phase and to build corresponding interaction diagrams. Wherever there is a step in the use case which involves a functionality from a new agent there must be some interaction from a previously involved agent to the newly participating agent. While it is not possible to automatically derive the interaction diagrams from the use cases, substantial consistency checking is possible. Figure 1 (left) shows an interaction diagram for a scenario of buying a book at our electronic bookstore. It depicts the user requesting a particular book from the sales assistant which checks the details with the warehouse then replies. The user decides to buy the book and places an order; the sales assistant checks for delivery options, confirms them with the user, checks the user's credit card details with the cashier, and then places the order and thanks the user. In addition to deriving interaction diagrams from use cases, each of the major environmental events should have an associated interaction diagram.

Interaction diagrams, like use cases, give only a partial picture of the system's behaviour. In order to have a precisely defined system we progress from interaction diagrams to **interaction protocols** which define precisely which interaction sequences are valid within the system.

Figure 1 (right) shows the protocol for the credit check portion of the interaction diagram shown in figure 1 (left). Because protocols must show all variations they are often larger than the corresponding interaction diagram and may need to be split into smaller chunks. We use the AUML notation [19] to specify protocols,

Consistency checking should be done between protocols and interaction diagrams, the system overview diagram, and use cases. With the appropriate tools, much of this consistency checking can be automated.

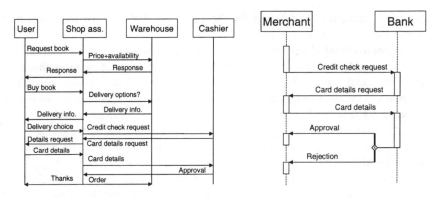

Fig. 1. Example Interaction Diagram (left) and Protocol (right)

4   Detailed Design

Detailed design focuses on developing the internal structure of each of the agents and how it will achieve its tasks within the system. It is at this stage of the design that the methodology becomes specific to agents that use user-defined plans, triggered by goals or events, such as the various implementations of Belief, Desire, Intention (BDI) systems (e.g. PRS, dMARS, JAM, or JACK). A number of details regarding the implementation platform also become evident at this stage when looking at any particular design. However, the principles are easily adapted to the specifics of whichever development platform has been chosen, as long as it is within the broad general category of agents which use plans and react to events.

The focus of the detailed design phase is on defining capabilities (modules within the agent), internal events, plans and detailed data structures. A progressive refinement process is used which begins by describing agents' internals in terms of capabilities. The internal structure of each capability is then described, optionally using or introducing further capabilities. These are refined in turn until all capabilities have been defined. At the bottom level capabilities are defined in terms of plans, events, and data.

The functionalities from the specification phase provide a good initial set of **capabilities**, which can be further refined if desired. Sometimes there is also functionality akin to "library routines" which is required in multiple places - either within multiple agents, or within multiple capabilities within a single agent. Such functionality should also be extracted into a capability which can then be included into other capabilities or agents as required.

Capabilities are allowed to be nested within other capabilities and thus this model allows for arbitrarily many layers within the detailed design, in order to achieve an understandable complexity at each level.

Each capability should be described by a capability descriptor which contains information about the external interface to the capability - which **events** are **inputs** and which events are **produced** by (as inputs to other capabilities). It also contains a natural language **description** of the functionality, a unique descriptive **name**, information regarding **interactions** with other capabilities, or **inclusions** of other capabilities, and a reference to **data** read and written by the capability. We use structured capability descriptor forms containing the above fields.

The **agent overview diagram** provides the top level view of the agent internals. It is very similar in style to the system overview diagram, but instead of agents within a system, it shows capabilities within an agent. This diagram shows the top level capabilities of the agent and the event or task flow between these capabilities, as well as data internal to the agent. By reading the relevant capability descriptors, together with the diagram, it is possible to obtain a clear high level view of how the modules within the agent will interact to achieve the overall tasks of the agent as described in the agent descriptor from the architectural design.

The agent overview diagram below is for a warehouse manager agent in the electronic bookstore. This agent has the capabilities of tracking stock, placing orders for new stock and organising delivery of books to clients.

A further level of detail is provided by capability diagrams which take a single capability and describe its internals. At the bottom level these will contain plans, with events providing the connections between plans, just as they do between capabilities and between agents. At intermediate levels they may contain nested capabilities or a mixture of capabilities and plans.

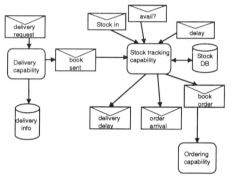

These diagrams are similar in style to the system overview and agent overview diagram, although plans are constrained to have a single incoming (triggering) event.

Just as the agent overview diagram should be checked for consistency with the system overview (in terms of incoming and outgoing events), so each capability overview diagram should be checked against its enclosing context - either the agent overview, or another capability overview.

The final design artifacts required are the individual plan, event and data descriptors. These descriptions provide the details necessary to move into implementation. Exactly what are the appropriate details for these descriptors will depend on aspects of the implementation platform. For example if the context in which a plan type is to be used is split into two separate checks within the system being used (as is the case in JACK) then it is appropriate to specify these separately in the descriptor. Fields regarding what information an event carries assumes that events are composite objects able to carry information, and so on.

The plan descriptors we use provide an **identifier**, the **triggering event type**, the **plan steps** as well as a short natural language **description**, a **context** specification indicating when this plan should be used and a list of **data** read and written.

Event descriptors are used to fully specify all events, including those identified earlier. The event descriptor should identify the **purpose** of the event and any **data** that the event carries. We also indicate for each event whether it is expected to be *covered* and whether it is expected to be *unambiguous*. An event is *covered* if there is always at least one handling plan which is applicable; that is, for any situation, at least one of the matching plans will have a true context condition. An event is *unambiguous* if there is always at *most* one handling plan which is applicable.

Data descriptors should specify the fields and methods of any classes used for data storage within the system. If specialised data structures are provided for maintaining beliefs, these should also be specified.

An additional artifact that is completed (and checked) at this point is the **data dictionary**. The data dictionary should be started at the beginning of the project and developed further at each stage. The data dictionary is important in ensuring consistent use of names (for example, what is called "delivery info" in one place in the design should not be called "deliv. information" elsewhere). One option is to organise the data dictionary into separate sections for agents, capabilities, plans, events and data, organised alphabetically within sections. The other option is to have a flat alphabetical structure. With tool support multiple views (automatically generated) can be provided.

5 Discussion and Conclusions

We have briefly described the key aspects of the Prometheus methodology. The methodology has been in use for several years and has been taught in industry workshops (most recently at the Australian AI conference, 2001). The methodology has been in use for several years as a teaching tool. The feedback we have received indicates that it provides substantial guidance for the process of developing the design and for communicating the design within a work group. With student projects it is abundantly clear that the existence of the methodology is an enormous help in thinking about and deciding on the design issues, as well as conveying the design decisions.

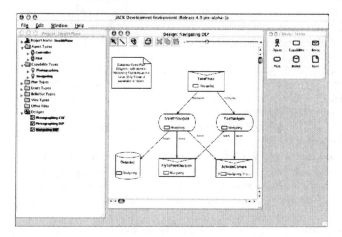

One of the advantages of this methodology is the number of places where automated tools can be used for consistency checking across the various artifacts of the design process. For example, the input and output events for an agent must be the same on the system overview diagram and on the agent overview diagram. Agent Oriented Software has constructed a support tool for the methodology that allows design diagrams to be drawn and generates corresponding skeleton code (in JACK).

We are also investigating how some of the design artifacts, such as the protocol definitions, and the capability diagrams, can be used for providing debugging and tracing support within the implemented system [21]. Having a design methodology which can be used through to testing and debugging is clearly advantageous in terms of an integrated and complete methodology.

Other areas for future work include: clearer integration of goals as a first class concept, extensions to the graphical notation to allow percepts, actions, goals, and (some) sequencing information to be specified; introduction of social concepts (teams, roles); and investigating the commonalities and differences with various extensions of UML to agents [19, 20]. Additionally, we intend to integrate Prometheus with the agent concepts we have identified [26].

Acknowledgements

We would like to acknowledge the support of Agent Oriented Software Pty. Ltd. and of the Australian Research Council (ARC) under grant C00106934. We would also like to thank James Harland and Jamie Curmi for comments on drafts of this paper.

References

1. F. M. T. Brazier, B. M. Dunin-Keplicz, N. R. Jennings, and J. Treur. DESIRE: Modelling multi-agent systems in a compositional formal framework. *Int Journal of Cooperative Information Systems*, 6(1):67–94, 1997.
2. B. Burmeister. Models and methodology for agent-oriented analysis and design. Working Notes of the KI'96 Workshop on AgentOriented Programming and Distributed Systems, 1996.
3. G. Bush, S. Cranefield, and M. Purvis. The Styx agent methodology. The Information Science Discussion Paper Series 2001/02, Department of Information Science, University of Otago, New Zealand., Jan. 2001. Available from *http://divcom.otago.ac.nz/infosci*.
4. G. Caire, F. Leal, P. Chainho, R. Evans, F. Garijo, J. Gomez, J. Pavon, P. Kearney, J. Stark, and P. Massonet. Agent oriented analysis using MESSAGE/UML. In M. Wooldridge, P. Ciancarini, and G. Weiss, editors, *Second International Workshop on Agent-Oriented Software Engineering (AOSE-2001)*, pages 101–108, 2001.
5. A. Collinot, A. Drogoul, and P. Benhamou. Agent oriented design of a soccer robot team. In *Proceedings of ICMAS'96*, 1996.
6. S. A. DeLoach. Analysis and design using MaSE and agentTool. In *Proceedings of the 12th Midwest Artificial Intelligence and Cognitive Science Conference (MAICS 2001)*, 2001.
7. S. A. DeLoach, M. F. Wood, and C. H. Sparkman. Multiagent systems engineering. *International Journal of Software Engineering and Knowledge Engineering*, 11(3):231–258, 2001.
8. A. Drogoul and J. Zucker. Methodological issues for designing multi-agent systems with machine learning techniques: Capitalizing experiences from the robocup challenge. Technical Report LIP6 1998/041, Laboratoire d'Informatique de Paris 6, 1998.
9. M. Elammari and W. Lalonde. An agent-oriented methodology: High-level and intermediate models. In G. Wagner and E. Yu, editors, Proc. of the 1st Int. Workshop. on Agent-Oriented Information Systems., 1999.

10. F. Giunchiglia, J. Mylopoulos, and A. Perini. The tropos software development methodology: Processes, models and diagrams. In *Third International Workshop on Agent-Oriented Software Engineering*, July 2002.
11. N. Glaser. The CoMoMAS methodology and environment for multi-agent system development. In C. Zhang and D. Lukose, editors, *Multi-Agent Systems Methodologies and Applications*, pages 1–16. Springer LNAI 1286, Aug. 1996. Second Australian Workshop on Distributed Artificial Intelligence.
12. C. Iglesias, M. Garijo, and J. González. A survey of agent-oriented methodologies. In J. Müller, M. P. Singh, and A. S. Rao, editors, *ATAL-98*, pages 317–330. Springer-Verlag: Heidelberg, Germany, 1999.
13. C. A. Iglesias, M. Garijo, J. C. González, and J. R. Velasco. Analysis and design of multiagent systems using MAS-commonKADS. In *Agent Theories, Architectures, and Languages*, pages 313–327, 1997.
14. E. A. Kendall, M. T. Malkoun, and C. H. Jiang. A methodology for developing agent based systems. In C. Zhang and D. Lukose, editors, *First Australian Workshop on Distributed Artificial Intelligence*, 1995.
15. D. Kinny and M. Georgeff. Modelling and design of multi-agent systems. In *Intelligent Agents III: Proceedings of the Third International Workshop on Agent Theories, Architectures, and Languages (ATAL-96). LNAI 1193*. Springer-Verlag, 1996.
16. D. Kinny, M. Georgeff, and A. Rao. A methodology and modelling technique for systems of BDI agents. In R. van Hoe, editor, *Seventh European Workshop on Modelling Autonomous Agents in a Multi-Agent World*, 1996.
17. H. Knublauch and T. Rose. Tool-supported process analysis and design for the development of multi-agent systems. In *Third International Workshop on Agent-Oriented Software Engineering*, July 2002.
18. J. Lind. A development method for multiagent systems. In *Cybernetics and Systems: Proceedings of the 15th European Meeting on Cybernetics and Systems Research, Symposium "From Agent Theory to Agent Implementation"*, 2000.
19. J. Odell, H. Parunak, and B. Bauer. Extending UML for agents. In *Proceedings of the Agent-Oriented Information Systems Workshop at the 17th National conference on Artificial Intelligence.*, 2000.
20. M. Papasimeon and C. Heinze. Extending the UML for designing JACK agents. In *Proceedings of the Australian Software Engineering Conference (ASWEC 01)*, Aug. 2001.
21. D. Poutakidis, L. Padgham, and M. Winikoff. Debugging multi-agent systems using design artifacts: The case of interaction protocols. In *Proceedings of the First International Joint Conference on Autonomous Agents and Multi Agent Systems (AAMAS'02)*, 2002.
22. S. Russell and P. Norvig. *Artificial Intelligence: A Modern Approach*. Prentice Hall, 1995.
23. O. Shehory and A. Sturm. Evaluation of modeling techniques for agent-based systems. In J. P. Müller, E. Andre, S. Sen, and C. Frasson, editors, *Proceedings of the Fifth International Conference on Autonomous Agents*, pages 624–631. ACM Press, May 2001.
24. L. Z. Varga, N. R. Jennings, and D. Cockburn. Integrating intelligent systems into a cooperating community for electricity distribution management. *Int Journal of Expert Systems with Applications*, 7(4):563–579, 1994.
25. G. Wagner. The agent-object-relationship metamodel: Towards a unified view of state and behavior. To appear in *Information Systems*, 2002. http://AOR.rezearch.info.
26. M. Winikoff, L. Padgham, and J. Harland. Simplifying the development of intelligent agents. In M. Stumptner, D. Corbett, and M. Brooks, editors, *AI2001: Advances in Artificial Intelligence. 14th Australian Joint Conference on Artificial Intelligence*, pages 555–568. Springer, LNAI 2256, Dec. 2001.
27. M. Wooldridge, N. Jennings, and D. Kinny. The Gaia methodology for agent-oriented analysis and design. *Autonomous Agents and Multi-Agent Systems*, 3(3), 2000.

Tool-Supported Process Analysis and Design for the Development of Multi-agent Systems

Holger Knublauch and Thomas Rose

Research Institute for Applied Knowledge Processing (FAW)
Helmholtzstr. 16, 89081 Ulm, Germany (+49-731 501 8918)
holger@knublauch.com,Thomas.Rose@faw.uni-ulm.de

Abstract. This paper introduces a methodology for the development of multi-agent systems, in particular multi-agent systems that optimize the collaboration of distributed work groups like clinical departments. A major difficulty with such systems is requirements elicitation, because intimate knowledge of the work processes is needed to identify the potential agent application scenarios. In the face of uncertain requirements, our methodology exploits some ideas from agile software development approaches such as Extreme Programming, namely the values of collaboration with domain experts and of human creativity driven by rapid feedback. We support collaboration by means of a tool-supported modeling approach that allows one to capture existing and agentified processes in a format that is sufficiently simple to be understood and maintained by domain experts. These process models can be automatically synchronized with executable agent source code, so that rapid feedback is ensured. We support creativity by means of a searchable repository of reusable agent design patterns and other types of process modeling knowledge.

1 Introduction and Overview

An *agent* [9] is an autonomous software entity that is able to interact with its environment and other agents in a flexible manner in order to solve tasks on behalf of human principals. Agents are a promising approach to support information-intensive tasks like those encountered in distributed work groups with significant communication and coordination needs. For example, we have developed a multi-agent system which supports clinical work groups by means of pro-active and context-sensitive information services [11, 10]. Our agents notify physicians about changing patient data, resolve conflicting operation schedules, and forward consultation requests to the currently available medical specialists. Such agents inhabit a relatively closed environment with a finite number of potential agent communication channels. However, the requirements of such systems are typically hard to elicit without intimate knowledge of the interaction patterns in the existing processes. A major question is therefore how to identify and design suitable agent types and their interaction scenarios in a way that enables domain experts to contribute their ideas and to understand how the agents will affect their daily work.

F. Giunchiglia et al. (Eds.): AOSE 2002, LNCS 2585, pp. 186–197, 2003.
© Springer-Verlag Berlin Heidelberg 2003

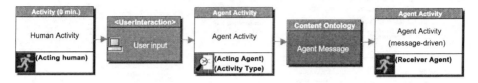

Fig. 1. Some of the symbols used in our process modeling approach.

In this paper, we introduce an agent development methodology that offers particular support for the collaboration between domain experts and engineers. Our approach transfers some ideas from agile software development methods like *Extreme Programming (XP)* [2] into the domain of agents. In contrast to systematic engineering methodologies, where developers typically step through a series of intermediate modeling artifacts before executable code is available, XP suggests to focus on very few models and to keep them as simple as possible. Our approach relies on a single modeling artifact, namely a process model, which is iteratively evolved into a multi-agent system design. These process models are sufficiently simple to be understood and maintained by domain experts and at the same time sufficiently formal to lead to executable code rapidly.

Our methodology is optimized for the design of agents that support the information flow between humans in existing work groups. The approach is most beneficial when the work group is ready to provide one or more domain experts who have a sufficiently deep understanding of the existing processes. The development team in our clinical case study comprised an anesthetist who was partially released from clinical routine to contribute to process analysis and design. In our approach, domain experts use an intuitive process modeling tool to capture the existing work flows. As illustrated in fig. 1, these process models mainly consist of *activities* (bright boxes) that are performed by a given *role* (either humans or agents). Activities process *media* (dark boxes): They can receive input media such as paper-based forms or user input, and produce output media such as *messages* to other agents (see section 2 for details on our process modeling metamodel).

The models of the existing processes, in which all activities are performed by humans, are fed into an evolutionary process analysis and agent design cycle. During the iterations, engineers and domain experts jointly identify process bottlenecks and design agents to optimize these processes. From the evolving agentified process models, the tool can automatically derive various other models such as agent life cycles, acquaintance diagrams and executable code (see section 3 for details). These models allow to cross-check the processes from different view points and thus support intuition and rapid feedback. In order to reveal most of the potential agent application scenarios, our approach supports the developers' creativity by means of an agent design pattern repository from which reusable solutions to recurring tasks can be identified (see section 4).

While this paper focuses on analysis and design, a matching implementation approach is described in our complementary papers [14, 10] which show how the process models that result from the design can be implemented in an XP style.

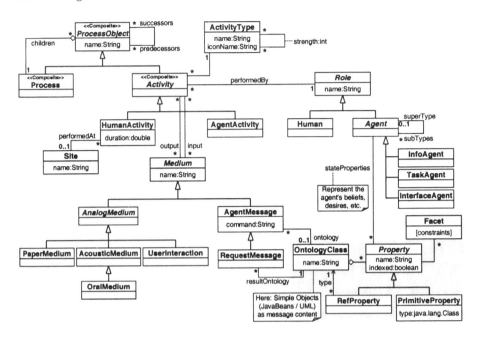

Fig. 2. Our metamodel for process and agent modeling.

Although this approach has been very successful in our clinical case study, it is certainly not the best choice for all types of multi-agent systems. Section 5 will therefore discuss our approach in comparison to related work, before the paper is summarized in section 6.

2   A Metamodel for Process and Agent Modeling

Fig. 2 illustrates a simple, adaptable metamodel which can be used to capture existing work processes and to design agents which optimize the information flow within these processes. In this metamodel, a `Process` consists of a network of sub-processes and activities, which can be temporally ordered by successor/predecessor relations. Each `Activity` represents a self-contained unit of work such as "Check blood pressure" and "Notify emergency unit". Each `Activity` can be annotated with an `ActivityType`, which classifies it into more general terms such as "Research", "Experiment" and "Decision making". These types serve as semantic tags which can be used to classify sub-processes for later reuse in agent pattern repositories (see section 4).

Each `Activity` is performed by an actor who takes a given `Role`. A `Role` can either be taken by `Humans` or software `Agents`. `Agents` are arranged in an inheritance hierarchy, so that they can reuse or overload behavior. Similar to Sycara et al. [19], we distinguish between three classes of `Agents`:

- `InterfaceAgents` are used to supply human actors with a pro-active user interface, potentially executable on mobile devices.

- `TaskAgents` fulfill asynchronous information processing activities.
- `InfoAgents` encapsulate data sources and legacy systems. A good agent oriented design should encourage developers to achieve the correct decomposition of entities into either agents or objects [20]. `InfoAgents` are very close to conventional objects but allow to model and access those objects in a convenient and uniform manner.

`Activities` can receive input `Media` and produce output `Media`. Various subclasses of `Medium` exist. Agents interact with humans by means of keyboard input and acoustic channels, and communicate with other agents through `AgentMessages` and `RequestMessages`. `RequestMessages` represent messages that are immediately responded to by the receiver. They allow to represent and implement *queries* very conveniently without the hassles of multi-threading, in particular to encapsulate legacy data sources through `InfoAgents`.

`AgentMessages` are identified by a `command` (or performative) and carry information content of a certain `ontology`. In our current implementation we represent ontologies by JavaBeans classes that are enriched by semantic metadata (facets) as described in the *KBeans* approach [13, 12]. This approach supports rapid coding because developers can consistently rely on object-oriented techniques such as UML editors and Java tools with industrial support (cf. [6, 3]). However, in cases when the agents require intelligent reasoning facilities that are not supported by hard-coded Java classes, completely different implementations based on other agent communication languages can be easily introduced by adding ontology meta classes to the above metamodel.

As a supplement to ontologies in agent messages, our metamodel also includes a technique to represent an agent's internal state (e.g., its beliefs and desires): An `Agent` can have a collection of `stateProperties` (slots), which can be compared to attributes in an object-oriented sense. For example, an agent that tracks a patient's position can have the patient's id and his or her position as `stateProperties`.

This metamodel can be used to build models of existing processes, and to incrementally introduce agents into them. The metamodel has shown to be sufficiently simple to be graphically visualized, understood and edited by domain experts such as clinicians. Although off-the-shelf drawing tools like Microsoft Visio can be used to edit these models, we have implemented an optimized process and agent modeling tool called AGILShell, which is described in the following.

3   Process Analysis and Agent Design with AGILShell

AGILShell[1] is a visual editor for process and agent models in the above metamodel. It has a desktop area on which various views can be arranged freely.

- **Process Graph** (Fig. 3, center). The main view of AGILShell is a graph in which domain experts and engineers can edit processes. Activities and

---

[1] AGILShell is freely available from `http://www.faw.uni-ulm.de/kbeans/agil`

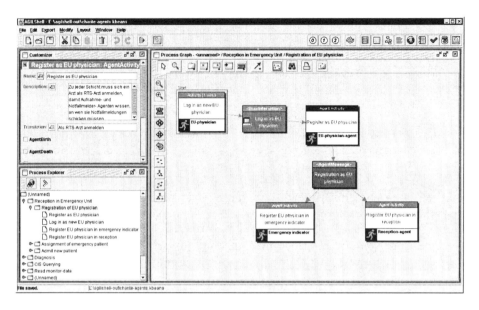

Fig. 3. The main editors of AGILShell are Process Graph and Customizer.

media are shown as nodes. For each activity, the name and the performing role are visualized. An icon shows the activity type. For each agent message, the command (performative) and content ontology are shown. The media flow and the sequence of activities are represented by means of edges.

– **Process Explorer** (Fig. 3, left, bottom). Complex process models can be quickly navigated along their hierarchy of (sub-) processes in a tree view.
– **Customizer** (Fig. 3, left, top). The properties of the currently selected activity, process, message, agent or ontology class can be edited in a Customizer.
– **Community Viewer** (Fig. 4). This graph displays the communication pathways between the roles in the system. The graph is automatically derived from the process graph at design time. The agents are shown as nodes which also display the role type (human, interface agent, etc.) and, for agents, the state properties. This view does not only provide a convenient overview of the implemented agent types, but furthermore allows to detect information bottlenecks. Nodes with many incoming and outgoing arrows represent roles that operate on a large accumulation of data. These focal points of information might particularly benefit from agent-based information services.
– **Life Cycle View** (Fig. 5). The temporal ordering of activities allows to extract a life cycle view in which only those activities that are performed by a given agent or human are shown. Such views allow to cross-check the design with the human process participants, who can – from their local point of view – assess whether their daily routine is sufficiently covered by the overall process. The view is also convenient to verify the implementation of the single agent types. Life cycles and all other graph views are equipped with comfortable layout algorithms that support their visual assessment (cf. [17]).

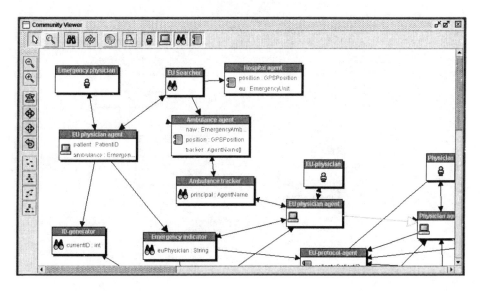

Fig. 4. The community viewer displays the communication links between the various humans and agents, and the agents' state properties.

In a typical development process, the agent designers use the process graph to capture the system design and switch to the other views to cross-check and clarify the agent specifications. Based on these specifications, AGILShell includes an incremental Java code generator of agent control classes, XP test cases and ontologies. This generator creates abstract base classes with handling methods for every incoming agent message. The programmers only need to overload these methods correctly and fill in the business logic. This mechanism makes sure that the design model is kept synchronized with the executable code because inconsistencies will be reported by the (Java) compiler. Beside code generators the tool offers a constraint checking mechanism, with the help of which syntactic modeling errors such as duplicate names can be detected. The open architecture of the tool furthermore allows one to write individual plug-ins such as views, analyzers or code generators for other agent platforms.

4   Example Process Models and Design Patterns

This section illustrates the evolution of a sample process model from our clinical multi-agent system, starting with a model of an existing process and ending with a general agent design pattern. The scenario illustrates a complex interaction between various humans and agents with the goal of finding a consultant. Consultants are specialized physicians such as gynecologists who are called by other physicians during the examination of a patient in the emergency unit (EU). In the original process (without agents, fig. 6), a physician has to phone the resident (head) of the desired department. The resident then has to go through a time-consuming series of telephone and pager calls to get hold of a consultant.

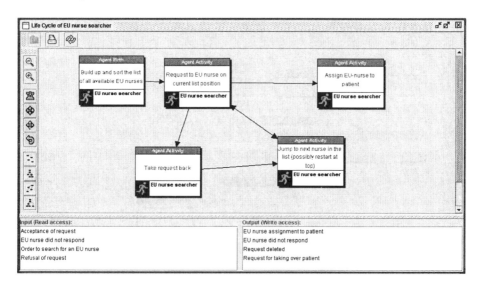

Fig. 5. A life cycle displays all activities a given role is involved in during its life.

In the "agentified" process (fig. 7), the physician only needs to enter the desired consultation expertise in his interface agent and a consultant finder agent will perform the search autonomously, without the need to contact a resident. The finder first gets a list of all potential consultants in service and then sends consultation requests to their agents until one of them delivers a positive response. Physicians who are busy can even configure their agent to reject incoming requests automatically. Furthermore, in contrast to the original scenario where the consultant must make a decision with only very little information about the patient, the new agents provide online access to the whole patient record.

A deeper analysis of the example from fig. 7 reveals a more general interaction pattern between agents. The consultant finder can be generalized to a generic search agent that continuously sends requests to other agents until one of them returns a predefined, positive response. Such agent application scenarios can be reused in other process segments and in other multi-agent projects. For example, the pattern above recurred three more times within our clinical processes. This clearly indicates that agent development can profit from libraries of reusable agent design patterns (cf. [15]). AGILShell is backed by such a library into which developers can conveniently copy excerpts of their process models for later reuse. The library thus serves as a repository of process and agent modeling knowledge (cf. [18, 17]). In order to provide intelligent access to this knowledge, the library has a search function which allows to filter only those processes in which certain *activity types* occur. The activity types form a taxonomy of semantically related types into which additional types can be added. For example, the type "find person" can be used to annotate all scenarios in which such a task is solved. Patterns can also be annotated and searched by non-functional con-

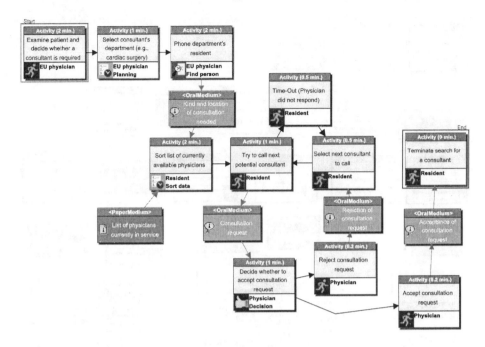

Fig. 6. A sample scenario from the clinical consultation process (without agents).

straints, e.g. security, potential, quality, and risks. Agent designers are thus able to browse through historical solutions and best-practices to recurring problems. Comparisons with existing solutions can also prevent expensive design mistakes.

5 Discussion

The main difference between our approach and most of the currently existing *Agent-Oriented Software Engineering (AOSE)* methods [20] is that we focus the whole analysis and design activities on only a single modeling artifact, namely a process model. AOSE methods like *Gaia* [21], *MaSE* [7] and *MESSAGE* [5], define a systematic sequence of activities that guide the developers through classical Software Engineering phases like requirements analysis, design, implementation, and test. A major goal of these rather waterfall-based approaches is to ensure that development processes become reproducible and that design models are not constrained by implementation details. However, their general weakness is the overhead when models need to be changed due to ill-defined requirements [2]. Furthermore, the domain experts are typically unable to contribute to the various formal modeling artifacts that are needed before executable code is available. While these various artifacts all cover specific views of the overall system, such as role models, agent life cycles, and organizational diagrams, we argue that a process model, from which many other types of views can be extracted, is often a more natural way of developing agents:

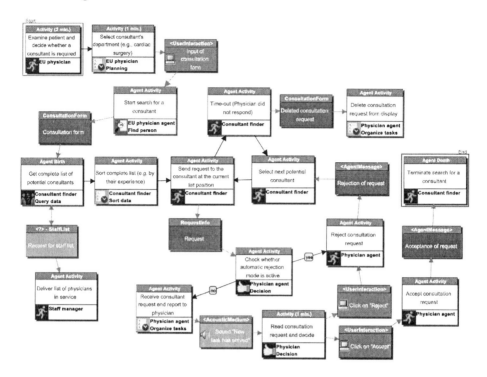

Fig. 7. An "agentified" version of the scenario from fig. 6.

- While methods like Gaia focus on the local perspective of the single roles, our approach takes a rather global view that enables domain experts to see their work flows in the overall context of process patterns. Role models and thus the mapping to implementable (Java) classes are in our approach a natural by-product.
- Process models integrate and keep together what is otherwise hard to synchronize. Developers using MESSAGE need to keep their various diagrams consistent [5] but the method provides little support to enforce this consistency. Developers using Gaia need to capture responsibilities, permissions, activities and protocols into semi-formal, textual models. Our approach enables developers to draw visual models in which all these information are embedded naturally. Models such as Gaia's acquaintance diagrams and agent life cycles can be updated with a single mouse click. While Gaia does not result in implementable design models, our approach allows to incrementally generate corresponding source code and thus offers excellent requirements traceability [8].
- The focus on only a single modeling artifact beside source code makes our approach very agile. Many AOSE methods rely on intermediate models that have little or no equivalent in the source code of the executable system, such as models which capture the static structure within an organization into departments and groups.

- While most of the existing AOSE approaches focus on agent analysis and design, they provide little support for the *identification* (cf. [4]) of these agent but rather assume the agent application scenarios are known in advance. Our development process commences one step earlier. Starting with a model of the existing processes, it is often straight-forward to gather ideas for agents. Backed by a "browsable" library of inspiring agent design patterns, further ideas emerge during the evolutionary process analysis in the collaboration of people with multiple view points. The agility of our approach with rapid turn-around times between analysis and code reduces the cost of change and thus explicitly welcomes experiments and evolution.

Despite the differences there are several similarities between our approach and other AOSE methods. Our modeling approach is similar to the *Protocol Diagrams* [3], which are based on *Collaboration Diagrams* in UML and allow to model the interactions between agents graphically without having to worry about formal agent semantics. Our process models have less expressive power than the linear swim lane diagrams of *Agent UML* [1]. However, these diagrams are hard to comprehend for people without formal training and can become unintelligible when more than two roles are involved in a conversation, while our process models exploit the freedom of full-fledged two-dimensional visualizations amid modeling tasks.

The methodology presented in this paper is certainly not the best choice for all types of projects. Here are some weaknesses and limitations that we would like to comment on.

- Like most of the AOSE methods, our approach is relatively new and therefore with little support beyond our research lab. In particular, the process-oriented modeling approach is incompatible to industrial standards such as UML and no tools support it beside AGILShell.
- The methodology is restricted to closed systems where agent interaction paths are predefined after the design. In other words, our approach is not optimized for completely flexible multi-agent systems in which agent types, ontologies, and collaborations come and go at runtime.
- Our approach shares the problems of other agile methods such as Extreme Programming. Among others [2], XP assumes that the project managers are ready to engage with a rather experimental, evolutionary method where much of the control is passed to the developers and customers. However, the management can monitor the team's progress from frequent intermediate results and prototypes.
- An assumption of customer collaboration is that motivated domain experts exist who are ready to participate in the project. Modeling the existing processes will also require the actual process participants to expose their daily routine transparently. However, practice necessarily operates with deception [16].
- A relatively open issue in our approach is how to find suitable activity types for the design pattern repository. This is a classical ontology problem and

as such demands for experience in semantic modeling. We are currently investigating along the lines of a generic classification of tasks and goals that might serve as a starting point for individual type schema.

6   Conclusions

This paper has introduced a methodology for the development of multi-agent systems, in particular multi-agent systems to optimize the collaboration of distributed work groups. Our approach relies on a simple process modeling metaphor which is just on the right level of abstraction to enable domain experts to participate in the analysis, design and test phases. While in most of the existing AOSE methods the developers must edit various intermediate models such as role and interaction diagrams, our approach focuses on the construction and analysis of process models, from which various other models such as agent life cycles, acquaintance diagrams and executable code can be derived automatically. The focus on only a single modeling artifact makes our approach agile and thus particularly suitable for projects with uncertain requirements. Our approach is supported by an intuitive process modeling tool. Beside graphical editors and views, this tool provides a repository of agent application scenarios which provides access to process modeling knowledge and best-practices of agent design and thus may guide the creativity of the developers into the right direction.

References

1. B. Bauer, J. P. Mueller, and J. Odell. Agent UML: A formalism for specifying multiagent software systems. In P. Ciancarini and M. Wooldridge, editors, *Agent-Oriented Software Engineering*. Springer-Verlag, 2001.
2. K. Beck. *Extreme Programming Explained*. Addison-Wesley, 1999.
3. F. Bergenti and A. Poggi. Exploiting UML in the design of multi-agent systems. In *Proc. of the ECAI Workshop on Engineering Societies in the Agents' World (ESAW)*, Berlin, Germany, 2000.
4. S. Bussmann, N. R. Jennings, and M. Wooldridge. On the identification of agents in the design of production control systems. In P. Ciancarini and M. Wooldridge, editors, *Agent-Oriented Software Engineering*. Springer-Verlag, 2001.
5. G. Caire, F. Leal, P. Chainho, and et al. Agent oriented analysis using MESSAGE/UML. In *Proc. of Ontologies in Agent Systems Workshop, Agents 2001*, Montreal, Canada, 2001.
6. S. Cranefield, S. Haustein, and M. Purvis. UML-based ontology modelling for software agents. In *Proc. of Ontologies in Agent Systems Workshop, Agents 2001*, Montreal, Canada, 2001.
7. S. DeLoach, M. Wood, and C. Sparkman. Multiagent systems engineering. *The International Journal of Software Engineering and Knowledge Engineering*, 11(3):231–258, 2001.
8. M. Jarke. Requirements tracing. *Communications of the ACM*, 41(12):32–36, 1998.
9. N. Jennings, K. Sycara, and M. Wooldridge. A roadmap of agent research and development. *Int. Journal of Autonomous Agents and Multi-Agent Systems*, 1(1):7–38, 1998.

10. H. Knublauch, H. Koeth, and T. Rose. Agile development of a clinical multi-agent system: An Extreme Programming case study. In *Proc. of the Third International Conference on eXtreme Programming and Agile Processes in Software Engineering (XP 2002)*, Alghero, Sardinia, Italy, 2002.

11. H. Knublauch, T. Rose, and M. Sedlmayr. Towards a multi-agent system for pro-active information management in anesthesia. In *Proc. of the Agents-2000 Workshop on Autonomous Agents in Health Care*, Barcelona, Spain, 2000.

12. H. Knublauch and T. Rose. Round-trip engineering of ontologies for knowledge-based systems. In *Proc. of the Twelfth International Conference on Software Engineering and Knowledge Engineering (SEKE)*, Chicago, IL, 2000.

13. H. Knublauch. KBeans: Implementing semantic transparency for components and domain models. Technical Report FAW-TR-01001, FAW Ulm, 2001.

14. H. Knublauch. Extreme Programming of multi-agent systems. In *Proc. of the First International Joint Conference on Autonomous Agents and Multi-Agent Systems (AAMAS 2002)*, Bologna, Italy, 2002.

15. J. Lind. Patterns in agent-oriented software engineering. In *(This book)*. 2003.

16. W. Rammert, M. Schlese, G. Wagner, J. Wehner, and R. Weingarten. *Wissensmaschinen: Soziale Konstruktion eines technischen Mediums. Das Beispiel Expertensysteme.* Campus Verlag, Frankfurt, Germany, 1998.

17. T. Rose. Visual assessment of engineering processes in virtual enterprises. *Communications of the ACM*, 41(12):45–52, 1998.

18. C. Rupprecht, M. Fünffinger, H. Knublauch, and T. Rose. Capture and dissemination of experience about the construction of engineering processes. In *Proc. of the 12th Conference on Advanced Information Systems Engineering (CAISE)*, Stockholm, Sweden, 2000.

19. K. Sycara, K. Decker, A. Pannu, M. Williamson, and D. Zeng. Distributed intelligent agents. *IEEE Expert*, 11(6), 1996.

20. M. Wooldridge and P. Ciancarini. Agent-oriented software engineering: The state of the art. In P. Ciancarini and M. Wooldridge, editors, *Agent-Oriented Software Engineering*. Springer-Verlag, 2001.

21. M. Wooldridge, N. Jennings, and D. Kinny. The Gaia methodology for agent-oriented analysis and design. *Journal of Autonomous Agents and Multi-Agent Systems*, 3(3):285–312, 2000.

Assembling Agent Oriented Software Engineering Methodologies from Features

Thomas Juan[1], Leon Sterling[1], and Michael Winikoff[2,*]

[1] Department of Computer Science and Software Engineering, The University of Melbourne
221 Bouverie Street Carlton, Victoria, 3010, Australia
{tlj,leon}@cs.mu.oz.au
[2] School of Computer Science and Information Technology, RMIT University,
GPO Box 2476V, Melbourne, 3001, Australia
winikoff@cs.rmit.edu.au

Abstract. In this paper we describe our effort to merge two existing AOSE methodologies, Prometheus and ROADMAP, by isolating a set of general-purpose common elements. The remaining parts of the two methodologies are componentized into special purpose "value-adding" features. This approach empowers the developer to assemble a methodology tailored to the given project (and the application domain) by adding appropriate features to the common elements. The assembled methodology can be modified during development to support changing aspects of the system.

1 Introduction

Many diverse Agent Oriented Software Engineering (AOSE) approaches and methodologies have been proposed [4, 14], including the AAII methodology, AUML, Gaia, MaSE, Tropos, Prometheus and ROADMAP [6, 8, 15, 3, 11, 10, 5]. Each of the methodologies has different strengths and weaknesses, and different specialized features to support different aspects of their intended application domains.

Clearly no single methodology is "one size fits all". However, as application complexity grows, we expect future projects to have an increasingly large number of aspects that cannot be addressed by a single methodology alone. To provide engineering support for such projects, specialized features to address different aspects must be brought together from different methodologies in a consistent fashion.

It is useful to identify and standardize the common elements of the existing methodologies. The common elements could form a generic agent model on which specialized features might be based. The remaining parts of the methodologies would represent "added-value" that the methodologies bring to the common elements, and should be "componentized" into modular features. The small granularity of features allows them to be combined into the common elements in a flexible manner. By conforming to the generic agent model in the common elements, we expect the semantics of the optional features to remain consistent.

---

* Michael Winikoff is supported by the Australian Research Council and Agent Oriented Software Pty. Ltd.

F. Giunchiglia et al. (Eds.): AOSE 2002, LNCS 2585, pp. 198–209, 2003.

As a step towards standardizing methodologies, we investigate two in detail. Prometheus and ROADMAP [10, 5] have rather different aims. Prometheus focuses on building agents using BDI platforms [12] and on providing explicit and detailed processes and deliverables suitable for use by industry practitioners with limited agent experience, or by undergraduate students. ROADMAP focuses on building open systems [7, 13, 16] and emphasizes the societal aspects of an agent system. Key concepts in ROADMAP are roles and environmental zones. These concepts are used to model and establish trust in open organizations of agents.

We introduce the two methodologies and discuss their respective applicability in Sections 2 and 3. We then identify a set of common modeling elements in Section 4 and show how both ROADMAP and Prometheus can be seen as adding to the common elements in Sections 5 and 6. An illustrating example is presented in Section 7. Section 8 outlines future work and concludes.

2   Prometheus

The Prometheus[1] methodology is a detailed and complete ("start-to-end") process for specifying, designing, and implementing intelligent agent systems, which has been developed over the last few years in collaboration with Agent Oriented Software[2] (A company which markets the agent development software platform JACK™ [2], as well as agent solutions). The goal in developing Prometheus is to have a process with defined deliverables, which can be taught to industry practitioners and undergraduate students who do not have a background in agents, and which they can use to develop intelligent agent systems.

The methodology consists of three phases: system specification, architectural design, and detailed design, as shown in Figure 1. The following description of the phases and deliverables is necessarily brief, for more information see [10].

System Specification: Actions and percepts define the interface between agents and the environment in which they are situated. Functionalities describe in a broader sense what the system should do (e.g. *"the robot will try to maintain an awareness of ball position"*). In this phase actions, percepts and functionalities are identified and specified. Use case scenarios are created to provide a more holistic view of the interaction between actions, percepts and functionalities.

Architectural Design: The major decision to be made during the architectural design is which agents should exist within the system, and what functionalities they should have. The artifacts of the previous phase are analyzed to suggest possible designs, which are evaluated according to the traditional software engineering criteria of cohesion and coupling.

---

[1] Prometheus was the wisest Titan. His name means "forethought" and he was able to foretell the future. Prometheus is known as the protector and benefactor of man. He gave mankind a number of gifts including fire. (*http://www.greekmythology.com/*)

[2] http://www.agent-software.com

During this stage of the design it is important to identify the events (significant occurrences) that the agent will respond to. Agent messages are also identified, forming the interface between agents. At this point interaction protocols are specified based on interaction diagrams (which in turn are based on use cases). If there are to be any shared data objects in the system, these should also be identified at this stage.

The system overview diagram ties together the agents, events and shared data objects. It is arguably the single most important artifact of the entire design process, although it cannot be understood fully in isolation.

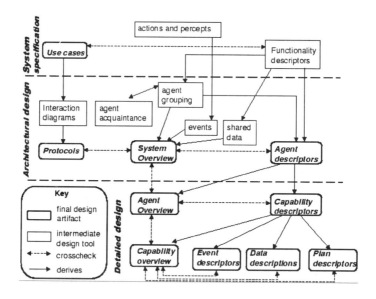

Fig. 1. Overview of 3 Phases in Prometheus

Detailed Design: Detailed design focuses on developing the internal structure of each of the agents and how it will achieve its tasks within the system. The focus is on defining capabilities (modules within the agent), in terms of internal events, plans and detailed data structures.

Because design in Prometheus is oriented towards systems of *intelligent* agents, each agent may well be quite complex, with a number of interacting responsibilities, and an ability to fulfil these responsibilities in a variety of ways. Capabilities can be nested which allows for arbitrarily many layers within the detailed design, in order to achieve an understandable complexity at each level.

Applicability: Prometheus supports the engineering of conventional closed systems with controlled and trusted agents. It specifically supports the BDI framework, and focuses on functionalities. Its concrete nature and detailed models and processes allow easy transition from the conventional OOSE approaches and make it very suitable for conventional applications such as an intelligent web server.

However, it lacks support for advanced properties for agent systems, such as openness and is not suitable for systems requiring these properties.

3   ROADMAP

The ROADMAP[3] methodology aims to support the engineering of large-scale open systems. It extends the Gaia methodology [15] by introducing use-cases for requirements gathering, explicit models of the agent environment and the domain knowledge, and an interaction model based on AUML interaction diagrams [8].

The original Gaia role model is also extended with a dynamic role hierarchy. This role hierarchy is carried into design and will have a run-time realization, allowing social aspects to be explicitly modeled, reasoned about and modified at run-time.

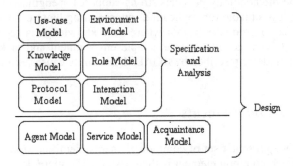

Fig. 2. Overview of ROADMAP

ROADMAP promotes the view of software systems as computational organizations. Agents in a system are similar to individuals in a human organization, while the roles in ROADMAP encapsulate regulations, processes, responsibilities and team roles by which individuals function within a human organization. They specify, support and constraint an agent's behaviors in the organization. When the expected behaviors in the organization are explicitly represented at run-time, agents can verify each other's behavior, and misbehaving agents can be identified, removed or replaced.

A useful level of trust can be established when new agents enter the system. If the new agent has the appropriate knowledge, and behaves according to its role in the correct environment zone, then the other agents in the organization can trust this agent to act to achieve the overall goal of the organization.

The relationship between roles and agents is similar to the relationship between interfaces and objects in an OO approach. Like interfaces, roles provide an abstract model of the system above concrete implementation of functionalities. However, unlike interfaces, roles can be changed at run-time given the correct authorization. Instead of an immutable contract of behavior, roles should be considered as a variable-term agreement of behavior that can be reasoned about and changed. This difference allows a computing organization modeled by roles to be more flexible.

For more information on ROADMAP, please see [5].

The Development Process: The ROADMAP methodology encourages an iterative approach and expects details of the models to be filled in when applicable. During the

---

[3] This is the acronym for Role-Oriented Analysis and Design for Multi-Agent Programming

analysis phase, the six analysis models are created to allow conceptualization of the system as an organization. During the design phase, the initial conceptualization of the system is optimized for the chosen quality goals, such as performance. The original models are modified and refined to reflect the design decisions. In addition, three new design models are created to populate the updated organization with member agents.

Applicability: Before adopting our feature-based approach, ROADMAP prescribes rich models to explicitly deal with roles of agents, the environment and knowledge in the system. The methodology provides strong support for engineering complex open systems, but is less suitable for applications not requiring these properties. Consider a stand-alone desktop productivity tool where little knowledge is required outside its functionalities. Given its static nature, simple environment and lack of knowledge, creating all the models prescribed by ROADMAP simply causes extra overhead.

4   The Common Elements

In this section we present a set of common elements identified from Prometheus and ROADMAP. Each common element is then described in more detail. The analysis to derive the common elements is straightforward and omitted here.

Overview

The common elements are independent of the implementation architecture and support analysis and architecture design of the system. It consists of six basic models as depicted in Figure 3. During the analysis stage, the models are created to conceptualize and document the system requirements. During the architecture design stage, the same models are refined and optimized for the given quality goals. During these two stages, agents are considered as black boxes. At the end of the architecture design phase, an implementation architecture, such as the BDI architecture, is chosen for each agent.

The common elements do not support detailed design, and rely on optional features from other architecture-dependent methodologies to fill the gap. In Figure 3, features derived from the Prometheus methodology are available to support the design of agent internals with BDI constructs.

The ROADMAP features are architecture-independent and can be added to the common elements to facilitate analysis and high-level design. Each feature can be introduced into a few models in the common elements, forming a thread of related additions to support a given quality goal.

The Common Elements

The common elements are organized as the following models:

1. The Use-case Model is adapted from the conventional OO use-case model [1, 9]. It contains graphical use-case diagrams and text scenarios. The main difference is that agents in the system are depicted. Figure 4 shows an example.

2. The Environment Interface Model lists and describes the percepts and actions possible in the environment of the agents.
3. The Agent Model lists agent classes, the services they provide, and the implementation paradigm chosen for them. This is similar to the class model in conventional OO approaches.
4. The Service Model contains basic descriptions, such as input, output and the processing, for each service in the system
5. The Acquaintance Model is a directed graph between agent types. An arc in the graph represents the existence of a communication link allowing messages to be sent. The purpose is to allow the designer to visualize the degree of coupling between agents. In this light, details such as message types and orders are ignored.
6. The Interaction Model contains sequence diagrams as proposed in AUML.

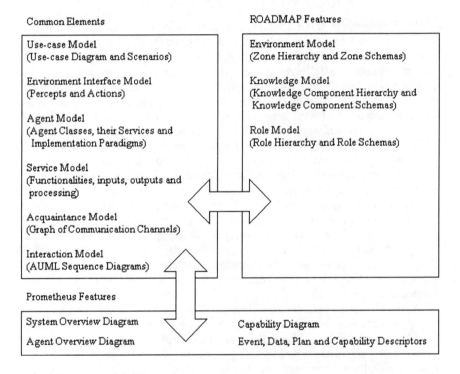

Fig. 3. Overview of the common elements and optional features from Prometheus and ROADMAP

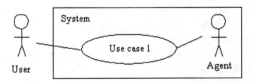

Fig. 4. An example use case diagram

Summary
The models in the common elements are designed to be simple and closely related to conventional OO models for two reasons. It allows developers without background in agent research to easily utilize the technology.

It also reduces the overhead from unused advanced features. For systems requiring low level of agency, the cost of development with the common elements is that similar to with OO methodologies. When additional agent properties are required, our approach enables the common elements to be consistently updated with given features. This enables a smooth transition to model different levels of intelligence and agency.

5   The Optional Features from ROADMAP

ROADMAP introduces three additional features to complement the common elements. They model environmental zones, domain knowledge and the roles in the system.

1. The environment model replaces the original environment interface model in the common elements. Instead of a uniform space, the environment can now be modeled in zones. The environment model contains a hierarchy of zones in the environment, and a set of zone schema to describe each zone in the hierarchy. The zone hierarchy is similar to an OO class hierarchy and uses inheritance and aggregation to relate zones and the objects in zones. See Figure 5 for an example.

   Percepts and actions are now modeled as read and write methods of objects in the zone controllable by the agents. Static objects model entities in the zone whose existence is known to the agents, but no direct interaction exists.

   Zones can be added to the use-case model, the agent model, the acquaintance model and the interaction model. Please see Figure 6 for an example use-case diagram and Figure 7 for an example interaction diagram.

2. The knowledge model formalizes the knowledge aspect of the system. By abstracting knowledge out of functionalities, we aim to facilitate sharing and re-using of knowledge. It will also encourage the system to be designed and implemented at a higher level.

   A knowledge component is a coherent block of knowledge. The knowledge model consists of a knowledge component hierarchy, and a set of schema for each knowledge component. Knowledge components can be added into the use-case model, where required knowledge components to achieve the scenarios are identified. Knowledge components can also be assigned to roles, to model knowledge distribution in the organization.

3. The role model allows the developer to express an abstract framework of the organization according to which its member agents behave. The role model consists of a role hierarchy and a set of role schemas for each role in the hierarchy. The roles define expected behaviors of the agents and provide verification services to any authorized agents at run-time.

   The agent model can include a list of roles taken by each agent. Agents interacting through roles can also be modeled in the use-case model, the acquaintance model and the interaction model. Please see Figures 6 and 7 for examples of roles in the use-case model and interaction model.

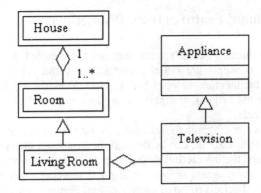

Fig. 5. An example of Zone Hierarchy with Objects

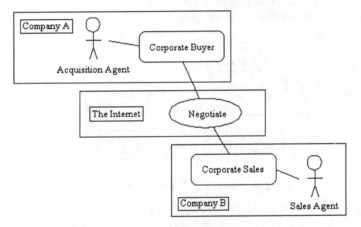

Fig. 6. An Example of a Use-case diagram showing Roles and Zones

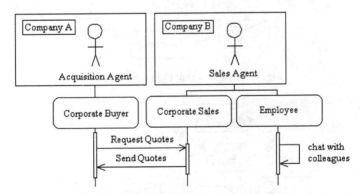

Fig. 7. An Example of an Interaction Diagram with Roles and Zones

6   The Optional Features from Prometheus

Prometheus introduces a set of related features for detailed design using BDI constructs. The key concepts are beliefs, events, plans and capabilities as outlined in Section 2. The architecture-independent models from the common elements were largely based on the original Prometheus models and can be refined directly to the BDI oriented models.

1. System overview diagram shows agents in the system and the events they send to each other. This diagram can be derived directly from the common element use-case model and the interaction model. Figure 8 shows an example.
2. Agent overview diagram shows the internal working of an agent as interacting capabilities and beliefs through event passing. Figure 9 shows an example.
3. Capability diagram shows the internal working of a capability as interacting plans through event passing. Figure 10 shows an example.
4. In addition to the above diagrams, Prometheus also defines descriptors for events, data, plans and capabilities in the system.

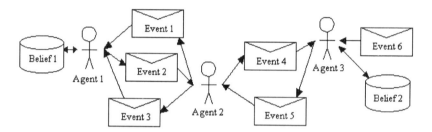

Fig. 8. Example System Overview Diagram

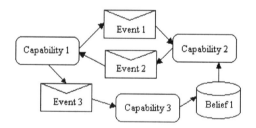

Fig. 9. Example Agent Overview Diagram

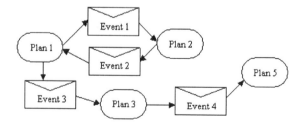

Fig. 10. Example Capability Overview Diagram

7 Illustrating Example: Extending an Intelligent Personal Assistant

We illustrate our proposed feature-based approach by a scenario. Consider a business attempting to boost employee productivity by providing an intelligent personal assistant. The assistant allows the users to communicate via instant messaging, e-mail, voice conversation and file sharing. It will also allow the users to publish and manage their timetables, and allow appointments to be made online.

Developers in the company are not familiar with the agent paradigm and used the common elements to model the functionalities. At the end of the architecture phase the BDI architecture is chosen for the implementation. The optional features derived from Prometheus are used to create the detailed design and translate easily into Jack code.

The prototype was a success and the company decides to integrate more aspects of its operation into the Personal Assistant. To accommodate the richer requirements, the development team extends the common elements with optional features derived from ROADMAP.

The employees want access to the Personal Assistant at home, from their PDAs and mobile phones. They also request integration of the Personal Assistant to the infrastructures, ie, task tracking, of various projects and departments they are involved in. Suppliers and clients of the company also requested to be included in the network. Environment zones and related features are therefore added into the development methodology to model the security and access control of various access locations and modes. Roles are used to model employee involvement in projects and departments. By structuring the system as an agent organization, the system can be modified and extended easily.

The knowledge modeling thread is also introduced to abstract domain knowledge out of functionalities. Business rules in projects and departments can then be shared and re-used.

The original analysis and design models were consistently extended with the optional features to handle the new requirements. The overhead to port project artifacts from Prometheus to ROADMAP is avoided by the use of common elements. The feature-based approach to build flexible methodologies significantly reduced the development risks in this example.

8 Conclusion and Future Work

We expect future software to require in addition to traditional quality goals such as performance, security or scalability, a new set of less precise quality goals such as privacy, politeness and good taste. These quality goals arise from our increasing reliance on software to decide and act on our behalf.

The engineering of these quality goals requires new methods. For example, we might need to analyze the distribution of knowledge in the system and answer questions like: does any agent have unnecessary knowledge that can be abused? What do we do to agents who know too much?

It is worth noting that in large-scale systems, the engineering of quality goals is mainly required on particular parts of the system. For example, politeness is important at the user interface. It is most cost effective to focus the engineering effort locally to the appropriate module, instead of the entire system.

The feature-based approach allows new techniques to be deployed into projects consistently, and applied accurately to the part of the system requiring the effort. The common elements could model the functionalities of the entire system, and form a foundation for specialized features to be added. The optional feature would support the engineering of quality goals important to local modules. For example, features supporting the engineering of politeness only need to be applied to models concerning the user interface.

In this paper we described our experience in merging two existing methodologies, Prometheus and ROADMAP. We presented a useful approach to isolate common elements from methodologies, and componentize the remainders of the methodologies into complementary features. We described the actual common elements and features obtained from applying this approach to Prometheus and ROADMAP, and illustrate the usefulness of this approach with an example.

In future we aim to formalize and standardize the agent model underlying the merged methodologies. The standard agent model could allow other methodologies to be componentized and merged with consistent semantics.

References

1. Booch, G. Object-Oriented Analysis and Design (2nd edition). Addison-Wesley: Reading, MA, 1994.
2. Busetta, P., Ronnquist, R., Hodgson, A and Lucas, A, Jack Intelligent Agents – Components for Intelligent Agents in Java. Agent Oriented Software Pty. Ltd, Technical Report tr9901, 1999. http://www.agent-software.com
3. DeLoach, S., Analysis and Design using MaSe and agentTool, Proceedings of the 12th Midwest Artificial Intelligence and Cognitive Science Conference (MAICS 2002), 2001.
4. Iglesias, C., Garijo, M., and Gonzalez, J. A Survey of Agent-Oriented Methodologies. In Intelligent Agents V - Proceedings of the Fifth International Workshop on Agent Theories, Architectures, and Languages (ATAL-98), Lecture Notes in Artificial Intelligence. Springer-Verlag, Heidelberg. 1999
5. Juan, T., Pearce, A. and Sterling, L., Extending the Gaia Methodology for Complex Open Systems, Proceedings of the First International Joint Conference on Autonomous Agents and Multi-Agent Systems (AAMAS), p3-10, Bologna, Italy, July 2002.
6. Kinny, D., Georgeff, M. and Rao, A., A Methodology and Modeling technique for systems of BDI agents. Proceedings of the 7th European workshop on modeling autonomous agents in a multi-agent world, LNCS 1038, p56-71, Springer-Verlag, Berlin Germany1996
7. Ladaga, R., Active Software, in Self-Adaptive Software, P. Robertson, H. Shrobe, and R. Lagada, Editors. 2000, Springer-Verlag: New York, NY. P.11-26
8. Odell, J., Parunak, H. and Bauer, B., Extending UML for agents. In the Proceedings of the Agent-Oriented Information System Workshop at the 17th National Conference on Artificial Intelligence, 2000.
9. OMG. OMG Unified Modeling Language Specification. 1999 http://www.rational.com/media/uml/post.pdf
10. Padgham, L. and Winikoff, M., Prometheus: A Methodology for Developing Intelligent Agents, Proceedings of the Third International Workshop on Agent-Oriented Software Engineering, at AAMAS 2002. July, 2002, Bologna, Italy.

11. Perini, A., Bresciani, P., Giunchiglia, F., Giorgini, P and Mylopoulos, J., A knowledge level software engineering methodology for agent oriented programming. Proceedings of Autonomous Agents, Montreal CA, 2001.
12. Rao, A. and Georgeff, M, BDI-agents: from theory to practice, Proceedings of the First Intl. Conference on Multiagent Systems, San Francisco, 1995.
13. Robertson, P., R. Ladaga, and H.Shrode, Introduction: The First International Workshop on Self-Adaptive Software, in Self-Adaptive Software, P.Robertson, H.Shrobe, and R. Ladaga, (eds). 2000, Springer-Verlag: New York, NY. P.11-26
14. Wooldridge, M. and Ciancarini, P. Agent-Oriented Software Engineering: The State of the Art. In Agent-Oriented Software Engineering. Ciancarini, P. and Wooldridge, M. (eds), Springer-Verlag Lecture Notes in AI Volume 1957, 2001.
15. Wooldridge, M., Jennings, N. and Kinny, D. The Gaia Methodology for Agent-Oriented Analysis and Design. Journal of Autonomous Agents and Multi-Agent Systems 3 (3). 2000, 285-312.
16. Yokote, Y. The Apertos Reflective Operating System: The Concept and its Implementation, Proc. OOPSLA '92, ACM, 1992, p414-434.

Agent-Oriented Software Technologies: Flaws and Remedies

Jörg P. Müller and Bernhard Bauer

Siemens AG, Corporate Technology, Intelligent Autonomous Systems
Otto-Hahn-Ring 6, D-81730 Munich, Germany
{joerg.p.mueller,bernhard.bauer}@siemens.com
www.ct.siemens.com

Abstract. Agent-Oriented Software Technologies, i.e., the engineering of agent systems, agent languages, development tools, and methodologies, are an active research area. However, the practical influence of AOST on what we call mainstream software technologies is very small. As of today, trends in software technologies are not made by agent researchers or companies, but rather by Microsoft and Sun Microsystems. In this position paper, we investigate basic questions: Why are agent-oriented software technologies currently not fully exploiting their potential? Is there another "CORBA syndrome" lurking behind the next corner? And what can we do to better position agent software technologies in the market, and to increase their practical impact?

We are convinced that the most severe problems in today's agent-oriented software technologies and in the way we market them are due to a few basic flaws. In this paper, we will try to identify and discuss these flaws. However, it is also our firm belief that agent-oriented software technologies have a huge potential, and that there are remedies that can be applied to cure the flaws. We shall also identify some of these potential remedies and formulate them as recommendations.

1 Introduction

A (software) agent is a computer system, situated in some environment, that is capable of flexible autonomous actions in order to achieve its design objectives [28]. Since the emergence of multiagent systems and intelligent agents as a research topic in the late 1980s, research on agent technologies has steadily grown, and developed into various strands of research. One of these research strands which emerged towards the end of the 1990s, is called agent-oriented software engineering (AOSE). Like the term *agent* itself, the scope of AOSE is fuzzy and subsumes a variety of approaches to investigate how existing software engineering approaches could be improved by introducing agent concepts, but also what software engineering concepts are required to support the design and development of (multi-)agent systems. What AOSE is about is well illustrated by a quote from the call for papers of the International Workshop on Agent-Oriented Software Engineering [6]:

F. Giunchiglia et al. (Eds.): AOSE 2002, LNCS 2585, pp. 210–227, 2003.

Just as we can understand many systems as being composed of essentially passive objects, which have state, and upon which we can perform operations, so we can understand many others as being made up of interacting, semi-autonomous agents.

Agent-oriented software engineering comprises a number of issues, including core aspects of software engineering (requirements engineering, analysis and design, development, testing and integration, lifecycle models), but also accompanying technologies such as specific programming languages for agents and agent systems, Integrated Development Environments (IDEs) and tools, as well as methodologies for agent development. Throughout this paper, we shall use the term *Agent-Oriented Software Technologies (AOST)* to denote the union of these topics, including core software engineering, languages, tools, and methodologies.

It appears that Agent-Oriented Software Technologies are an active research area. However, it is also undeniable that today the practical influence of AOST on what we call mainstream software technologies (MSST) is very small. As of today, trends in software technologies are not made by agent researchers, but rather by the ones of Sun Microsystems and Microsoft. Figure 1 provides a strongly simplifying illustration of the current status of AOST. Agent researchers and providers of agent-oriented software technologies are competing with Mainstream Software Technologies for a scarce and difficult to obtain resource: the attention of professional software architects and application developers. A simple comparison, e.g., of the number of downloads of one of the most successful agent platforms, the Java Agent Development Framework (JADE, [26]), with those achieved by Sun's J2SE leaves no doubt in who is ruling this market today: JADE has achieved some ten thousand downloads (mostly by universities and research institutes), while Java has a world-wide circulation with millions of downloads, in particular by industrial companies.

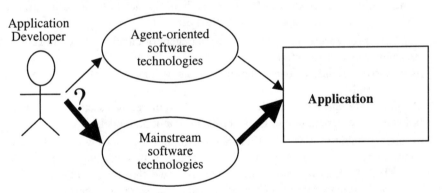

Fig. 1. The software technologies market

This situation may remind some of those agent researchers who have been in the field for a while to the situation in the mid-nineties, which we call the *CORBA syndrome*: at that time, mainstream software technologies such as CORBA started offering software infrastructures that promised software interoperability and dynamic discovery of services (e.g., Trading Services), leaving some agent researchers wondering and angry that (at least from their perspective) some of the good ideas originating from agent technology were taken up from mainstream software technologies without giving the (multi-)agent community credit.

In this paper, we shall investigate some basic questions: Why are agent-oriented software technologies currently not fully exploiting their potential? Is there another CORBA syndrome lurking behind the next corner? And what can we do to better position agent-oriented software technologies in the market, and to increase their practical impact?

We are convinced that the problems in today's agent-oriented software technologies and in the way we market them are due to a few basic flaws. In this paper, we will try to identify and discuss these flaws. However, it is also our firm belief that agent-oriented software technologies have a huge potential, and that there are remedies that can be applied to cure the flaws. We shall also identify some of these potential remedies and formulate them as recommendations.

This paper is structured as follows: In Section 2, we describe the context of agent-oriented software technologies. In Section 3, we investigate the structure of today's' research on AOST. Section 4 provides a critical analysis of the relationship between AOST and mainstream software technologies. In Section 5, we identify what we believe are the essential flaws of AOST with respect to application development. Finally, Section 6 concludes and gives some basic recommendations how the position and impact of AOST can be improved.

2   Setting the Context

Agent technology interconnects various research disciplines [30]; in particular, agents are closely related to and appear in the context of:

- *software engineering*, in particular viewing agent oriented software development as a new way of abstraction;
- *distributed systems*, in particular multi-agent systems are inherently distributed systems; and
- *artificial intelligence*, in particular models for autonomy based on planning and knowledge representation (e.g., belief-desire-intention models)

Thus, and as stated in [28], agent technology implies a new view on understanding and modelling as well as implementing complex, self-organising, and distributed systems. Therefore, as we said in the introduction, we chose the term *agent-oriented software technologies* to subsume agent-oriented software engineering as a whole, including tools, methodologies, platforms, and languages.

We want to clarify this context by using a model originally proposed by Douglas Engelbart and adapted in [37] to agent technology (shown in Figure 2).

The *A-Level* provides the perspective of the application developer, i.e. the end-users of agent technology, who usually are not agent experts and mostly unfamiliar with the latest agent technologies. However, these users are often accustomed to and sometimes highly skilled in state-of-the-art software technologies like J2SE/EE,

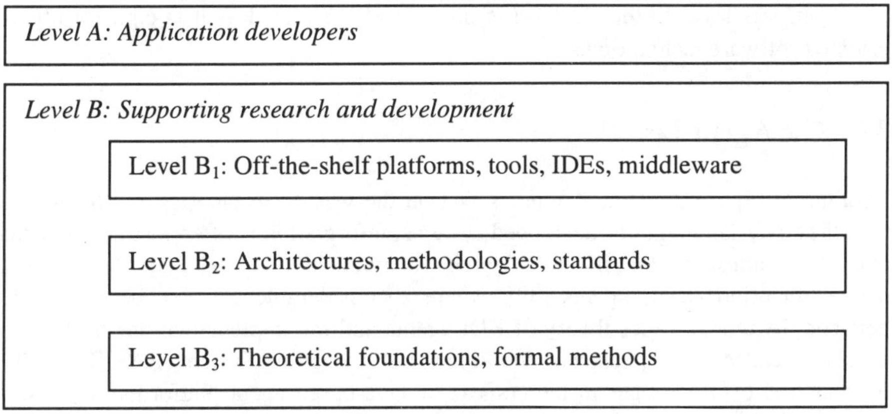

Level A: Application developers

Level B: Supporting research and development

> Level B$_1$: Off-the-shelf platforms, tools, IDEs, middleware

> Level B$_2$: Architectures, methodologies, standards

> Level B$_3$: Theoretical foundations, formal methods

Fig. 2. A layered view of software technologies

WebServices and XML standards[1]. In any case, they recognise and appreciate tools that help them do their job more quickly or more conveniently.

The *B-Level* sums up the support that Software Technologies can provide the *A-Level* users. It is divided into three sub-levels:

The *B1-Level* provides off-the-shelf platforms and components, integrated development environments, test-beds, and other tools (e.g. for debugging or system analysis and design), but also infrastructures and middleware services, applied by the *A-Level* end-users. However in the case of AOST, commercially usable platforms and integrated development environments are still rare (see e.g. [2] for an overview of available platforms and [4] for a wider overview of agent related software); the market for programming languages and development environments is small and developing such tools is therefore unattractive from a business perspective (i.e., unprofitable). Hence, a common business model for agent platform providers (like Tryllian [46] or LivingSystems [34]) is to market applications built using their platforms.

The *B2-Level* sub-services the *B1-Level* with architectures, abstractions, methodologies, and standards. This is another point where agent technology misses out. At the moment, and very much alike in the early phases of object-oriented programming, no unified underlying formal model exists (since there is not even a unified shared notion of an agent); also there is no unified architectural approach to building agent platforms and agent applications. Methodologies exist (see e.g., [6], [30]) but refer to different underlying agent models, are hence not standardised and usually not supported by good-quality tools.

Finally, the *B3-Level* comprises theories, formal frameworks, and methods. In this area a considerable amount of research has been done and good results were accomplished, e.g., as documented by the ATAL workshop series [3]. However the transi-

---

[1] Note, that this strongly depends on the market sector. In some areas of industry, application developers are working on mainframes or developing mostly assembler, COBOL or C/C++ code.

tion from this level to the *B2 level* is not as well-described as it is e.g., for object-oriented software technologies.

3   The Agent Level

Looking at Figure 2 again, it appears that on the way from theories and formal approaches over languages to developed systems, information is often lost in a way that is hard to control and that is – to a degree – unavoidable. A good example are belief, desire, intention (BDI) agents [39], where a considerable gap can be observed - between the modal logics theory of BDI agents and the implementations of this theory, such as dMars [17] based on the Procedural Reasoning System (PRS, [24]). This mismatch is even stronger in the context of Java-based agent platforms, like JADE [26] or FIPA-OS [22], where the underlying BDI theory is maintained (if at all) merely at a folk-psychological level. Similar observations hold for reactive agent architectures (see [49] for an overview) that are being implemented e.g., using rules engines such as JESS [29]. JESS, however, is connected with Java-based platforms without defining formal semantics concerning internal state of the agent and its external behavior. So there is an easily recognizable (and undisputed) gap between theories and implementations of languages (model-theoretical and operational semantics) as well as platforms. This fact alone is not peculiar to agents; similar is true e.g., for object-oriented languages. There is to our knowledge no complete formal semantics for Java and all its packages (although there is active research on this topic, see e.g. [5][23]).

However, since it is argued that the major benefit of agent technology stems from the ability to describe and use the semantics of communication, and from describing complex systems by using concepts such as beliefs, desire and intentions, allegedly the consequence of the gap between theories and platforms is critical for AOST than it is for e.g., object-oriented software technologies. One could argue that at least these parts of agent technology that create the unique selling point of this software technology should be provided in a clean and formally rigid way. This mismatch becomes obvious when looking at the FIPA 97 specification part 2 on Agent Communication Languages[2] [21] there, a formal semantics is given for the library of communicative acts; however, when it comes to the specification of interaction protocols, the same document states ([21], p. 50):

A designer of agent systems has the choice to make the agents sufficiently aware of the meanings of the messages, and the goals, beliefs and other mental attitudes the agent possesses, [...]. This, however, places a heavy burden of capability and complexity on the agent implementation, [...]. An alternative, and very pragmatic, view is to pre-specify the protocols, so that a simpler agent implementation can nevertheless engage in meaningful conversation with other agents, simply by carefully following the known protocol.

In addition the implementation of the communicative acts as well as the interaction protocols are pragmatic (i.e., they do not rigidly follow a formal model) in all cur-

---

[2] Note, that no major revisions were made on this topic since 1997.

rently available FIPA-compliant agent platforms. Another lapse in the FIPA specification is between the semantics of communicative acts on the one hand and the agent architecture on the other: The basis for the formal semantics of communicative acts is a modal logic model similar to the one used for BDI; in particular the definition of the semantics of the communicative act implies some kind of BDI architecture of the agent. However, FIPA leaves the choice to the platform providers which kind of agent architecture (e.g. BDI, re-active, hybrid) their platform supports. Therefore, the semantics of communicative acts imposes constraints on the agent architecture, which are not enforced by the standard.

4   AOST and Mainstream Software Technologies

As Figure 1 illustrates, the main purpose of agent-oriented and mainstream software technologies is to support application developers in writing applications. Hence it is natural that AOST and MSST have certain challenges and solutions in common, and that they compete in the market for acceptance.

4.1   Infrastructure and Middleware

A major flaw of today's AOST is that the actual usefulness of introducing agent concepts in software engineering (defined e.g., by a cost-benefit ratio) is not sufficiently clear. To one end, there is a strong overlap between the functionality supported by work done in AOSE and that provided by mainstream programming. For instance, considerably-sized agent infrastructure projects over the past ten years spent considerable efforts to enable two computers to exchange character sequences.

This negative impact of this tendency is increased from a different direction, i.e., by the convergence of distributed and object-oriented middleware. Many features that the agent community believed to be agent-specific were simply done quicker, better, and more professionally by the ones of Sun, Microsoft, Rational, or OMG. Examples are the different directory services, like LDAP [33] and UDDI [47], the development of middleware supporting distributed programming like CORBA [12] or Java RMI and last but not least the recent hype of WebServices [48] (with the implementations .net [1] and SunOne [45]). For agent researchers, focusing on the platform development and not building agents to extend existing standards and technologies has the inherent risk of running into another CORBA syndrome, i.e., for agents to stay an experimental science or become a niche market – a fate similar to that of functional or logic programming. This concern holds in particular for proprietary agent specific programming languages like APRIL [7] and Congolog [31]. These new programming languages only have a chance to take off if a large player will push them, like it was the case for Java with the same concepts as Smalltalk, but with a better marketing strategy and the right language at the right time. More likely though, and as it was witnessed in the case of functional and logic programming, the concepts underlying these agent-based programming languages will be taken up by large players in the more distant future.

Clearly, agent technology is (or: should be) more than middleware and infrastructure, but provides additional functionality and a valuable abstraction layer on top of these mainstream technologies.

From the multi-agent system point of view, the abstraction layer is very much compliant with the view taken by the Web Services approach, in that different (web) service provider agents can be used by different requester agents in a distributed environment. The crucial add-on of agent technology to this web services view, the capability of flexible interaction, is discussed in detail later on.

From the point of view of an individual service / agent, there is an additional abstraction process: describing the behavior of an agent based on goals, tasks and autonomous and rational decision-making, based on techniques such as planning, decision theory, game theory, and machine learning. This abstraction layer should be taken up by the agent community and has to be integrated in or build on top of mainstream technologies to be part of them in the future. We are aware that underlying a strict formal model to an agent is likely to put constraints on the freedom of the developer. For instance, many developers find the threaded behavior model underlying JADE [26] an awkward restriction rather than a helpful tool. However, if and when we argue that these concepts are the unique selling point for agent technology, we need to tackle these issues and find a way to offer agent developers access to advanced agent architectures and concepts without limiting their choice where to use them and where not. A possible starting point to overcome the coding effort for JADE behaviors is the approach presented by Martin L. Griss et al. in this volume, where JADE behaviors are generated from hierarchical state diagrams.

4.2   Benefits of Agent Technologies

We strongly believe that to be successful in the software technologies market, agent-oriented software technologies will need to focus on the essentials of agency and to clearly market themselves based on this added value. In our view, agent technology has an opportunity to prove its unique selling point in four major directions:

Expressing and Exploiting Semantics

The usage of semantics, where agent scientist have done respectable work, in contrast to pure syntax, as it is the standard today, combined with mainstream approaches from the SemanticWeb initiative, like DAML-OIL [14] or DAML-S [15], will bring additional benefit to the customers, thus resulting in increased funding for research on this topic, focusing on two aspects in particular:

- *Ontologies* and in particular the definition, maintenance and usage of large ontologies is a hot topic. Starting points could be standards from the W3C consortium like RDF(S) [40] and DAML-OIL which are already applied in the context of agent platforms (for instance, the JADE agent platform supports the import of ontologies defined using the ontology tool Protégé [38]).
- Self-organization, self-description and self-configuration of software based on semantic information of the agent itself, its environment and the services available

in its surroundings are other key functions that agents can provide to main stream technologies. This insight is the main background behind what IBM calls *autonomic computing* [25]. First steps in this direction are undertaken by DAML-S allowing a semantic description of the interfaces of software components.

Enabling Flexible Interaction

Flexible interaction within multi-agent systems is mainly based on communicative acts and interaction protocols. They are the basis for negotiation and the development of specific negotiation strategies, but also for the usage of market mechanisms for dynamic resource scheduling. In this context an open issue is the interworking of loosely coupled agents.

- *Communicative acts* or *speech acts* and the *interaction protocols* that are created on top of them have to be defined with a pragmatic semantics for advanced communication between distributed services or agents. A possible starting point could be WSCL [50]. WSCL allows us to define the abstract interfaces of web services, i.e., the business level conversations or public processes supported by a web service. In its current version, it defines a number of "primitive" speech acts called *interactions*, namely *Send* (the service sends out an outbound document); *Receive* (the service receives an inbound document); *SendReceive* (the service sends out an outbound document and then expects to receive an inbound document in reply); *ReceiveSend* (the service receives an inbound document and then sends out an outbound document); and *Empty*.
- Based on the interaction protocols negotiations can be established, e.g. in electronic market places or for optimization purposes. Specification and adaptation of negotiation strategies are fields that have long been studied in the agent domain and that can be usefully propagated to electronic market places or supply chain management. The necessity of distributed problem solving and the relationship and benefit compared with central solutions have to be outlined and detailed. One large benefit of market-based resource management and optimization is that it does not require global knowledge but can work with reasonable results even under the assumption of local, incomplete and possibly inconsistent knowledge. This setting seems to accurately describe the problem of optimizing virtual organizations. However, given what has been said before, it should be clear that research activities in this area should build on generic standards and business standards like BizTalk [10], ebXML [19], or RosettaNet [42].
- The ability of components designed by different designers to find a common way to communicate meaningfully is hard to achieve. Two aspects have to be considered, namely the formal description of the systems to allow an automatic interworking and combination of the components (e.g. using DAML-S) and the specification of system to allow other developers to use existing components, comparable with a semantically grounded version of UDDI.
- The ability of ensuring global properties of loosely coupled systems is a key property of multi-agent systems when it comes to understanding and designing decentralized, self-organized systems that share a common environment and where

certain global constraints and global welfare functions need to be enforced. Market mechanisms design is a powerful tool to analyze, design, and build these types of systems.

Expressing, Implementing, and Controlling Autonomy

Autonomy is one of the key features of agents, which need to be filled with life. Doing this includes a number of issues:

- The ability to sense, reason, decide and act in a dynamic environment, e.g. for delegation of routine tasks. This can be achieved by pragmatic knowledge representation, i.e. not developing an agent for arbitrary environments but for specific tasks and services. Using planning and goal-oriented reasoning to allow agents to react to unforeseeable events to some extent constitutes a value-added functionality with comprehensible benefit. Generic components based on standards for e.g. knowledge representation should be easily integratable into existing mainstream software such as libraries for constraint satisfaction.
- The ability to adapt the behavior of a system to its situation. When a situation changes, or the environment of an agent undergoes longer-term changes, the agent should be able to reflect upon its behavior, about causal relationships between its behavior and its environment, and about changes necessary to adapt its behavior to the new settings.
- The ability to make rational decision about actions and courses of action, by assigning utilities to actions or world states, enables an agent to perform well, but also to reflect and recognize opportunities for adaptation or optimization.

Supporting Individualization

We characterize individualization as customization of e.g. services and goods to the needs of a person. Individualization takes into account the specific context or situation of a user and can be applied at different levels.

- *User context:* The needs of a person are situation-aware, i.e. in different situations the user may have different needs, e.g. in a desert a glass of water may seem more appealing to a person than a large amount of money. Based on personal profiles and preferences and adaptation of them, situation awareness can depend on factors, like geographical context (e. g., positioning), social context (am I talking to my friend? my colleague? my boss?), users preferences and roles (e.g. at home/work), process context (e.g. workflows), temporal context (e.g. night / day), physical environment (e.g. raining), organizational context (e.g. chief / assistant), and emotional context (e.g. hungry, happy).
- *Levels of individualization*: Individualization can occur at different levels: At the *service level* (e.g., preferred hotel categories or travel type (like private or business trip) can be taken into consideration to support the customer with the optimal service or information in the current situation). As a special case of service level individualization, the *content* provided through a service can be prepared to match the user's need. The *user interface level* deals with individualization issues, e.g.

depending on the end-user device, preferred user's look and feel, or physical context (e.g., level of noise). The individual handling of tasks and workflows needs easily customizable *processes*. In addition, *infrastructure level* personalization is of interest for several reasons, e.g. paying for a high quality of service may be relevant for commercial use, while cheaper communication channels may be preferred for private usage.

4.3   Bridging the Gap between AOST and MSST – A Proposal

As already stated there is not only a gap between AOST and MSST, but also a large overlap between the two areas. The agent community deals more and more with topics of MSST, like infrastructures, software engineering methodologies for distributed systems, and vice versa, e.g. directory services (e.g. UDDI), some kind of interaction protocols (e.g. WSCL). Thus effort is invested twice.

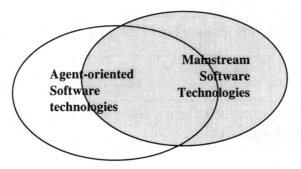

Fig. 3. Overlap between AOST and mainstream software technologies

Therefore we also believe that in order to exploit its potential, AOST needs to establish precise interfaces to mainstream software technologies and build on important standards (like middleware, business, and ontology standards). This will enable agent research not to lose much energy in developing basic technologies and standards, thus re-inventing wheels, but to focus on its unique selling points, i.e., semantics, flexible interaction, and autonomy.

We do believe that these well-defined interfaces need to be created in three directions, as shown in Figure 4: infrastructure and components, system description and specification, knowledge representation and ontologies. Fortunately, for each of these directions, promising standards are available upon which advances in agent technology can build: WebServices, UML, and ontologies. Let us have a closer look at these three aspects:

- *Infrastructure and components*: Based on the WebService infrastructure with directory services and communication channels, new functions could be added to build scalable and smart WebServices based on flexible interaction and autonomy. Based on standards, interaction protocols could be defined and smart components, like planning and learning can be added to present a real add-value.

- *System description and specification*: People in industry are familiar using object oriented analysis and design tools and are not familiar with the latest agent technology. Therefore a starting point is the usage of UML for the specification of agent-based systems, see e.g. [8] for several papers on this topic[3]. However the results are not yet fully convincing and some unification and revisions are necessary, but a migration path is pointed out.
- *Knowledge representation and ontologies*: Looking at current practice in software development the internal object oriented structure, containing to some extend semantic information, are serialized to flat XML structures without semantic information for communication between different systems. This loss of semantics can be overcome with the upcoming SemanticWeb standards, like RDF(S) and DAML-OIL. Using knowledge representation, modeling and reasoning mechanisms can also result in overcoming the bottleneck of standardization of domain specific ontologies, which are time consuming and not fitting the goals of all participants.

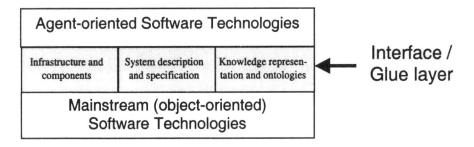

Fig. 4. Providing clear interfaces between AOST and MMST

Note that we do not argue that agent technology should flow into mainstream technologies. But the results, already commercially usable, have to be brought to market by adding it to mainstream technologies. Further research has to be done in variety of directions, see e.g. the AgentLink agent technology roadmap for details [41]. Let us highlight just one aspect that has to be studied in more details: we are still very bad in managing decentralization. More research is necessary in studying interrelationships and dependencies in and between decentralized, loosely coupled systems. While there are some areas which are well-investigated, e.g., market-based interactions (e.g., Sandholm[43]), or coordination (most prominently covered by the work of Lesser [32] and Decker [16]), the link from these theoretical results to practical software engineering is not yet very well explored.

---

[3] A small success story: parts of UML extension, originally developed for agents in the context of the agent standardization FIPA will be part of the upcoming UML 2.0 specification.

5 Building Applications with AOSE

Application areas for agent technology are wide-spread, like e-/m-business (e.g. marketplaces, SCM), industry (e.g. MES, production), consumer sector (e.g. games, smart mobile services), public services (e.g. human resource market, e-democracy), and telecommunication networks (e.g. network management, QoS provisioning). Looking at today's agent-based applications allows us to learn from a handful of existing, more or less successful examples, as well as from a large number of research prototypes that somehow never manage to get to the state of practical usefulness.

For one, it is still very early days talking about flaws of AOST in terms of application development; for the other we argue that it is a marketing issue rather than a technological issue.

One major flaw here is that agent researchers hardly think about how to bring their solutions together with existing IT landscapes. In the previous sections we pointed out how AOST and MSST can fit together. Migration is crucial for the success of agent technology, and protects companies' hardware and software investments. Don't wait until the killer application will be found. Start small and useful.

A second important issue is that a new technology or solution will only succeed if there is some tangible benefit attached to it. I.e., the first thing to worry about when trying to convince a business to take up agent technology is a business plan. An example of a successful commercially deployed agent-based solution is the manufacturing control system of DaimlerChrysler [11][13]. A precondition to success in this case was not to start with technology, but with the commercial and technical problems in a production line. It was only after these aspects had been analyzed when the necessary technologies were identified; then, a business case was set up showing how a double-digit increase in productivity was within reach using the agent-based solution — a convincing argument for managers.

Bringing agent technology to market requires investigating three different issues:

- *Technical issues*: *Hardware migration* can be a critical part of the investment in introducing agent technology. Looking at the DaimlerChrysler example again, it turned out that all the hardware, and in particular the machines for manufacturing the cylinder heads had to be exchanged to flexible CNC machines. Another point is the *operating system migration* (does the agent system run in the considered environment?). For example, in the manufacturing domain, using a Java-based platform was not an option, putting new restrictions on the agent infrastructure. In particular, the aspects of *performance*, *availability*, and *scalability* are success criteria for industrial application of agent technology. Can the agent platform handle 1000 requests in a minute and run throughout 365 days a year with a reliability of 99.9%? At the moment these are severe problems with agent software. Is the agent platform just „*yet another piece of infrastructure*" competing with well-established products?
- *Cultural issues*: The problem of *cultural acceptance* of new technologies for people facing these technologies for a first time must not be neglected. Humans are used to think in specific patterns and have their mentalities and mindsets. Thus

new technologies need to change their mental attitudes to work productive in the new area. Moreover some people are in fear of new techniques. In particular with agents performing tasks in an automated fashion and threatening to organize peoples' schedule the lives, acceptance problems almost seem pre-programmed. No need to say that standard usability levels for software tools and solutions are also valid for agent-based software.

- *Economical issues*: Beyond technical and cultural issues the economic issues have to be considered. The cost of migration must not be underestimated, as already stated in the technical issues. Introducing a complete new hardware infrastructure is expensive and has to be calculated well. The benefit of successful migration can be measured in different ways. The direct (short-term) benefits include e.g. productivity and process efficiency increases, but also downtime decrease, throughput increase, etc. Indirect (longer-term) benefits can result e.g., in increased process or product flexibility. Usually management will be easier accessible to business plans based on direct benefits than on indirect benefits.

In summary, the introduction of agent based applications has to cope with technical, social and cultural as well as economical issues. In particular migrations paths need to be provided to deal with these issues, ensuring a smooth transition of existing applications to agent-based applications.

6   Summary and Recommendations

In this paper, we started by identifying and discussing what we believe are some major flaws of agent oriented software technologies — problems that today prevent AOST from being commercially successful. After describing the context of AOST and showing the structure of today's research on AOST, we gave a critical analysis of the relationship between AOST and mainstream software technologies and pointed out how the gap between both can be overcome. We finished our considerations with an investigation of the essential flaws of AOST with respect to application development. We will finish this paper with some basic recommendations on how the position and impact of AOST can be improved.

Recommendation 1:
Play to your strengths

We believe that the concepts of agent technology will play an important role in the development of the next generation solutions and systems over the next few years. In a nutshell, *agent-oriented software technologies is all about building and managing decentralized systems consisting of intelligent components.* We identified a number of core capabilities that agents can provide in comparison with related software technologies:

- Providing enriched, higher level communication (agent communication languages, based on existing transport encoding and underlying networking protocols, co-ordination of tasks, collaboration based on semantics and ontologies)

- Enabling more intelligent service provision and process management e.g. by personalization and integration of different services to value-added services (service wrapping, brokering, matchmaking, negotiation, auctioning, preference modeling, adaptive behavior by learning mechanisms)
- Dealing with the enlarging amount of information and functions (agent mobility, intelligent knowledge/information management, personalization, presentation)
- Allowing self-organizing of systems and processes (autonomous, flexible and pro-active behavior by planning, scheduling, and learning functionality)

As stated several times throughout this paper the strength of agent technology is based on these items and it would be desirable to see research focus more clearly around them. In this context, emerging standards and technologies must be used and applied within the agent community; no wheels must be re-invented. In particular the results and the strengths of AOST have to be marketed to the MSST community. But consider the second recommendation in this context!

Recommendation 2:
Prove Economic Benefits or Sell Solutions not Technologies

The economic benefits have to be shown to management to keep on attracting funding for technology development. I.e., technology is not the key factor: usually you do not sell technology, but solutions that must have an evident benefit for your customer. Thus the following aspects have to be taken into consideration:

- A good business plan is the key for bringing agent technology to your enterprise, especially in the current general depression in trade and industry. However do not overestimate the usefulness of indirect or deferred savings (e.g., the argument of saving money at a later point in time when introducing new product generations by increased product flexibility) as an argumentation for a corporate decision maker, but show that there is a tangible direct, short-term benefit.
- For several areas ideally fitting agent technology, like mobile commerce, telematics or optimization of processes in virtual enterprises, new business models are necessary for the success of these applications. At the moment the business models for these kinds of applications / solutions are weak and not promising for investors. So when thinking of agents, also think about business models for them.
- Build your business ideas on innovative scenarios and markets and show the applicability and benefit in real-world studies. Do not re-invent Microsoft Exchange when e.g., trying to model personal assistance for appointment scheduling (as one example), but rather analyze the shortcomings of commercial products and find out how the strengths of AOST can best be used (see Recommendation 1).

Recommendation 3:
Provide Migration Paths

In our view a main reason for the lack in industrial take-up for AOST is the absence of migration paths for the implementation of agent-based features, solutions, or products. We cannot hope to establish agent technology radically and from scratch. Rather we need to show industry how they can migrate to agent-based solutions gradually, hence protecting existing investments in hardware, software, and skills. Four important characteristics of industrial software development have to be addressed in this context:

- The scope of industrial software projects is much larger than typical academic research efforts, involving many more people and a higher financial investment across a longer period of time. Thus, collaboration among developers and high quality tools are essential;
- Industrial software development is focused more on preserving existing know-how, setting up development methodologies, and managing the development processes than on tracking the latest agent techniques. Thus, codifying best practice is essential;
- Industrial projects have clear success criteria. Thus, traceability between initial requirements and the final deliverable is essential. In particular the switch to agent technology has to be profitable. (see Recommendation 2).
- Business and technical considerations aside, issues of culture and mentality are key for a successful project. If you do not understand the requirements and specific concerns of users, you are likely to run into problems. This is true in particular if you are developing solutions or products for decision-support or personal assistance. There are plenty of psychological issues involved in providing humans with automated assistance, such as straight fears of being made redundant. While some of these problems are outside of your control, they will affect your work, and they will have a deep effect on whether your work will be a success.

Be aware that migration of agent technology towards applications is the most important factor of the ones we discussed here; very likely, whether you manage migration or not will be ultimately responsible for the success or failure of the solution, product, or system that you build.

Recommendation 4:
Promising Foci of Research

From our view several research areas are of main interest for industry:

- As we stated above (see Recommendation 1), the one main challenge for AOST is dealing with decentralized systems. We still know fairly little about how to deal with decentralization, and basic research on the topic seems in place, i.e. How can these systems be to understood, analyzed, designed, built, tracked and traced, monitored, tested, integrated, migrated, operated, and administered? What is the role of self-organization, self-configuration, and self-management in this context? How can these techniques be instrumentalised e.g., in the way Dorigo et al. [18] instrumentalised the concept of Ant Colony Optimization to solve combinatorial optimization problems?
- The current research activities in the context of the SemanticWeb [9] and in particular, their combination with currently emerging WebServices infrastructure,

should be strengthened. How can the SemanticWeb concepts be applied in real-world application? How can large ontologies be maintained and the interoperability of ontologies be assured? Business ontologies like ebXML or RosettaNet are useful and should be used wherever possible; however, difficult to achieve and practical experience shows that there is a necessity to allow more flexibility in defining data structures and to support their interchange. Closely related with the first bullet is the combination of the semantic web and the web services activities, allowing a flexible finding, matching and interoperation of services on a semantic level. Preliminary results on this topic were presented by Sycara et al. in [36], describing how an ontology-based matchmaker can be implemented on top of the UDDI service directory. A more visionary approach is the autonomic computing initiative of IBM [25].

- A third point where agents can add benefit is in the area of mobile and ubiquitous computing. Context recognition and interpretation in mobile and ad-hoc environments, tracing, tracking, monitoring and analyzing information and supporting the user by routine tasks, are examples of difficult problems that will need to be mastered. Here, the ability to take user or group preferences and profiles into consideration in a situation-aware fashion will be crucial.

Successfully bringing agent technology to market ultimately requires us to produce techniques that reduce the perceived risk inherent in any new technology, by showing the benefit and economic profitability, by presenting the new technology as an incremental extension of known and trusted methods, and by providing explicit engineering tools to support proven methods of technology deployment.

As a final note, we would like to state that the opinions and analysis stated in this paper constitute our subjective view; they are based on our experience of using agent technology in commercial environments. It is the nature of a position paper that readers may agree or disagree, and, by disagreeing, new positions will emerge. In writing this paper, our main hope is to encourage agent researchers think about how to position their work — either by agreeing or by disagreeing with our analyses.

References

1. .net: http://www.microsoft.com/net/
2. Agent Platforms: http://www.agentbuilder.com/AgentTools/commercial.php
3. Agent Theories, Architectures, and Languages (ATAL)- International Workshop Series: http://www.atal.org
4. Agentlink Software Report: http://www.agentlink.org/resources/software-report.html
5. Alves-Foss, J., editor, *Formal Syntax and Semantics of Java*, LNCS 1523, Springer, Berlin, 1999.
6. AOSE 2002: http://www.jamesodell.com/aose2002
7. APRIL: http://sourceforge.net/projects/networkagent/
8. AUML: http://www.auml.org/
9. Berners-Lee, T., Hendler, J., Lassila, O.: *The Semantic Web*. In: Scientific American, Issue 05/01, online available at http://www.sciam.com/2001/0501issue/0501berners-lee.html, 2001.

10. BizTalk: http://www.microsoft.com/biztalk/default.asp
11. Bussmann, S., Schild, K.: *An Agent-based Approach to the Control of Flexible Production Systems.* In: Proc. of the 8th IEEE Int. Conf. on Emergent Technologies and Factory Automation (ETFA 2001), pp.481-488 (Vol.2). Antibes Juan-les-pins, France, 2001.
12. CORBA: http://www.corba.org/
13. DaimlerChrysler Produktion 2000+ Project: http://www.agentlink.org/agents-london/presentations/Daimler Ch.ppt
14. DAML-OIL: http://www.w3.org/TR/daml+oil-reference
15. DAML-S: http://www.daml.org/services/
16. Decker, K.: http://www.cis.udel.edu/~decker/ (Homepage)
17. d'Inverno, M., Kinny, D., Luck, M. and Wooldridge, M.: *A formal specification of dMARS.* In: Intelligent Agents IV: Proceedings of the Fourth International Workshop on Agent Theories, Architectures, and Languages, LNAI 1365, pp. 155-176. Springer, Berlin, 1998.
18. Dorigo, M.: *Ant algorithms solve difficult optimization problems.* in: Advances in Artificial Life, 6th European Conference, ECAL 2001, LNAI 2159, pages 11-22, Springer, Berlin, 2001.
19. ebXML: http://www.ebxml.org/
20. FIPA (Foundation of Physical Intelligent Agents): http://www.fipa.org
21. FIPA 97, part 2: http://www.fipa.org/specs/fipa00003/
22. FIPA-OS: http://fipa-os.sourceforge.net/
23. Formal Semantics for Java: http://www-sop.inria.fr/oasis/java/
24. Georgeff, M.P., Lansky, A.L.: *Procedural Knowledge.* In: Proc. Of the IEEE Special Issue on Knowledge Representation, volume 74, pp. 1383-1398, 1986.
25. IBM's Autonomic Computing Initiative: http://www.ibm.com/research/autonomic
26. JADE Agent Platform: http://sharon.cselt.it/projects/jade/
27. Java RMI: http://java.sun.com/products/jdk/rmi/
28. Jennings, N.R, Sycara, K., Wooldridge, M.J.: *A roadmap of agent research and development.* In: International Journal of Autonomous Agents and Multiagent Systems, 1, pp. 275-306, 1998.
29. Jess: http://herzberg.ca.sandia.gov/jess/
30. Kinny, D., Georgeff, M.P.: *Modelling and Design of Multi-Agent Systems.* In: Müller, J.P., Wooldridge M.W., Jennings, N.R., editors, Intelligent Agents III, pp. 1-20, Springer, Berlin, 1997.
31. Lesperance, Y., Levesque, H.J., Lin, F., Marcu, D., Reiter, R., Scherl, R. B.: *Foundations of a logical approach to agent programming.* In: Intelligent Agents II, pp. 331-346, LNAI 1037, Springer, Berlin, 1996.
32. Lesser, V.: http://dis.cs.umass.edu/lesser.html (Homepage)
33. Lightweight Directory Access Protocol (LDAP): http://www.openldap.org/
34. Living-Systems: http://www.living-systems.com/
35. Müller, J.P.: *The Design of Intelligent Agents.* LNAI 1177. Springer, Berlin, 1996.
36. Paolucci, M., Kawamura, T., Payne, T., Sycara, S.: *Semantic Matching of Web Services Capabilities.* In: Proc. of the 1st International Semantic Web Conference, online available at http://www-2.cs.cmu.edu/~softagents/daml_Mmaker/daml-s_matchmaker.htm, 2002.
37. Petta, P., Müller, J.P.: *Guest Editorial*, Engineering Agent Systems: Best of 'From Agent Theory to Agent Implementation (AT2AI) 3', Applied Artificial Intelligence, 16, 2002, forthcoming.
38. Protégé: http://protege.stanford.edu/index.shtml

39. Rao, A.S., Georgeff, M.P.: *Modeling rational agents within a BDI architecture*. In: R. Fikes and E. Sandewall, editors, Proc. of the 2ⁿᵈ International Conference on Principles of Knowledge Representation and Reasoning, pp. 473-484, Morgan-Kaufmann,1991.
40. RDF(S): http://www.w3.org/RDF/ and http://www.w3.org/TR/rdf-schema/
41. Roadmap AgentLink on Agent Technology to be published on http://www.agentlink.org/
42. RosettaNet: http://www.rosettanet.org/
43. Sandholm, T.: http://www-2.cs.cmu.edu/~sandholm/ (Homepage)
44. SemanticWeb: http://www.semanticweb.org/
45. SunOne: http://wwws.sun.com/software/sunone/
46. Tryllian: http://www.tryllian.com/
47. UDDI: http://www.uddi.org/
48. WebServices: http://www.webservices.org/
49. Wooldridge, M.J.: *An Introduction to Multiagent Systems*. John Wiley&Sons, 2002.
50. WSCL: http://www.w3.org/TR/wscl10/

Author Index

Lecture Notes in Computer Science

For information about Vols. 1–2505

please contact your bookseller or Springer-Verlag